▶COUNTERPOINTS◀

—FOUR VIEWS—
ON
SALVATION
IN A
PLURALISTIC
WORLD

John Hick
Clark H. Pinnock
Alister E. McGrath
R. Douglas Geivett
W. Gary Phillips

Dennis L. Okholm
Timothy R. Phillips

General Editors
Previously titled *More Than One Way?*

ZondervanPublishingHouse
Grand Rapids, Michigan

A Division of HarperCollins*Publishers*

Four Views on Salvation in a Pluralistic World
Copyright © 1995, 1996 by Dennis L. Okholm, Timothy R. Phillips, John Hick, Clark H. Pinnock, Alister E. McGrath, R. Douglas Geivett, and W. Gary Phillips

Previously titled *More Than One Way?*

Requests for information should be addressed to:

▟ ZondervanPublishingHouse
Grand Rapids, Michigan 49530

Library of Congress Cataloging-in-Publication Data

More than one way?
    Four views on salvation in a pluralistic world / John Hick . . . [et al.] ; Dennis L. Okholm & Timothy R. Phillips, editors.
       283 p. ; 21 cm. — (Counterpoints)
    Originally published: More than one way. Grand Rapids, Mich. : Zondervan Pub. House, 1995.
    Includes bibliographical references and indexes.
    ISBN: 0-310-21276-6
    1. Salvation outside the church.   2. Christianity and other religions.   3. Religious pluralism—Christianity. I. Hick, John.   II. Okholm, Dennis L. III. Phillips, Timothy R. (Timothy Ross), 1950– .   IV. Title.   V. Series: Counterpoints (Grand Rapids, Mich.)
BT759.M67 1996
261.2—dc 20   96–19860
                                                    CIP

Edited by Verlyn D. Verbrugge

Printed in the United States of America

98 99 00 01 02 /❖ DH/ 10 9 8 7 6 5 4

#3470505

CONTENTS

INTRODUCTION

Dennis L. Okholm and Timothy R. Phillips

THE CHALLENGE OF RELIGIOUS PLURALISM

Susan had just returned to campus after a semester of social work in Nigeria. "How could anyone believe that the Yoruba are not saved?" she blurted out in her Christian theology course. "They are more giving and caring than I!"

Dr. Smith, an American college professor, spends a summer teaching Christians in Muslim-dominated Sudan and wonders how God could so arrange a world that he, the professor, has the "advantage" of growing up in a Christian-dominated culture where the gospel is readily heard, whereas thousands of Muslims in Sudan never hear the gospel. Is it all a matter of historical accident or of some mysterious divine providence?

Every summer hundreds of Chicago restaurants pitch their tents in Grant Park to host a smorgasbord of culinary delights—from the everyday to the exotic. The curious and the hungry can sample the feast without guilt or commitment. The recent "World Parliament on Religions" in the same windy city offered a similar "Taste of Chicago" for religion. And increasingly, major cities across America offer festivals of diverse religions and spiritualities that highlight our pluralistic culture in a splay of booths.

Are the moral adherents to the African traditional religions, virtuous Hindus, and Buddhists really outside a salvific relationship to God? Do Muslims and Jews—who know the God of Abraham and follow his commands—need to hear the gospel? No other issue is so defining of the contemporary religious landscape.

This haunting question is not new. Christianity was born in a religiously pluralistic world. But throughout its history the church has proclaimed that Jesus Christ is the only Savior and that salvation is found only in communion with him, specifically in the church. The point is not simply that Christ is *sui generis*, for here alone God assumed flesh and lived among us, but that his salvific benefits require personal communion with him. As a result, Cyprian's famous dictum, *extra ecclesiam nulla salus*, found wide acceptance throughout church history in both Catholic and Protestant circles, even though the focus shifted to the church as the instrument of the gospel. Consequently, Christian leaders have perceived their religious competition to be in need of conversion to Jesus Christ, despite knowing many truths regarding God. In fact, this vision has propelled Christian missions in a variety of forms from St. Paul to Gregory the Great, from Francis Xavier to Philippe de Corguilleray, from William Carey to Jim Elliot.

Christianity's historical particularity was confronted with the question of fairness and justice during the Enlightenment: How could a loving God fail to offer salvation to all? Friedrich Schleiermacher in the early nineteenth century sought to answer this question by applying his innovative theological method— correlating Christianity as the fulfillment of public truths—to the problem of religious diversity. God, Schleiermacher argued, is salvifically available in some degree in all religions, but the gospel of Jesus Christ is the fulfillment and highest manifestation of this universal religious awareness. Classically, liberal Christianity has held that God's immanent and saving revelation is available to all ages and cultures but exemplified in the final degree in Jesus Christ. That is, Christianity is the all-inclusive and final religion.[1]

By the late nineteenth century, historicism, with its heightened awareness of cultural and religious relativities, challenged the inclusivists' normative claim that Jesus Christ is the fulfillment of religion. As Ernst Troeltsch provocatively argued, since we are at every moment purely historical creatures, religious claims can only be viewed as our culturally conditioned apprehension of the divine. Unable to make normative religious judg-

---

[1]Friedrich Schleiermacher, *Christian Faith*, Par. 7–9; Paul Tillich, *Christianity and the Encounter of the World Religions* (New York: Columbia Univ. Press, 1962), 27–36.

ments, Troeltsch espoused pluralism. While confessing that Christianity possesses "a mighty spiritual power and truth," even "a manifestation of the Divine Life itself," he concluded that this judgment has "validity *for us*" alone. While Christianity is the currently supreme revelation for Western Europeans, other civilizations have their own independent salvific access to the divine life.[2]

The late twentieth century has heightened the dialogue regarding other religions. While the three views of particularism, inclusivism, and pluralism still have their advocates, Western culture has significantly impacted and narrowed the acceptable alternatives. The distinctive feature of our contemporary world is not Christianity's heralded competition with other religions, but the way Western cultures deal with the reality of religious pluralism. Gandhi expressed the rationale a half century ago. When questioned why he proselytized in the political arena but precluded this among the religions, Gandhi replied, "In the realm of the political and social and economic we can be sufficiently certain to convert, but in the realm of religion there is not sufficient certainty to convert anybody, and therefore there can be no conversions in religions."[3]

Simply put, the specter of historicism has corralled religious claims into the private sphere, isolated from political and social discourse. And Western societies demand that everyone assume this relativistic attitude so that each religion must treat the others as if they also have salvific access to God. Popularly we call this political correctness. Everyone is to have an equal voice, especially the marginalized and disenfranchised. That is why the chief virtue in our society is never having to say you're wrong, letting the other have his or her opinion. Religious beliefs amount to little more than matters of personal taste, on a par with one's preference for ice cream or movies.[4]

---

[2]Owen C. Thomas, ed., *Attitudes Toward Other Religions: Some Christian Interpretations* (New York: Harper & Row, 1969; reprint ed., New York: Univ. Press of America, 1986), 86.

[3]Quoted in H. A. Evan Hopkins, "Christianity—Supreme and Unique," in H. A. Evan Hopkins, ed., *The Inadequacy of Non-Christian Religion: A Symposium* (London: Inter-Varsity Fellowship of Evangelical Unions, 1944), 67.

[4]See Lesslie Newbigin, *Foolishness to the Greeks: The Gospel and Western Culture* (Grand Rapids: Eerdmans, 1986).

In this pluralistic politically correct environment, normative religious claims are increasingly difficult to maintain. The recent ebbing of inclusivism in mainline theological circles evidences this. Historicism shattered its attempts to retain the particularity of Christ while affirming the universality of his salvific benefits. Today in mainline circles, Jesus Christ is usually reconstructed as a symbol pointing to God's universal salvific presence. As one contemporary theologian concludes, Christianity is simply "one paradigm of the divine-human relationship among many others," and thus "arguments for the absoluteness, superiority or uniqueness of Christianity become difficult if not impossible."[5] Now the difference between liberal inclusivists and pluralists appears to be only a matter of degree. And during the past two decades some of the most prominent liberal leaders have crossed the theological Rubicon and embraced religious pluralism. Some theologians are boldly heralding the end of classical Christianity and the beginning of a new millennium in religion.[6] That may not be too far off the mark, given the level of political correctness within mainline churches.

But pluralistic ideologies pervade the conservative Christian constituency to no less degree. James Davison Hunter's sociological analyses a decade ago documented the inroads that modernity's "ethic of civility"—which seeks to be tolerable to others—was making in evangelicalism. While this ethic promoted evangelicalism's public legitimacy and a new engagement in the scholarly arena, it also muted such theologically "offensive" beliefs as God's judgment on sin, the sole authority of Scripture, and salvation through Christ alone.[7] And so with the "deghettoization" of evangelicalism has come a loss of sharp and fixed boundaries. Theological proposals are only hesitating

---

[5]Sallie McFague, "An Epilogue: The Christian Paradigm," in Peter C. Hodgson and Robert H. King, eds., *Christian Theology: An Introduction to its Traditions and Tasks*, 2d ed. (Philadelphia: Fortress, 1985), 381.

[6]Paul F. Knitter, *No Other Name? A Critical Survey of Christian Attitudes Toward the World Religions* (Maryknoll, N.Y.: Orbis, 1985), 230–31; Paul F. Knitter and John Hick, eds., *The Myth of Christian Uniqueness: Toward a Pluralistic Theology of Religions* (Maryknoll, N.Y.: Orbis, 1987), vii–xii.

[7]James Davison Hunter, *Evangelicalism: The Coming Generation* (Chicago: Univ. of Chicago Press, 1987), 34–40, 150–54, 180–86; *American Evangelicalism: Conservative Religion and the Quandary of Modernity* (New Brunswick, N.J.: Rutgers Univ. Press, 1983), 84–91.

and tentative; uncertainty regarding Scripture's truth-claims fogs the evangelical mind. The "fact" of ambiguity has replaced the so-called "myth of certainty." Refrains such as "everyone is entitled to his or her opinion" or "let's not judge" increasingly triumph over God's Word. The current jeremiads from prominent evangelical leaders have finally recognized the devaluation of traditional evangelical distinctives. They have taken evangelicalism to the woodshed, reprimanding her theology as "made in America," "sold out" to the "gods of the age," a "wasteland" with "no place for truth."[8]

Undoubtedly Western culture has dramatically affected evangelical distinctives. Long known for its evangelistic zeal, the number of missionaries supported by North American agencies in the 1990s has begun declining for the first time since the 1940s. Foreshadowing this reversal for more than a decade, monetary contributions have not matched inflation.[9] The apparent reason is not difficult to discern: The new willingness to subject revelation to contemporary sensibilities has eroded the theological underpinnings for a missionary faith. Hunter's questionnaire found that only two-thirds of the students in evangelical colleges believe that the sole hope for heaven is through a personal faith in Jesus Christ. Increasingly students in Christian colleges are affronted when hearing the traditional claim that salvation is found in Jesus Christ alone.

Within the academy the classical evangelical position is under severe attack. While the quandaries arising from the particularity of salvation have always been recognized, previously they were employed to evoke a missionary praxis, not to question evangelicalism's theological foundation. But in the mid-

---

[8]Carl F. H. Henry, *Gods of this Age or—God of the Ages?* (Nashville: Broadman & Holman, 1994); Os Guinness and John Seel, eds., *No God but God: Breaking with the Idols of Our Age* (Chicago: Moody, 1992); Michael Scott Horton, ed., *Power Religion: The Selling Out of the Evangelical Church?* (Chicago: Moody, 1992); Michael Scott Horton, *Made in America: The Shaping of Modern American Evangelicalism* (Grand Rapids: Baker, 1991); David F. Wells, *No Place for Truth, or, Whatever Happened to Evangelical Theology?* (Grand Rapids: Eerdmans, 1993), and *God in the Wastelands: The Reality of Truth in a World of Fading Dreams* (Grand Rapids: Eerdmans, 1994).

[9]John A. Siewert and John A. Kenyon, eds., *Mission Handbook USA/Canada: Christian Ministries Overseas. 1993–1995 Edition* (Monrovia, Calif.: MARC, 1993), 55–58.

1980s, Clark Pinnock rejected traditional particularism, insisting that God's grace is sufficiently available in every culture to lead the unevangelized to salvation. In the subsequent decade, through conferences, articles, and books, Pinnock, John Sanders, and Robert Brow have mounted a severe critique of particularism, which they label "restrictivism" or "exclusivism." If salvation is available only through a knowledge of Jesus Christ, they ask, does not this privilege some people over others? Is such a God the merciful and loving one whom we see in Jesus Christ? Should not we be optimistic about God's salvific grace, even outside the church's proclamation?[10]

The debate within the evangelical academy regarding salvation and the unevangelized is intense and fierce, dominating all other discussions. And it should be, for this debate is momentous. In large measure the future of evangelical theology and world missions will be shaped by its outcome.[11]

HOW THIS BOOK CAME TO BE

This book grew out of the 1992 Wheaton Theology Conference, which brought together younger evangelicals to discuss the challenges posed by normative pluralism and inclusivism. The theological vitality and initiative witnessed at that conference encouraged us to engage the key parties in dialogue, including nonevangelical pluralists. This work does not attempt to advance the current frontier of the debate, but it introduces the basic positions within evangelicalism and the wider theological world, and brings these participants into an interchange

---

[10]Clark H. Pinnock, "The Finality of Jesus Christ in a World of Religions," in Mark A. Noll and David F. Wells, eds., *Christian Faith & Practice in the Modern World: Theology from an Evangelical Point of View* (Grand Rapids: Eerdmans, 1988), 152–68; "Toward an Evangelical Theology of Religions," *Journal of the Evangelical Theological Society* 33 (1990): 359–68; *A Wideness in God's Mercy: The Finality of Jesus Christ in a World of Religions* (Grand Rapids: Zondervan, 1992). John Sanders, *No Other Name: An Investigation into the Destiny of the Unevangelized* (Grand Rapids: Eerdmans, 1992). Robert Brow, "Evangelical Megashift," *Christianity Today* 34 (Feb. 19, 1990): 12–14. Clark H. Pinnock and Robert C. Brow, *Unbounded Love: A Good News Theology for the 21st Century* (Downers Grove, Ill.: InterVarsity, 1994).

[11]For a similar assessment see John G. Stackhouse, Jr., "Evangelicals Reconsider World Religions: Betraying or Affirming the Tradition?" *Christian Century* 110 (September 8–15, 1993): 858–65.

so that the layperson can understand the gravity of these issues. Some of the best-known advocates for their respective positions within and outside evangelicalism have graciously agreed to be participants in this discussion.

John Hick towers over all other pluralists in influence and renown. Beginning with his 1972 call for a Copernican Revolution in dealing with the world religions, John Hick has raised the questions, pushed the boundaries, coined the paradigmatic phrases, and thereby prepared the fertile ground for normative pluralism. Recognizing his pivotal role in contemporary theology, Hick's *An Interpretation of Religion* (Yale) received the 1991 Grawemeyer Award for the most significant new thinking in religion. Currently John Hick is Fellow at the Institute for Advanced Research in the Humanities, Birmingham University (U.K.), and Professor Emeritus at Claremont Graduate School.

Among evangelicals, Clark Pinnock is the most prominent inclusivist. Currently at McMaster Divinity College in Hamilton, Ontario, Pinnock has taught at leading evangelical institutions over the years. Throughout this period, he has courageously led evangelicalism in not only reflecting on such diverse topics as biblical authority and socio-political engagement, but also in dialoguing with mainline thinkers. In the last decade, amidst bitter attacks, he has faced his critics and pioneered the current debate on other religions among evangelicals.

Alister McGrath has established himself as one of the leading young evangelical theologians in the English-speaking world. Principal of Wycliffe Hall, McGrath teaches at both Oxford in England and Regent College in Vancouver, British Columbia. A prolific writer, McGrath's academic work ranges across the theological disciplines; his studies on the history of justification, Luther's theology of the cross, and contemporary Christology have received critical recognition. Concerned that the academy assists the church, McGrath also writes on apologetics and spirituality for the layperson in the tradition of C. S. Lewis.

R. Douglas Geivett and W. Gary Phillips are younger evangelicals who presented distinguished papers at the Wheaton Theology Conference and have published in the area of religious pluralism. Both are trained broadly in theology and philosophy, but specialize in different disciplines. Geivett teaches philosophy at the School of Theology at Biola University, while Phillips teaches Bible and theology at Bryan College. Seeing the similarity in their position and approach, the editors asked them to work together, since the issues raised regarding religious pluralism encompass both their specialties. For the sake of convenience, we have coined the composite name Geivett/Phillips in referring to them.

The following procedure was strictly followed in producing this book. Each participant was asked to write a chapter defending his stance on other religions. Then this chapter was critiqued by each of the other participants, to which the original author rejoined with a concluding response. There is a fair amount of repetition within the critiques because the respective participants worked independently of each other. However, in this way the reader is able to discern the perspective of the individual writers more clearly.

THE CATEGORIES AND THE RHETORIC

Many categories have been used to classify religions. The Reformers pitted the true against the false; the Deists distinguished natural religion from the positive religions; the Romantics wrote of the concrete manifestations of religion's identical essence. From a distance their theological agendas are patently self-evident. Throughout the twentieth century the debate regarding other religions has been cast as discontinuity (Hendrik Kraemer), fulfillment (John Farquhar), and mutual appreciation (William Hocking).[12] But after the path-breaking works by Alan Race and Gavin D'Costa in the 1980s, the threefold typology of exclusivism, inclusivism, and pluralism defines the debate.[13] As before, these categories are rhetorical instruments that frame the debate through their often hidden theological agendas. Clearly, terms are rhetorical tools; they aid in selling a case to the audience by linking their vocabulary with the culture's sensitivities,

---

[12]Hendrik Kraemer, *The Christian Message in a Non-Christian World* (New York: Harper & Brothers, 1938); John Nicol Farquhar, *The Crown of Hinduism* (London: Oxford, 1913); William Hocking, *Re-thinking Missions: A Layperson's Inquiry After 100 Years* (New York: Harper & Brothers, 1932).

[13]Alan Race, *Christians and Religious Pluralism: Patterns in the Christian Theology of Religions* (Maryknoll, N.Y.: Orbis, 1982); Gavin D'Costa, *Theology and Religious Pluralism: The Challenge of Other Religions* (Oxford: Blackwell, 1986).

thereby suppressing certain questions. Indeed, the harsh attacks and caricatures in the current theological debate regarding other religions feature all the color of a political campaign, where rhetoric is just as important as substance. Before compliantly accepting these categories, one needs to expose them as rhetorical devices.

Pluralism, which argues that many religions are salvific, on first glance appears to be an accurate and appropriate label. However, does the pluralists' definition of salvation reflect every specific religion's understanding of this condition? At times Troeltsch appears to verge on this sort of relativism, but most contemporary pluralists do not. In order to escape relativism, John Hick defines saving religions as those involving a "transformation of human existence from self-centeredness to God- or Reality-centeredness." Yet this definition contradicts a more traditional Christian or Muslim understanding of salvation. As a result, the term *pluralism* conceals its own normative truth-claims regarding religion.

The term *inclusivism* is appropriate insofar as it connotes that salvation encompasses all cultures. But a curious twist occurs here as well. Gender-inclusive language refuses to affirm that either male or female are intrinsically superior to the other, but Christian inclusivism does not use the term in the same manner. Instead, Christian inclusivists affirm that Jesus Christ is the normative fulfillment of all religion. Again, inclusivism hides a normative truth claim. Political correctness encourages selective hearing at this point. That selectivity was uncovered by Hans Küng in his retort to Karl Rahner's suggestion that Buddhists were really "anonymous Christians." Why not say instead that Christians are "anonymous Buddhists"?

The rhetoric regarding *exclusivism*, however, cuts in a decidedly different direction. In our politically correct environment, exclusivism is akin to flapping a red flag before a bull. The history of associating exclusivism with arrogance, intolerance, dogmatism, and close-mindedness is well established.[14] The very term fosters hostility and caricature. Surveying the newest batch of books by pluralists and inclusivists, Francis Clooney laments that

---

[14]See Arnold Toynbee, "What Should Be the Christian Approach to the Contemporary Non-Christian Faiths?" in Owen C. Thomas, ed., *Attitudes toward other Religions*, 161; Knitter, *No Other Name?* 164–65.

exclusivists are generally presented unsympathetically, as fiercely ruling out the truth of other religions, proclaiming (sometimes arrogantly) Christian superiority, having naive views on world history, etc. But this is of course a caricature... ; it is unfortunate that the exclusivist position is not presented in the best possible light. .... [15]

As a result, an obligatory disclaimer has become standard practice in the conservative literature:

Exclusivism should be understood in terms of *theological* and not *social* exclusivism. .... It should not be understood as restricting association with adherents of other faiths, nor as encouraging intolerance or disrespectful behavior toward those of other faiths.[16]

These observations and requisite disclaimers speak volumes. Clearly the label *exclusivism* is so prejudicial that it precludes true dialogue.

Restrictivism is commonly used as a synonym for exclusivism.[17] When contrasted with inclusivism, it obscures the breadth of options in the classical exclusivist position. In addition, this prejudicial term gives the impression of an arrogant elitist club and carries the suggestion that fewer are saved in it than in inclusivism. But as William Lane Craig has astutely pointed out, just because "salvation is *available* to more people under inclusivism ... does not imply that more people actually *avail* themselves of salvation. ... It seems perverse to call a view inclusivistic if it does not actually include any more people in salvation" than does so-called restrictivism.[18]

As editors, we believe that in our current politically correct environment, the terms *exclusivism* and *restrictivism* preclude a fair hearing. We propose *particularism*—which was used inter-

---

[15]Francis X. Clooney, "Christianity and World Religions: Religion, Reason, and Pluralism," *Religious Studies Review* 15 (July 1989): 200.

[16]Harold Netland, "The Uniqueness of Jesus in a Pluralistic World," *Religious and Theological Studies Fellowship Bulletin* 5 (November/December 1994): 8, 20.

[17]Clark Pinnock and John Sanders have invented this term for those who will not definitively assert that salvation is available outside special revelation. Pinnock, *Wideness*, 14–15; Sanders, *No Other Name*, 37.

[18]William Lane Craig, "Politically Incorrect Salvation," in Timothy R. Phillips and Dennis Okholm, eds., *Christian Apologetics in the Postmodern World* (Downers Grove, Ill.: InterVarsity, 1995), 84.

changeably with exclusivism before the current discussion—as a more appropriate term.[19] The question under discussion is this: Where is salvation found? Particularists argue that salvation is available only through faith in God's special acts in history, culminating in Jesus Christ. The other options by contrast construe salvation pluralistically, as being independently available in many cultures and religions, or inclusively, where Jesus Christ is the normative fulfillment of the salvation available throughout other cultures. Hopefully, shifting the weight of rhetoric will help prevent any one view from controlling the terms of the debate and open the discussion.

PLURALISM

Pluralism, or more accurately, normative religious pluralism, maintains that the major world religions provide independent salvific access to the divine Reality. The contemporary case for pluralism is argued on several grounds: (1) ethically, as the only way to promote justice in our intolerant and oppressive world; (2) in terms of the ineffability of religious experience, so that no religion can claim an absolute stance; and (3) through the historicist thesis that varying cultural and historical contexts preclude absolutist religious claims.[20] John Hick has helped formulate most of these arguments. Developing the historicist thesis in his essay, Hick argues that the world religions relate to Ultimate Reality, but in differing ways. While the cultural and historical settings of the world religions have produced varying conceptions of the Real (Hick's term for what some might call "God") and even of the salvation sought, there is a common soteriological structure in all religions, namely, turning humans from self-centeredness to a new orientation to the Real. But there is no public evidence that any one religion is soteriologically unique or superior to others and thus has closer access to Ultimate Reality.

---

[19]Tillich, *Christianity and the Encounter of the World Religions*, 35, 44; Gerald H. Anderson and Thomas F. Stransky, C.S.P., eds., *Christ's Lordship and Religious Pluralism* (Maryknoll, N.Y.: Orbis, 1981), 148ff., 152.

[20]John Hick and Paul F. Knitter, *The Myth of Christian Uniqueness*, vii–xii.

At this point Hick effectively taunts evangelicals with that haunting question: If Christians really do have a more direct connection with God—the unique reality of the Holy Spirit and his fruits—should they not be morally superior to believers in other religions? Hick hopes to place his opponents in a beguiling dilemma. If one affirms the moral superiority of Christian civilizations, Hick easily assails this as a historically misguided and self-deluded assertion. But if there is no moral advantage to Christianity, then Hick concludes pluralism is true. In addition, Hick repudiates Christianity's normative confession of Christ's deity, arguing that this claim is historically dubious and intellectually incoherent. While Hick still identifies himself as a Christian, Jesus is unique only for him and fellow Christians. Others have their own independent insight into God.

The other essayists challenge Hick's claim that his theory is grounded in ordinary and public experience instead of an a priori claim. Geivett/Phillips ask: Is this theory, which "has such strong affinity with Eastern pantheistic conceptions of reality," really as religiously neutral as it claims? Similarly, Hick's argument for the moral parity of the religions appears to equate religion with moral development, a thesis no world religion accepts. Is Hick not imposing an a priori claim on all religion here? In addition, evangelicals are suspicious of his distinction between the phenomenal and the noumenal Reality. How can Hick know that the unknowable, noumenal Ultimate Real stands behind religious phenomenon? As McGrath notes, the nature of salvation and other religions' respective notions of God differ at such a basic level that a commonality cannot be established. But if this Kantian stance is, as he argues, not a claim to know but a theoretical explanation of religious phenomenon, then Hick seems to espouse a form of agnosticism or even unbelief, in that every religious belief is transformed into a mere phenomenal apprehension of the unknown noumenal.

On the other hand, the discordant responses to Hick's attacks on biblical authority and a traditional Christology demonstrate higher criticism's deep inroads within the evangelical academy. Only Geivett/Phillips attempt to counter directly Hick's attacks on biblical authority, once a hallmark of evangelical distinctives. More agreement exists on Christology. Each evangelical essayist affirms that Jesus' own claims and deeds entail Christological affirmations. But their understandings of Jesus' person and work differ widely. Geivett/Phillips defend a more traditional understanding of Jesus' person and work. Pinnock employs a Logos Christology and rejects the propitiatory element in the atonement, focusing solely on a recapitulation theory of Christ's work. McGrath looks to Pannenberg, Moltmann, and Jüngel (who are critical of the traditional metaphysical concepts of God) as providing resources for contemporary Christological formulations.

PARTICULARISM

Particularism is a hallmark of the salvation-history scheme, the oldest enduring tradition in Christian theology. Key to this scheme is a sharp division between general and special revelation. Even though God makes himself generally known through creation, after the Fall humankind is corrupted, guilty, and fearful of a holy God; consequently, humans misuse this revelation to keep God within their control. But as Scripture narrates, God has freely demonstrated through word and deed his mercy—the reality of salvation and the promise of a new heaven and earth—which was fulfilled in Jesus Christ. Jesus does not express an immanent process. Rather, this is God's personal act supernaturally intervening to reverse the Fall, change the very destiny of creation, and constitute our salvation. This offer of salvation in Jesus Christ allows the sinner to trust God. Through faith in Jesus we can "approach God with freedom and confidence" (Eph. 3:12), for we know that God views us in terms of Christ's righteousness. Since God desires the salvation of all humankind, the church is mandated to carry this message of salvation throughout the whole world until Christ reestablishes his kingdom.

This position, as the others, includes a range of options within the general scheme. Admittedly, many who hold this position maintain that only those who hear the gospel of Jesus Christ and explicitly trust in him in this life can be saved, while all others are swept into a lost eternity. Harold Lindsell baldly states, "God does not reveal Himself redemptively through other means than ... through His children's missionary activity to a lost world."[21] This version of particularism is appropriately labeled *hard restrictivism*. But this is not the only possible stance

---

[21]Harold Lindsell, *A Christian Philosophy of Missions* (Wheaton: Van Kampen Press, 1949), 117.

a particularist can take. One can also be a pessimistic agnostic toward the unevangelized, acknowledging that special revelation is necessary for salvation but choosing to go no further than Scripture (which admittedly does not seem to offer much hope to those who have not heard). This leaves the difficult question of salvation in the hands of God, who is righteous and merciful. But this agnostic stance toward the unevangelized can also be construed optimistically, though such optimism can only be held tentatively and as a secondary theme, never to encroach on or revise the salvation-history scheme.

Some of the most prominent figures in evangelical missiology have espoused an agnostic stance. For instance, Arthur T. Pierson, leader in early fundamentalist institutions and editor of the *Missionary Review of the World*, repeatedly insisted on worldwide evangelism as the church's duty. How can they be saved, unless we be sent? Yet Pierson did not conceive the church as tying God's hand.

> This does not limit the power or grace of God. If there be anywhere a soul feeling after God, following the night of nature and of conscience, in hope and faith that the Great Unknown will somehow give more light, and lead to life and blessedness, we may safely leave such to His fatherly care.[22]

While Pierson was pessimistic about the fate of the unevangelized, he was ultimately agnostic, leaving their fate in God's hands.[23]

Other evangelical leaders have advocated a more optimistic form of this agnostic stance. A leading Presbyterian missions theorist and historian at the turn of the century, James Dennis acknowledged the perceived difficulty of reconciling "the justice and love of God with the condemnation of a heathen soul."[24] He dismissed romantic portrayals of the unevangelized

---

[22]Arthur T. Pierson, *The Crisis of Mission: or, The Voice out of the Cloud* (New York: Baker & Taylor Co., 1886), 297.

[23]Other evangelicals at the turn of the century held this position. See Samuel Henry Kellogg, *Handbook of Comparative Religion* (New York: Student Volunteer Movement For Foreign Mission, 1908), 174; William G. T. Shedd, *Dogmatic Theology* (New York: Charles Scribner's Sons, 1889), 2:706ff.

[24]James S. Dennis, *Foreign Missions After a Century* (London: Oliphant, Anderson & Ferrier, 1894), 202–3.

and ad hoc theories (such as probation after death) as alien to "fundamental biblical teachings." But he was not willing to conclude that the unevangelized are without hope. For God

> has nowhere declared that in cases where Christ's mediation is absolutely unrevealed there *is no hope* whatever of obtaining its benefits. . . . There seems to be nothing, however, in the divine character, or in the revealed Word, which forbids the hope that God in His sovereignty *is able*, if He wishes, to exercise His mercy, . . . in cases where the object of mercy is in such an attitude of humble, childlike self-renunciation and dependence upon divine help. . . . Who of us would dare to close this door of hope, and to decide *ex cathedra* that God is helpless. . . ?[25]

But Dennis refused to "advance this message of hope as an essential doctrine of Christian theology," for this is not a "clear and specific teaching of the divine Word."[26] Whether some of the unevangelized are eventually saved, as well as how and who are included, is unknown. And so the missionary imperative is not diminished one bit.

This breath of legitimate options within the particularist position was maintained in evangelicalism throughout the twentieth century. For over forty years one missions text dominated the Bible Institutes—Robert H. Glover's *The Progress of World-Wide Missions*.[27] After forthrightly stating his traditional stance on the "condemnation of the heathen," Glover acknowledged other acceptable views, and in particular recommended James Dennis' "most helpful treatment of the subject."[28]

This agnostic form of particularism has repeatedly been affirmed at major evangelical conferences, from the 1974 Lausanne

---

[25]Ibid., 207–10.

[26]Ibid., 211.

[27]Glover's credentials earned him respect: He had spent eighteen years as a missionary to China, served eight years as the North American director of the China Inland Mission, and finally directed the missionary curriculum at Moody Bible Institute.

[28]Robert Hall Glover, *The Progress of World-Wide Missions* (New York: George H. Dorna Company, 1924), 25. When Glover's text was updated and revised by Herbert Kane, again the legitimacy of this optimistic form of agnosticism was acknowledged. Robert Hall Glover, *The Progress of World-Wide Missions*, rev. by J. Herbert Kane (New York: Harper & Brothers, Publisher, 1960), 6.

Congress to the 1989 Evangelical Affirmations Consultation.[29] At the latter conference, J. I. Packer argued that while the cases of Melchizedek, Naaman, Cyrus, and the sailors in Jonah's boat offer some basis for optimism, "many of our questions ... are left unanswered by the Word of God." As a result, these optimistic hints can never become a first-order control belief. "We have no warrant from Scripture to expect that God will act thus in any single case where the Gospel is not yet known," and so we cannot presume upon God. "Living by the Bible means assuming that no one will be saved apart from faith in Christ, and acting accordingly."[30] Simply put, particularism encompasses a range of positions—a point acknowledged by evangelicals but seldom by others.

In the present work, two very different particularist viewpoints are offered. Neither Geivett/Phillips nor McGrath are Lindsellian in their approach. While Pinnock attempts to hang the restrictivist label on Geivett/Phillips, they are properly classified as pessimistic agnostics, for they forthrightly acknowledge the possibility of exceptions "in very special circumstances" to the rule that "people are not saved apart from explicit faith in Jesus Christ." But Geivett/Phillips refuse to speculate any further, and their reserve is tied to Scripture's silence on this issue. McGrath, on the other hand, is more optimistic regarding these exceptions, and he freely speculates on the possibility of special revelation given through visions. Nevertheless, in both instances these exceptions have a secondary place and never overthrow

---

[29]Harold Lindsell's hard restrictivist version of particularism has often been highlighted, ignoring if not suppressing other legitimate options. But after his address at the 1974 Lausanne Congress, the universalism study group remained unconvinced. They responded with questions regarding infants, the mentally retarded, and "those who have never heard or known of Christ in their lifetime." They diplomatically concluded, "We feel that some of these questions are covered under ... this report." J. D. Douglas, ed., *Let The Earth Hear His Voice: International Congress on World Evangelization, Lausanne, Switzerland* (Minneapolis: World Wide Publications, 1975), 1206–15. At the 1989 Evangelical Affirmations Consultation, J. I. Packer affirmed that in theory the unevangelized could be saved by throwing themselves on God's mercy (see his "Evangelicals and the Way of Salvation: New Challenges to the Gospel—Universalism, and Justification by Faith," in Kenneth S. Kantzer and Carl F. H. Henry, eds., *Evangelical Affirmations* [Grand Rapids: Zondervan, 1990], 121–23).

[30]James I. Packer, "Evangelicals and the Way of Salvation," 121–23.

the classic salvation-history scheme, where God's special revelation is necessary for salvation.

Using an evidentialist strategy, Geivett/Phillips argue that natural theology leads one to expect a special revelation, such as God has established in Jesus Christ and in Scripture, which is their real authority. They perceive natural theology as an important contested field in the debate regarding other religions, for one's interpretation of Scripture is frequently shaped by these background beliefs. Even though their respondents remain unconvinced of their specific proposal, their argument is an insightful contribution and calls for needed attention to this area.

In the second stage of their essay, Geivett/Phillips carefully present a classic biblical case for particularism. The responses to their exegesis clearly demonstrate that background beliefs shape one's conception and interpretation of Scripture—even one's definition of proof-texting. But their initial use of natural theology must eventually confront them with the question of theodicy. As Pinnock asks, What if God gives a powerful general revelation, but sends no grace along with it? Can this be the loving God found in Jesus Christ? Perhaps their natural theology needs to attend to the phenomenon of unbelief and sin's horrible reality. Relatedly, Hick's denial of the empirical moral superiority of Christianity comes back to haunt, despite Geivett/Phillips' (and McGrath's) objections that morality and Christian soteriology are not synonyms. Hick's denial should at least give Christian particularists pause, especially in the application of words such as "superior."

Instead of beginning with natural theology, McGrath repudiates any attempt to ground knowledge on a universal foundation as reminiscent of the Enlightenment's pretense. Indebted to the postmodern turn, McGrath delights in the particularity of Christianity. Because Jesus Christ and the salvation he has constituted for us stands as the heart of Christianity, there is an ineradicable Christological cast to Christian salvation. Similarly, each religion is distinctively and irreducibly particular in its understandings, practices, and affections. Contrary to Hick's thesis that the world religions are phenomenal apprehensions of the noumenal, McGrath notes that the deeper one examines Christianity and Buddhism, the more they differ. This stance allows McGrath to mount a powerful attack on Hick's assumption that a common Ultimate Reality underlies the religions' varying apprehensions.

Affirming God's desire that all repent, McGrath is agnostic yet optimistic regarding the unevangelized, insisting that God cannot be frustrated by human failure. However, Geivett/Phillips question the source of McGrath's optimism and especially his apparent hope that every human being, in all times and ages, can receive Jesus' salvific benefits. As Pinnock and Geivett/Phillips recognize, here McGrath tends toward inclusivism. Has he at this point softened his prior analysis regarding the particularity of Christian salvation and faith? Does not his analysis mandate an understanding of salvation that is Christologically cast and confined?

INCLUSIVISM

Dissatisfaction with particularism, especially with its inability to speak more definitively regarding the universal availability of salvation, has produced a massive theological shift—a paradigm change—in modern theology. Liberal Protestant theologians and Catholic theologians after Vatican Council II have made this a well-trodden path. Agnosticism is now replaced by a definitive optimism: The salvation offered in Jesus Christ is available not only for those who hear his name; saving grace *must be* universally available in all cultures, without regard to geography or age. The old qualitative distinctions between general and special revelation—between God's universal presence and his personal action in Jesus Christ —are undercut. However, the final expression and norm for this immanent revelation is still Jesus Christ.

Inclusivists demonstrate the coherence of these two principles—the universal accessibility of saving grace and the finality of Jesus Christ—by their explanations of how God's saving grace is operative in every culture, place, and time. But as in the prior categories, there is no one definitive shape to the inclusivist proposal. For many Christian inclusivists, other religions mediate salvation. But Pinnock openly resists that move. By contrast, he insightfully notes that religions are mixtures of truth and error and are often pathways to damnation. On the other hand, God's Spirit can use positive aspects of other religions and a variety of other elements—specifically, the conscience, the human religious quest, angels, social interaction—as a means of grace. The requirement for salvation is simply trust in God—under whatever form God is known—and obedience. Perhaps some believers will receive an explicit knowledge of Jesus Christ and the basis of their salvation only later, after death.

The other essayists are skeptical whether the salvation Pinnock is describing is Christian. The evangelicals ask: Does not inclusivism inherently denigrate the particularity of salvation in Jesus Christ? McGrath's thesis, namely, that Christian salvation is ineradicably Christological, poses a masterful challenge to Pinnock's argument that salvation is available without regard to cultural and historical requirements. Is not the particularity of the salvation established by Jesus Christ lost in this proposal? Given the ineradicable worldviewish nature of every culture, is it even possible to distinguish so sharply between truth and error, God's Spirit and human distortion?

On the other hand, Hick charges that this theory regarding the universal availability of Christian salvation fails to acknowledge the distinctive religious lives of non-Christians. Is it meaningful to identify historical non-Christian saints as "believers awaiting messianic salvation"? Would Mohammed, Gandhi, or the Dalai Lama accept such a description? If every culture is distinctively religious at its core, can Pinnock escape the implication that other religions are salvific? At this point, Pinnock appeals to God's mysterious work. But when agnostic particularists used this ploy, Pinnock labeled it a theological cop-out.[31] Is not this criticism even more decisive for the inclusivist? For its coherence depends on the ability to explain how God is offering salvation outside the proclamation of Jesus Christ.

In addition, the other evangelical essayists perceive as problematic the lack of a qualitative distinction between God's personal action in Jesus Christ and his universal presence. For inclusivists, God's saving grace has pervaded the cosmos from the beginning, always offering love. Consequently, Jesus is viewed as the one who perfectly acts out God's ever-present love for creation, mirroring the nature of God reaching out to a rebellious humanity through the cross. This has important theological

---

[31]Pinnock, *Wideness*, 152.

effects. The biblical emphasis on God's holiness is replaced with an ever-forgiving love. Indeed, Pinnock rejects the propitiatory view of Christ's atoning work. Furthermore, while Jesus Christ is the clearest expression of God's universal grace, is he also for Pinnock the one who establishes God's grace by his unique work in his life, death, and resurrection? Admittedly, Pinnock insists on a "high" Christology, but for him does Jesus actually constitute our salvation or just express it? Inclusivism's inability to distinguish between God's presence and God's personal act in Jesus Christ appears to treat Jesus as just "the sent one" and not as the actual Savior of the world. Can inclusivism view Jesus Christ as *sui generis* and not simply as final?

OUR HOPE

If the editors have tipped the introduction toward the particularist, it is not necessarily because they agree with their view. That is beside the point, and the interchange among the four essayists must speak for itself. Rather, it is because theological discussions must sometimes act as thermostats, reversing tendencies which, if allowed to go on too long, will cause us to forget something of our heritage. As we have pointed out, in our culture "inclusivism" and "pluralism" are hot words; "particularism" leaves many cold. Perhaps when—and if—the pendulum swings back toward restrictivism and presumptive superiority, then the thermostat might have to be turned in the other direction, so as, again, not to lose something of our rich Christian heritage.

These essays raise many important issues for advocates of all views of religious pluralism and salvation. Indeed, these are issues of life and death. We thank our five contributors for the conviction, courage, forthrightness, and care with which they presented their positions and their responses to each other. We hope this work is instructive for all readers. More importantly, we hope that they will not find in these pages support merely for the views they bring to the text, but that this interchange will spur the Christian church to think through the ramifications of the beliefs it holds in this incredibly challenging but exciting time.

Chapter One

A PLURALIST VIEW

John Hick

A PLURALIST VIEW

John Hick

The other writers in this book represent either conservative or very conservative theological standpoints. I do not at this stage know whether any of them accept the label "fundamentalist," and so I shall not use it. But in contrast to their positions I represent a much more liberal point of view and am therefore pleased to be included in the discussion. The plan of the book suggests that it is addressed primarily, but not of course exclusively, to a conservative Christian constituency, and I shall therefore be addressing primarily readers with conservative presuppositions. It seems appropriate to begin by telling you, our readers, of my own conservative background.

MY CONVERSION EXPERIENCE AND SPIRITUAL PILGRIMAGE

I began my Christian life as a fundamentalist. I was baptized as a baby in the Church of England and was taken as a child and teenager to its services, which were to me a matter of infinite boredom. The whole Christian "thing" seemed to me utterly lifeless and uninteresting. But I was nevertheless conscious of being in some kind of long-term state of spiritual dissatisfaction and search. My unformed worldview was broadly humanist. At the age of sixteen I was thrilled by the writings of Nietzsche and greatly enjoyed reading Bertrand Russell.

But as a law student at University College, Hull, at the age of eighteen, I underwent a powerful evangelical conversion under the impact of the New Testament figure of Jesus. For several days I was in a state of intense mental and emotional turmoil, during which I became increasingly aware of a higher truth and greater reality pressing in upon me and claiming my recognition and response. At first this was highly unwelcome, a disturbing and challenging demand for nothing less than a revolution in personal identity. But then the disturbing claim became a liberating invitation. The reality that was pressing in upon me was not only awesomely demanding but also irresistibly attractive, and I entered with great joy and excitement into the world of Christian faith. Some of my fellow students were members of the InterVarsity Fellowship, the evangelical campus organization; and throwing in my lot with them, I accepted as a whole and without question the entire evangelical package of theology—the verbal inspiration of the Bible; Creation and Fall; Jesus as God the Son incarnate, born of a virgin, conscious of his divine nature, and performing miracles of divine power; redemption by his blood from sin and guilt; Jesus' bodily resurrection, ascension, and future return in glory; heaven and hell.

Intending now to enter the ministry of the Presbyterian Church of England, mainly because my InterVarsity friends were Presbyterians, I moved to Edinburgh University to study philosophy, with which I was already fascinated, before going to seminary. The regular meetings, prayer meetings, and Bible study groups of the Evangelical Union at Edinburgh occupied a good deal of my time, and I also engaged in its other activities, such as conducting ward services in the Edinburgh Royal Infirmary.

However, this was 1941—my second academic year, with World War II, of course, having already begun in Europe. Previously in Hull I had taken part along with other students in "fire watching" and was on duty during the three nights when almost the entire center of Hull was destroyed by bombing. In the summer of 1942, I was due for military service. Although nearly all my fellow students joined the forces, I felt called to be a conscientious objector on Christian grounds. The way I thought about it then was simply that the teachings of Jesus were utterly incompatible with the mass violence of war. I would now add that, regardless of the justification at the time for any particular conflict—and World War II was, in the cir-

cumstances of the Nazi threat to Europe, probably as well justified on the Allied side as almost any war could be—war
between nations is a collective insanity of killing, maiming, and
destroying our common human assets. An observer from outer
space would say that in a "world war" the human race goes
temporarily mad, kills off much of the best of its present generation, undermines the degree of civilization it has achieved, and
may even eventually destroy itself. The only way to communicate this as other than an unheard bleat was actually to refuse to
take part in war. I saw this refusal as a vocation for some of us,
while others had a vocation to take part in what was to them the
lesser of two evils. However, I could not opt out of the war itself,
but only out of the willingness to kill; thus, I joined the Friends'
(i.e., Quakers') Ambulance Unit, and this option was endorsed
by a Conscientious Objectors' Tribunal. I served in the F.A.U. for
the last three years of the war—first in hospitals in London and
Edinburgh, then in a variety of places in Egypt, Italy, and Greece.

INTELLECTUAL DOUBTS

After the war I returned to Edinburgh University for the
remaining three years of my philosophy course. I rejoined the
Evangelical Union, but soon found that I was no longer fully in
tune with it. My philosophical training was leading me to ask
awkward questions. How, for example, could one understand
the sun standing still for about a day as recounted in Joshua
10:13? In the light of our modern knowledge of astronomy, we
would have to say that the earth, which rotates at a speed of
about a thousand miles an hour, suddenly ceased to rotate; but
taken seriously, this is mind-boggling. Again, can biological evolution responsibly be rejected just because it is contrary to the
book of Genesis? Are there not numerous contradictions
between this biblical text and that? And could it really be an
expression of infinite love to send the majority of the human
race to eternal torment in hell? And so on. But instead of such
questions being honestly confronted, there seemed to me to be a
distinct reluctance on the part of the student and faculty leadership to face them, a feeling that they were dangerous and ought
not to be raised, and that they constituted a temptation to back-
sliding. Thus I drifted apart from the conservative evangelical

student movement, though continuing for many years to be what I would now describe as theologically conservative.

The year I graduated a new scholarship came into existence to support an Edinburgh philosophy graduate to do research at Oxford. I received this award and became the first Campbell Fraser scholar at Oriel College, Oxford, working for the D. Phil. degree under Professor H. H. Price and writing my thesis on "Faith and Belief," later revised as *Faith and Knowledge*.[1] After Oxford I studied for three years at the Presbyterian seminary, Westminster College, Cambridge. There I remember being profoundly shocked by a graduate student who argued that Jesus was not God incarnate but a remarkable human being. At the end of the seminary course I was ordained to the ministry of the Presbyterian Church of England (subsequently, after union with the Congregationalists, the United Reformed Church). At the same time I was married and for the next three years served a rural congregation just south of the Scottish border. I greatly enjoyed the work, the congregation flourished, and our first child was born.

However, one day a totally unexpected letter arrived from the Philosophy Department at Cornell University, asking if I would be interested in going there as an assistant professor teaching philosophy of religion. We went there and enjoyed Cornell enormously. While there, I published my first article, in the *Scottish Journal of Theology* (March 1958), criticizing D. M. Baillie's "paradox of grace" Christology for departing, more than he seemed to recognize, from Chalcedonian orthodoxy. In other words, I had not yet proceeded very far from the conservative theology with which I started. The first noticeable departure occurred in 1961, while teaching at Princeton Theological Seminary, when I questioned whether belief in the Incarnation required one to believe in the literal historicity of the Virgin Birth.

THE NECESSITY FOR AN INTELLECTUAL APPROPRIATION OF THE CHRISTIAN FAITH

I have recounted this piece of autobiography to help conservative readers to appreciate that I have some understanding

---

[1] John Hick, *Faith and Knowledge*, 2d ed. (Ithaca: Cornell Univ. Press, 1966 / London: Macmillan, 1966; reprint, London: Macmillan, 1988; orig. ed. 1957).

of their position, because it was once my own. My departure from it was gradual and was partly the result of further reflection prompted by a philosophical training, partly of reading the works of the New Testament scholars, and partly of trying to preach the gospel in a way that made sense to ordinary twentieth-century men and women, both young and old. My conversion experience, with its powerful awareness of a divine presence that was both profoundly challenging and at the same time profoundly creative and life-giving, remains basic; but the particular fundamentalist intellectual package that came with it has long since crumbled and disappeared. I can, however, recognize—as some liberal Christians do not—that the conservative evangelical wing of Christianity sometimes serves a vital purpose in challenging young people and jolting them out of the pervasive secular humanism of our culture. It can in many cases be good to undergo a "fundamentalist" conversion, so long as one later sorts out the intellectually acceptable and unacceptable and is able eventually to discard the latter.

THE RELIGIOUS WAY OF EXPERIENCING-AS AND REVELATION

Having done that sorting out, I ought at this point to make clear to a conservative readership how I differ from them on the questions of revelation and the authority of Scripture. I do not think that it is possible to settle theological issues with "The Bible says. . . ." The Bible is a collection of documents written during a period of about a thousand years by different people in different historical and cultural situations. The writings are of a variety of kinds, including court records, heavily edited and slanted history, prophetic utterances, hymns, letters, diary fragments, memories of the historical Jesus, faith-created pictures of his religious significance, apocalyptic visions, etc. The human authorship and historical setting must always be taken into account in using the Scriptures. We do not, for example, need today to take over the prescientific beliefs and cultural assumptions of people living in the remote past in a much different human world. If they thought that the earth is flat and that physical diseases are caused by demons, we do not have to follow them in that. It is their religious experience that is important.

God is always and everywhere present to us—above, beneath, around, and within us. And when a human being is exceptionally open to the divine presence, he or she has a vivid awareness of God, which is then called revelation.

Usually within our Judeo-Christian tradition, this awareness takes the form of experiencing some event in one's own life, or in the wider history of which one is part, as mediating or revealing the presence and activity of God. Thus the Old Testament prophets characteristically experienced events in the history of Israel as occasions of God's presence in the form of guidance, aid, warning, or punishment. For example, Jeremiah saw the Chaldean army advancing on Jerusalem as God's instrument to punish faithless Israel. This was not, I believe, a retrospective theological interpretation, but an expression of the way in which the prophet actually experienced the event at the time. No doubt others experienced the same event as having a purely political or economic significance. The religious way of experiencing-as does not negate these secular ways but adds another layer of meaning to the experience. Thus the Chaldeans had their own purely human purposes; but Jeremiah experienced this moment of history, including those human purposes, as serving a divine purpose. The difference between the religious and secular modes of experiencing-as occurs in the interpretive element within the formation of the experience. Religious faith is this uncompelled interpretive element within religious experience.[2]

THE NEW TESTAMENT'S CONFESSION OF JESUS

And what of the New Testament? This is a selection of Christian documents from the first century A.D., which takes us as far back to the historical Jesus and the origins of Christianity as we can get. The earliest document, Paul's first letter to the Thessalonians, is probably dated about 50 A.D., and the earliest Gospel, that of Mark, about 70 A.D. We should not think of the four Gospels as if they were eyewitness accounts by reporters on the spot. They were written between forty and seventy years

---

[2]For more about this, see my *Faith and Knowledge*, 2d ed., or "Religious Faith as Experiencing-as," in my *God and the Universe of Faiths* (1973; reprint, London: Macmillan, 1988 / Chatham, N.Y. and Oxford: One World Publications, 1993).

after Jesus' death by people who were not personally present at the events they describe; for all are dependent on sources in a way in which an eyewitness would not be. Furthermore, intensive developments had taken place within the Christian community during those formative decades.

However, the documents are all documents of faith. They all see Jesus as one who mediated God's presence and God's call to live now as citizens of the coming kingdom. The earliest conceptualization of this faith response to Jesus seems to have been as a Spirit-filled prophet and healer; in the words attributed to Peter in Acts, "a man attested to you by God with mighty works and wonders and signs which God did through him in your midst" (Acts 2:22).[3] This God-inspired man seems to have understood his own role as that of the final prophet, proclaiming the imminent coming of the kingdom on earth. And the early church lived in the fervent expectation of his return as God's agent to inaugurate the kingdom. As this expectation gradually faded, Jesus was exalted in communal memory from the eschatological prophet to a divine status. The New Testament documents were written during the early stages of this development and contain both flashbacks to the human Jesus of history and anticipations of the divine Christ of later official church doctrine.

I am not sure whether it is generally known to students in the evangelical world that many human beings were called "son of God" in the ancient world. At least, I did not know this when I was a student in that world. Today, in our science-dominated secular society it would take earth-shaking miracles to cause us to regard a man or a woman as being also divine. But in the ancient world, the concept and language of divinity was much looser. Emperors, pharaohs, and great philosophers and religious figures were sometimes called "son of God" and regarded as divine in the broad sense that "divine" then had. Further, the "son of God" designation was familiar within Judaism. Israel as a whole was called God's son (Hos. 11:1); angels were called "sons of God" (Job 38:7); kings were enthroned as sons of God (2 Sam. 7:14; Ps. 2:7). The Messiah, being of the royal line of David, would be in this sense a son of God. Indeed, any outstandingly pious Jew could be called a son of God, meaning one

---

[3]The Scripture quotations in this essay are taken from the Revised Standard Version.

who was close to God, served God, and acted in the spirit of God. In terms of our modern distinction, this was clearly intended as metaphor. No one thought that King David, to whom God said at his coronation, "You are my son; today I have begotten you" (Ps. 2:7), was literally God's son. And it would be entirely natural that Jesus, as a great charismatic preacher and healer, should be thought of as a son of God.

However, this idea was sometimes less clearly metaphorical in the Gentile world. And when Paul took the gospel into that world, this "son of God" metaphor began to change. As Jesus was gradually deified in the minds of Christians, he became the semimetaphorical, semiliteral Son of God, and then finally, after several centuries, the literal God the Son, the Second Person of a divine Trinity. All this was the work of the church as it lived through new situations, and particularly as it became in the fourth century the official religion of the Roman empire.

I thus see theology as a human creation. I do not believe that God reveals propositions to us, whether in Hebrew, Greek, English, or any other language. I hold that the formulation of theology is a human activity that always, and necessarily, employs the concepts and reflects the cultural assumptions and biases of the theologians in question. As an example, the successive atonement doctrines that have become prominent during the history of Christian doctrine have reflected the states of society within which they were produced.[4]

THE CHALLENGE OF OTHER RELIGIONS

Returning to the personal story that I was recounting, there is at least one major difference between my own experience, now more than half a century ago, and that of the present younger generation. Whereas the question of other religions and the challenge that their existence poses to a conservative Christian faith were hardly on the agenda at that time, both aspects have today become prominent and unavoidable. At seminary I learned little about other faiths, though I did take one course from H. H. Farmer along the lines of his subsequent book *Revelation and*

---

[4]For details, see my *The Metaphor of God Incarnate* (Louisville: Westminster/John Knox, 1994 / London: SCM, 1994), ch. 11.

Religion, in which he saw Christianity as fulfilling what was partially available in the other world religions. And apart from an occasional Jew, I did not meet anyone who was not at least nominally a Christian. I shared the general Christian assumption that it was God's will that the whole world be evangelized and that humanity was in fact slowly but surely becoming Christian. At that time this belief was not problematic to me, and I remember being shocked when Reinhold Niebuhr declared that the mission to the Jews was a mistake.

How, then, have I come to adopt a "pluralist" understanding of the relation between Christianity and the other great world faiths? And what is this "pluralist" understanding? I can answer these questions by continuing the narrative. After teaching at Cornell, then at the fairly conservative Princeton Theological Seminary, and then at Cambridge University, I moved to the H. G. Wood Chair in the Theology Department of the University of Birmingham. This city, in the middle of England, is an industrial center, which was one of the main receivers of immigration during the 1950s and 1960s from the Caribbean islands and from the Indian subcontinent. There was thus a sizable presence of several non-Christian traditions, consisting of the new Muslim, Sikh, and Hindu communities, as well as a small but long-established Jewish community; subsequently there have come to be several Buddhist groups. Immigration was then a hotly debated issue, and the neo-Nazi National Front was active in the area, generating prejudice and hatred and promoting violence against black and brown people and against Jews. It was a challenging time and place in which to find oneself.

During my fifteen years at Birmingham I became deeply involved in a variety of "community relations" organizations. I was one of the founders and the first chair of the activist AFFOR (All Faiths for One Race), based in the largely black area of Handsworth, and chair of the Birmingham Inter-Faiths Council, chair of the Religious and Cultural Panel of the governmentally sponsored Birmingham Community Relations Committee, and chair of the coordinating committee of the Statutory Conference convened under the 1944 Education Act to create a new agreed-upon syllabus of religious education in the city's schools. The latter operation lasted two years and produced a new multifaith curriculum to replace the previous exclusively Christian one.

This was a busy and sometimes exciting period. The first director of AFFOR was violently assaulted several times by National Front thugs; the Jewish investigative journalist with whom I collaborated in a published exposure of the records of the National Front leaders—many of whom had been in prison for violent offenses—was knifed; and others of us received threats. In all this I found myself in active comradeship with Muslims, Jews, Hindus, Sikhs, Marxists, and humanists, as well as with fellow Christians. It has to be said that in the 1970s—the situation is happily very different today—the British churches, so far from leading the opposition to racial prejudice and discrimination, were largely uninterested in the issue and also unready to face the theological issues raised by the fact of religious plurality.

In the course of this work I went frequently to Jewish synagogues, Muslim mosques, Sikh gurudwaras, Hindu temples, and, of course, a variety of churches. In these places of worship I soon realized something that is obvious enough once noticed, yet momentous in its implications. This is that although the language, concepts, liturgical actions, and cultural ethos differ widely from one another, yet from a religious point of view basically the same thing is going on in all of them, namely, human beings coming together within the framework of an ancient and highly developed tradition to open their hearts and minds to God, whom they believe makes a total claim on their lives and demands of them, in the words of one of the prophets, "to do justice, and to love kindness, and to walk humbly with your God" (Mic. 6:8). God is known in the synagogues as *Adonai*, the Lord God of Abraham, Isaac, and Jacob; in the mosques as *Allah rahman rahim*, God beneficent and merciful; in the Sikh gurudwaras as God, who is Father, Lover, Master, and the Great Giver, referred to as *war guru*; and in the Hindu temples as Vishnu, Krishna (an incarnation of Vishnu), Rama, Shiva, and many other gods and goddesses, all of whom, however, are seen as manifestations of the ultimate reality of Brahman; and in the Christian churches as the triune God, Father, Son, and Holy Spirit. And yet all these communities agree that there can ultimately only be one God!

If there is indeed only one God, maker of heaven and earth, two obvious possibilities present themselves. One is that God as known within one particular religion, namely one's own, is the real God and that all the others are unreal. The other is that God as known to Christians, Jews, Muslims, Hindus, Sikhs, and others represent different manifestations in relation to humanity, different "faces" or "masks" or *personae* of God, the Ultimate Reality. But there is also a third, intermediate position, adopted today by the majority of mainline theologians, that God as known within Judaism, Islam, Hinduism, and Sikhism are partial or distorted glimpses of the real God, who is fully known within Christianity. This range of options seems to cover the field.

Why, then, do I opt for the pluralistic view that the God-figures of the great theistic religions are different human awarenesses of the Ultimate, rather than for the traditional Christian view that we alone have a true knowledge of God? The answer still lies in the realm of personal experience and observation, though expanding beyond multifaith Birmingham to a year filled with visits to Hindu, Muslim, Sikh India, Buddhist Sri Lanka, and Japan, and with involvement in Jewish-Christian-Muslim and Buddhist-Christian dialogues.

MORALITY IN THE MAJOR WORLD RELIGIONS

Coming to know both ordinary families, and some extraordinary individuals, whose spirituality has been formed by these different traditions and whose lives are lived within them, I have not found that the people of the other world religions are, in general, on a different moral and spiritual level from Christians. They seem on average to be neither better nor worse than are Christians. Clearly in saying this, I am presupposing a common criterion, a general sense of what we mean by the human goodness that reflects a right relationship to God. This is the universally recognized sense of goodness as consisting in concern for others, kindness, love, compassion, honesty, and truthfulness.

The basic ideal of love and concern for others and of treating them as you would wish them to treat you is, in fact, taught by all the great religious traditions. Jesus said, "As you wish that men would do to you, do so to them" (Luke 6:31). Confucius said, "Do not do to others what you would not like yourself" (*Analects*, XII:2). Taoism says that the good man will "regard [others'] gains as if they were his own, and their losses in the same way" (*Thai Shang*, 3). Zorastrianism declares, "That nature only is good when it shall not do to another whatever is not good for its own self" (*Dadistan-i-dinik*, 94: 5). In the Hindu *Mahabharata* we read, "One should never do that to another which one regards as injurious to one's own self. This, in brief, is the rule of Dharma" (*Anushana parva*, 113: 7). The Jain scriptures tells us that one should go about "treating all creatures in the world as he himself would be treated" (*Katanga Sutra*, Bk. I, lect. 11: 33). The Buddhist scriptures contain many injunctions to compassion and loving-kindness, such as this: "As a mother cares for her son, all her days, so towards all living things a man's mind should be all-embracing" (*Sutta Nipata*, 149). The Jewish Talmud tells us that "what is hateful to yourself do not do to your fellow man. That is the whole of the Torah" (*Babylonian Talmud*, *Shabbath* 31a). And in the Hadith of Islam we read the prophet Muhammad's words, "No man is a true believer unless he desires for his brother that which he desires for himself" (*Ibn Madja*, Introduction 9; cf. other hadiths).

In each case, for both Christian and non-Christian, this is of course an ideal. The important question is the extent to which the ideal is put into practice. The honest answer, in each case, is that it has been practiced imperfectly. Each tradition has its great saints and great sinners, and in the lives of ordinary believers is a wavering attempt to live up to the ideal, but with human behavior all too often sliding into a loveless and selfish treatment of others. We have no way of accurately recording the individual actions of hundreds of millions of people within the great world religions over the centuries or today. It is, of course, easy to pick out some manifest example of gross injustice or cruelty within some non-Christian community and contrast it with some manifest example of true goodness within a Christian community. But such a procedure could easily be reversed, and in each case it is manifestly unfair. We can only go on personal observation and the reports of others, both contemporary and historical, and on this basis form a global impression, though one that we cannot claim to prove. My own global impression, based inevitably on having known a limited number of families and individuals and having read a limited amount of history and travelers' accounts, is that the virtues and vices seem to be spread more or less evenly among human beings, regardless of whether they are Christians or—to confine ourselves for the moment to the "great world religions"—Jews, Muslims, Hindus (including Sikhs), or Buddhists.

But is this what we would expect if Christians have a more complete and direct access to God than anyone else and live in a closer relationship to him, being indwelt by the Holy Spirit? Should not the fruit of the Spirit, which according to Paul is "love, joy, peace, patience, kindness, goodness, faithfulness, gentleness, self-control" (Gal. 5:22–23), be more evident in Christian than in non-Christian lives? It would not, of course, be fair to expect that any randomly selected Christian be morally superior to any randomly selected non-Christian. But surely the *average* level of these virtues should be noticeably higher among Christians than among non-Christians. Yet it does not seem to me that in fact Christians are on average noticeably morally superior to Jews, Muslims, Hindus, Sikhs, or Buddhists. Rather than suggest a comparative quantification of a kind that is not in fact possible, I propose the more modest and negative conclusion, that it is not possible to establish the moral superiority of the adherents of any one of the great traditions over the rest.

And when we turn to the large-scale expressions of religion in human societies and civilizations over the centuries, I find that we are led to a similar conclusion. Christian, Muslim, Hindu, Buddhist, Chinese, African, and other "primal" cultures have each been a mixture of good and evil. But the goods and the evils are often incommensurate. How does one weigh the evil of the Indian caste system—which, incidentally, operates in the Christian as well as in the Hindu communities in India— over the centuries against the evil of the European class system over the same centuries? How does one weigh the poverty of many Muslim, Hindu, and Buddhist countries against the greedy use of the earth's nonrenewable resources and the heedless destruction of the environment by the Western Christian countries? How does one weigh the social problems of Calcutta or Bangkok or Cairo against those of some of our own inner cities, with their daily murders, violent crimes, destructive drug use, poverty, deprivation, and despair? Or how do we weigh the cruelties of some Eastern regimes against the virulent anti-Semitism of Christian Europe, culminating in the Holocaust of the 1940s?

It is, of course, once again easy to pick out some manifestly good aspect of our own civilization and compare it with some manifestly evil aspect of another. But as before, this is not a just way of proceeding. Again I conclude that it seems appropriate to come to the modest and negative conclusion that one cannot establish the unique moral superiority of any one of the great world religions.

Some will disagree with this estimate. Unfortunately, any debate about it is likely to be inconclusive. But it is worth at this point posing the question to my fellow writers in this book whether their positions require that the moral fruits of Christian faith are superior to those of any other faith, and if so, whether this is an a priori claim or one they believe can be demonstrated?

THE PHENOMENON OF SALVATION

Assuming, however, that my negative conclusion is correct—namely, that it cannot properly be claimed that the fruits of Christian faith in human life, both individual and corporate, are superior to those of the other major world religions—what then? A conservative might be tempted to reply that morality is something different from salvation. To see Jesus as God incarnate—more precisely, as God the Son, the second Person of the Holy Trinity, incarnate—and to take him as one's Lord and Savior, pleading his atoning death to cover one's sins, is to be justified in God's sight; this is what it means to be saved. The sanctification that follows is a long process. We are not immediately perfected, and Christians can be found in all stages of sanctification, from miserable sinners to devout saints. Thus it is not fair to expect Christians generally to be morally superior to non-Christians generally.

But is such a reply adequate? Surely the work of the Holy Spirit within us should have the effect of raising the general moral level of the Christian community above that of the surrounding world. Jesus called men and women to turn round in their lives and to begin to live the life of the coming kingdom. He called them to love their neighbors, to turn the other cheek, to overcome evil with good, to trust wholly in God rather than secure themselves by power or possessions, and to give without expecting any reward. And the criterion of judgment in his parable of the sheep and the goats was not a theological but a practical one: Have they given food and drink to the hungry, welcomed strangers, clothed the naked, and visited the sick and those in prison (Matt. 25:31–46)? Such behavior is the natural fruit of true religion: "Are grapes gathered from thorns, or figs from thistles? So, every sound tree bears good fruit" (Matt. 7:16–17). But if the fruit of Christian faith seems in general to be neither better nor worse than the fruit of Jewish, Muslim, Hindu, or Buddhist faiths, should this not lead us to think further about those other great Ways?

This path of thought, reflecting both personal observation and a fair amount of reading, suggests to me that we should think of salvation in more universal terms than has been customary in Christian theology. This in turn leads to a new understanding of the function of the world religions, including Christianity. If we define salvation as being forgiven and accepted by God because of Jesus' death on the cross, then it becomes a tautology that Christianity alone knows and is able to preach the source of salvation. But if we define salvation as an actual human change, a gradual transformation from natural self-centeredness (with all the human evils that flow from this) to a radically new orientation centered in God and manifested in the "fruit of the Spirit," then it seems clear that salvation is taking place within all of the world religions—and taking place, so far as we can tell, to more or less the same extent. On this view, which is not based on theological theory but on the observable realities of human life, salvation is not a juridical transaction inscribed in heaven, nor is it a future hope beyond this life (although it is this too), but it is a spiritual, moral, and political change that can begin now and whose present possibility is grounded in the structure of reality.

This salvific transformation is conceived in different sets of terms within the different religions. *Salvation* is primarily a Christian term. *Redemption* is common to Christians and Jews. Muslims think in terms of a *total submission to God*, who is the giver of life and who is ever gracious and merciful to humankind. The Eastern religions do not always experience the ultimate reality we call God as a personal being and do not think primarily in terms of guilt and forgiveness. Rather, this transformation is experienced as *liberation* or *enlightenment*, that is, the dispelling of the spiritual blindness of *avidya* and the discovery of ultimate oneness with Brahman, the eternally real. Another characteristic Eastern term is *awakening*, that is, awakening to the true nature of reality when experienced from a universal rather than an ego-centered point of view; this transformed consciousness, whose expression is compassion for all of life, is *nirvana*. These are very different experiences, formed by very different conceptualities and integral to very different religious totalities. But they are all forms of the same fundamental human transformation from self-centeredness to a recentering in the ultimately Real as variously thought and experienced within the different ways of being human that constitute the great religious cultures of the earth. When trying to think on the global scale, I have therefore become accustomed to using the hybrid term *salvation/liberation*.

The process of reasoning in which I find myself engaged is thus inductive, in the sense of proceeding upwards from observable data, rather than being deductive, in the sense of starting with a priori premises and deducing conclusions from them. I start from within the circle of Christian faith, committed to the fundamental conviction that Christian religious experience is not, as the skeptics believe, purely imaginative projection, but is our response to an ultimate transcendent reality, the reality we call God. The Christian totality, by which my own religious experience is shaped, is a complex historical process covering now twenty centuries, and it includes both great goods and great evils; but the tradition as a whole, "warts and all," constitutes my spiritual home. I then notice that there are also in the world other more or less equally ancient, vast, and complex streams of religious thought and experience, each likewise including both great goods and great evils. But looking at the good within them all, including my own, I see them as imperfect contexts of salvation/liberation. They are contexts within which men and women have been transformed, in varying degrees, from self-centeredness to Reality-centeredness. Their soteriological power can only be humanly judged by their human fruits, and, as indicated above, these fruits seem to me to be found more or less equally within each of the great traditions.

It therefore seems logical to me to conclude that not only Christianity, but also these other world faiths, are human responses to the Ultimate. They see the Divine/Sacred/Ultimate through different human conceptual "lenses," and they experience the divine/sacred/ultimate presence through their different spiritual practices in correspondingly different forms of religious experience. But they seem to constitute more or less equally authentic human awarenesses of and response to the Ultimate, the Real, the final ground and source of everything.

Let me now relate this to the central focus of the book, namely, the fate of non-Christians. For a traditionally orthodox theology, this is a grave problem, for the eternal destiny of the large majority of the human race is at stake. The unacceptable aspect of the old exclusivist view that non-Christians are eternally lost, or eternally tormented in hell, is its dire implication concerning the nature of God. Is it compatible with the limitless divine love that God should have decreed that only a minority of human beings, those who have happened to be born in a Christian part of the world, should have the opportunity of eternal life?

Taking up this issue elsewhere, I have argued on Christian grounds for a doctrine of universal salvation.[5] But from the point of view of religious pluralism, the issue takes a different form. It is no longer specifically a question of the fate of non-Christians, but of the fate of Christians and everyone else alike. Will all, or some, or none of the human race—whether they be Christian, Buddhist, Muslim, or humanist—eventually reach their final fulfillment in relation to the divine Reality? In my view, the cosmic optimism of the great traditions—their proclamation that a limitlessly better existence is available to all because it is rooted in the ultimate structure of reality—strongly suggests that all will in the end, perhaps after many lives in many worlds, attain to this. But the point to stress is that this is distinct from the issue of religious pluralism as such. Pluralism maintains that the question of limited or universal salvation/liberation applies equally to the people of all religions and even to those without one. It is not, as traditional orthodoxy holds, a different question for Christians as opposed to others.

---

[5]John Hick, *Death and Eternal Life* (1976; reprint, London: Macmillan, 1985; Louisville: Westminster/John Knox, 1994), ch. 13.

PLURALISM AS A PHILOSOPHICAL EXPLANATION OF RELIGIOUS PHENOMENA

This pluralist picture raises immense questions. How can we understand the situation of a plurality of great religious traditions that conceive and experience the Ultimate, the Real, in such different ways with such different and incompatible belief systems, but which nevertheless seem to be more or less equally effective contexts of human salvation/liberation?

Some will be content just to acknowledge that this is apparently how things are, without seeking to make intellectual sense of it. But the philosophically minded will want to understand the situation. And I suggest that philosophically the answer lies in an epistemological principle that was propounded long ago by Thomas Aquinas when he wrote, "Things known are in the knower according to the mode of the knower."[6] That is to say, the human mind is not a passive screen on which the world imprints itself. On the contrary, it is continuously involved in interpreting the data of perception in terms of the conceptual systems within which we live. In other words, the perceived world is partly, but only partly, constructed by the activity of perception. There is a reality there, but the form in which we are conscious of it comes from ourselves. This is the critical realist epistemology.

Thus, we must distinguish between the world as it is in itself, unperceived, and that same world as humanly perceived. For example, what I am conscious of as the continuous, brown, hard, heavy surface of my desk, which makes a sound when I bang it, is, according to the physicists, a region of mostly empty space within which infinitesimally minute packets of discharging energy are moving about at immense speed. These "particles"—currently identified as "quarks"—do not have color, weight, hardness, sound, or fixed position. But for a human perceiver, located where we are on the macro-micro scale and endowed with our particular kind of perceptual machinery and conceptual systems, the physical world appears as it does. It must be something very different for a microbe, or a horse, or a bird, or a fish. We therefore have to distinguish, as Immanuel

---

[6]Thomas Aquinas, *Summa Theologica*, II/II, Q. 1, art. 2.

Kant did, between a thing as it is in itself and that thing as humanly perceived—that is, as phenomenon. This understanding of our cognitive situation is well supported today not only by strong epistemological considerations, but also by research in cognitive psychology and the sociology of knowledge.

If, then, it is a general truth about the human mind that we become aware of our environment and are able to act and react appropriately within it through a continuous interpretive activity, this will also be true of religious awareness. We must expect there to be a human contribution to the forms in which we are aware of our ultimate environment, the universal presence of the Divine. To apply Aquinas' insight, the ultimate Reality is known in accordance with the cognitive mode/nature/state of the knower; and this varies, in the case of religious awareness, from one religio-cultural totality to another. If, then, we distinguish between the Real/Ultimate/Divine in itself and that Reality as humanly perceived, recognizing that there is a range of modes of human cognition, we can at once see how there is a plurality of religious traditions constituting different, but apparently more or less equally salvific, human responses to the Ultimate. These are the great world faiths.

THE REAL IN ITSELF AND AS EXPERIENCED BY HUMANS

I have been using a variety of terms—the Ultimate, the Real, the Transcendent, Ultimate Reality—where normally in Christian discourse we would simply say God. From this point on I will use the term "the Real," partly because it conforms to our Christian way of thinking of God as that which alone is fully and absolutely real, but also because it corresponds sufficiently to the Sanscrit *sat* and the Arabic *al Haqq*. For when we acknowledge the other great world religions as different but, so far as we can tell, more or less equally effective contexts of salvation/liberation, we have to think beyond the anthropomorphic God-figure of theistic piety. We have to recognize, with virtually all the greatest Christian thinkers, that the reality we call God exceeds the scope of human thought. Thus one of the Church Fathers, Gregory of Nyssa, insisted that no human words or ideas can grasp the *ousia* of God. He wrote:

The simplicity of the True Faith assumes God to be that which He is, namely, incapable of being grasped by any term, or any idea, or any other device of our apprehension, remaining beyond the reach not only of human but of angelic and all supramundane intelligence, unthinkable, unutterable, above all expression in words, having but one name that can represent His proper nature, the single name being "Above Every Name."[7]

Augustine declared that "God transcends even the mind."[8] Anselm defined God as that than which no greater can be thought, adding that God is even "something greater than can be thought."[9] If we think we know what God is, then what we are thinking of is not God! Thomas Aquinas echoed this when he wrote that "then only do we know God truly when we believe him to be above everything that it is possible to think about him," and "by its immensity the divine substance surpasses every form that our intellect reaches."[10]

Other classic Christian thinkers who have said essentially the same include Lactantius, Dionysius the Areopagite, John Scotus Erigena, St. John of the Cross, and the writer of the *Theologia Germanica*. Martin Luther, who once said that he owed more to the *Theologia Germanica* than to any other book apart from the Bible and Augustine's works, rejected attempts to know God's essence in distinction from God's purpose, that is, God in relation to us. God is *deus absconditus*, the hidden God, in God's own infinite nature. Karl Barth, in the twentieth century, likewise stressed the absoluteness and transcendence of God when he spoke of God as the "Wholly Other." And Paul Tillich spoke of "the God above the God of theism," echoing Meister Eckhart's distinction between the Godhead (*deitas*) and God (*deus*).

This apophatic strand running through Christianity from the earliest times is the basis within our own tradition for a distinction that also occurs in all of the other great world faiths. In its Christian form it is the distinction between God *a se*, God in God's eternal self-existent reality, "prior to" and independent of the creation, and God *pro nobis*, God in relation to humankind

---

[7]Gregory of Nyssa, *Against Eunomius*, 1.42.

[8]St. Augustine, *De Vera Religione*, 36.67.

[9]St. Anselm, *Proslogion*, 15.

[10]Thomas Aquinas, *Summa contra Gentiles*, 1.5.3.; 1.14.3.

as our creator, redeemer, and inspirer. Our Christian theologies are perforce concerned with God as known to us, acknowledging that God in God's own infinite being lies beyond the range of our finite thought. The Catholic thinker Nicholas of Cusa in the fifteenth century developed some of the implications of this when he wrote:

> As creator, God is three and one; as infinite, he is neither three nor one nor any of the things which can be spoken. For the names which are attributed to God are taken from creatures, since he in himself is ineffable and beyond everything that can be named or spoken.[11]

I mentioned that this distinction between, on the one hand, the Real *a se*—or in Kant's German *an sich*, or, using the neuter, "in itself" (which the English language requires if we are to avoid speaking of the Real as either male or female)—and, on the other hand, the Real as humanly known, occurs within all the major traditions. The great Jewish philosopher Maimonides distinguished between the essence and the manifestations of God; and both Jewish and Muslim mystics have distinguished between *Ein Sof* (the Infinite) in Jewish Kabbalah or *al Haqq* (the Real) in Islamic Sufism, and the self-revealing God of the Hebrew Bible or the Qur'an. The Taoist scripture, the *Tao Te Ching*, begins by declaring that "the Tao that can be expressed is not the eternal Tao." In Hindu thought the distinction is between *nirguna* Brahman (i.e., Brahman without attributes as beyond the range of human conceptuality) and *saguna* Brahman (i.e., Brahman as humanly experienced as a personal God). And in the Mahayana Buddhist tradition there is the distinction in the Trikaya doctrine between the Dharmakaya (the ultimate, absolute, ineffable reality that cannot be expressed in human thought forms) and the Sambhogakaya (consisting of the heavenly Buddha figures that incarnate within human history as the Nirmanakaya). In its generic form the distinction is between the Real as it is in itself and the Real as variously humanly conceived and experienced as the personal God-figures and the nonpersonal "absolutes" of the world religions.

The pluralistic hypothesis, offered as a religious understanding of religion around the world and across the centuries,

---

[11]Nicholas of Cusa, *De Pace Fidei*, 7.21.

is based on this distinction, together with the epistemological principle that there is an interpretive contribution to all human cognition. The hypothesis is that in order to account for the existence of the different religio-cultural totalities that we call, in rough historical order, Hinduism, Judaism, Buddhism, Taoism, Confucianism, African primal religion, Christianity, Islam, Sikhism, as apparently more or less equally effective contexts of salvation/liberation, we have to postulate an ultimate transcendent reality, the source and ground of everything, that is in itself beyond the scope of human conceptuality but is variously conceived, therefore variously experienced, and therefore variously responded to in life, from within these different religious totalities.

A qualification has to be made to the idea of the Real *an sich* as the ultimate reality that is ineffable in that it transcends our human thought forms. This is that purely formal statements can be made even about the ineffable—such as, for example, that it is ineffable! But this is a logical triviality. We cannot attribute to the Real *a se* any intrinsic attributes, such as being personal or nonpersonal, good or evil, purposive or nonpurposive, substance or process, even one or many, though the limitations of our language compel us to speak of it in the singular rather than the plural. For example, we are not affirming that the Real is impersonal by denying that it is in itself personal. This polarity of concepts simply does not apply to it, and likewise with the other polarities. Our systems of human concepts cannot encompass the ultimately Real. It is only as humanly thought and experienced that the Real fits into our human categories.

How then can we worship the Real, if it is beyond all human characterization? The answer is that we do not worship the Real in itself but always one or other of its manifestations to humanity—as the heavenly Parent of Jesus' teaching, or as the Qur'anic Allah, or as the Adonai (the Lord) of rabbinic Judaism, or as Vishnu, or as Shiva, or as *pratitya samutpada* (for one who orients oneself in meditation towards Nirvana in nontheistic Buddhism), or as the universal Buddha nature (*sunyata*). Or in nontheistic advaitic Hinduism one orients oneself in meditation to the universal reality of Brahman, which in the depths of our being we all are. These are all ways of referring to the ultimate reality, to awaken to which is peace and joy and compassionate kindness towards all life. In other words, the pluralistic hypothesis is not a new religion seeking to supplant the existing religions. It is a philosophical interpretation of the global religious situation. It leaves each tradition as it is, though opening it in dialogue with other traditions to both mutual criticism and mutual enrichment. Acceptance of some form of the pluralistic view does, however, make a difference that is more important to some traditions than others; for it prompts each to deemphasize and eventually winnow out that aspect of its self-understanding that entails a claim to unique superiority among the religions of the world.

IMPLICATIONS OF PLURALISM FOR CHRISTIANITY

What does this pluralistic hypothesis involve for Christianity? It is here, and also in Islam, that the claim to unique superiority is most deeply rooted in the belief-system, and where the pluralistic vision is therefore most challenging and most troublesome. And for this reason it is difficult, if not impossible, to avoid giving offense to conservative believers and to appear to be undermining faith and even, in the eyes of some ultraconservatives, doing the work of the devil. I can only say that having once been within that thought world, I can appreciate its fears. I have, however, discovered that there is nothing to fear in a greater openness to God's presence within the religious life of all humankind; on the contrary, there is a release from an artificially restricted vision into a greater intellectual honesty and realism and a more mature Christian faith.

As I have been suggesting, conservatives' claims regarding the unique superiority of Christianity are belied by the observable facts. But in what way does conservative theology entail the unique superiority of Christianity? Traditional orthodoxy says that Jesus of Nazareth was God incarnate—that is, God the Son, the Second Person of a divine Trinity, incarnate—who became man to die for the sins of the world and who founded the church to proclaim this to the ends of the earth, so that all who sincerely take Jesus as their Lord and Savior are justified by his atoning death and will inherit eternal life. It follows from this that Christianity, alone among the world religions, was founded by God in person. God came down from heaven to earth and launched the salvific movement that came to be known as Christianity. From this premise it seems obvious that God must wish all human beings to enter this new stream of saved life, so that Christianity shall supersede all the other world faiths. They may perhaps have some good in them and be able to function to some extent as a preparation for the gospel, but nevertheless Christianity alone is God's own religion, offering a fullness of life that no other tradition can provide; it is therefore divinely intended for all men and women without exception.

All this follows logically from the central dogma of the deity of Jesus. And the other traditionally central doctrines of Trinity and Atonement in turn follow logically from this one. For when God was on earth as Jesus Christ, there was at the same time God in heaven; and when we add the Holy Spirit—which was not, however, distinguished in the earliest strata of the New Testament from the spirit of Jesus and was not originally hypostatized as a third entity—we have the Trinity. The traditional Atonement doctrines, whether the early ransom theory, the later Catholic satisfaction theory, or the Reformed penal-substitutionary theory, presuppose the deity of Jesus. Thus the three pillars of traditional orthodoxy inevitably come under criticism in any attempt to develop our theology in the light of the realization that Christianity is not the one and only salvific path, but is one among others.

To revise the traditional doctrine of the Incarnation is thus, by implication, to revise also the traditional Trinity and Atonement doctrines. This has in fact already been effected in the minds of many Christians, quite independently of the pressures of religious pluralism. Many have found that they can love, revere, and seek to follow Jesus of Nazareth as he is known to us through the New Testament documents, without having to believe that he was literally God incarnate. For there are two main problems with the traditional dogma.[12]

The first problem is that the historical Jesus did not teach this doctrine. It is a creation of the church, one that Jesus himself would probably have regarded as blasphemous. Here we are on the edge of the "bottomless pit" of biblical interpretation, for virtually nothing that any scholar has said in this field has

---

[12]There is an extensive literature about this, some of which I have summarized in *The Metaphor of God Incarnate*.

remained uncontradicted by some other scholar. We must, however, distinguish between biblical fundamentalists, who hold to the verbal inerrancy of the Bible, and mainstream biblical scholars, such as those teaching in academically accredited universities and colleges. For fundamentalists, the Incarnation issue can be settled by such texts as "I and the Father are one" (John 10:30) and "He who has seen me has seen the Father" (John 14:9); and the pluralism issue by such texts as "I am the way, and the truth, and the life; no one comes to the Father, but by me" (John 14:6). But among mainline New Testament scholars, both conservative and liberal, Catholic and Protestant, there is today a general consensus that these are not pronouncements of the historical Jesus but words put into his mouth some sixty or seventy years later by a Christian writer expressing the theology that had developed in his part of the expanding church. To create speeches in this way for famous or revered figures of the past, embodying the writer's sense of the real significance of that past figure, was standard practice in the ancient world; and the discourses attributed to Jesus in the Fourth Gospel are seen today by most contemporary scholarship as examples of this.

However, not everyone within the evangelical wing of Christianity is aware of this. Therefore, I shall quote from one or two conservative New Testament scholars who wholeheartedly believe in the Incarnation doctrine but who acknowledge that it was not taught by Jesus himself. C. F. D. Moule, a pillar of orthodox Christology, wrote, "Any case for a 'high' Christology that depended on the authenticity of the alleged claims of Jesus about himself, especially in the Fourth Gospel, would indeed be precarious."[13] The late Archbishop of Canterbury, Michael Ramsay, another pillar of orthodoxy and, like Moule, a New Testament scholar, wrote, "Jesus did not claim deity for himself," and, "The title 'Son of God' need not of itself be of high significance, for in Jewish circles it might mean no more than the Messiah or indeed the whole Israelite nation, and in popular Hellenism there were many sons of God, meaning inspired holy men."[14] Professor James Dunn, a distinguished conservative New Testament

---

[13]C. F. D. Moule, *The Origins of Christology* (Cambridge: Cambridge Univ. Press, 1977), 136.

[14]Michael Ramsay, *Jesus and the Living Past* (Oxford: Oxford Univ. Press, 1980), 39, 43.

scholar who defends an orthodox Christology, concludes in a widely used book on Christian origins that "there was no real evidence in the earliest Jesus tradition of what could fairly be called a consciousness of divinity."[15]

This judgment is today so generally accepted that conservative theologians defending the traditional incarnation doctrine now accept it among the basic data of which they must take account. Thus Canon Brian Hebblethwaite, in a major defense of the traditional incarnation doctrine, acknowledges that "it is no longer possible to defend the divinity of Jesus by referring to the claims of Jesus."[16] And Professor David Brown, another conservative theologian, writes that "there is good evidence to suggest that [Jesus] himself never saw himself as a suitable object of worship," and that it is "impossible to base any claim for Christ's divinity on his consciousness once we abandon the traditional portrait as reflected in a literal understanding of St. John's Gospel."[17]

That Jesus himself did not claim to be God cuts the ground from under the feet of the old apologetic—which I myself used effectively several times as an evangelical student at Edinburgh—that one who claims to be God must be either mad, or bad, or God, and that since Jesus was obviously neither mad nor bad he must have been God. For it now seems clear that Jesus did not claim to be God. Upholders of a literal incarnation doctrine have thus had to retreat from a dominical authority for their belief to the highly debatable argument that Jesus' words and actions *implicitly* claim deity. Certainly Jesus declared God's forgiveness to individuals, as indeed priests and ministers do. And according to Mark, he said that "the Son of Man has authority on earth to forgive sins" (Mark 2:10); but while there are various theories concerning the meaning of "Son of Man," none of them suggests that he is more than either an intermediary being or simply a son of man, that is, a man.

---

[15]James Dunn, *Christology in the Making* (Louisville: Westminster/John Knox, 1980 / London: SCM, 1980), 60.

[16]Brian Hebblethwaite, *The Incarnation* (Cambridge: Cambridge Univ. Press, 1987), 74.

[17]David Brown, *The Divine Trinity* (LaSalle, Ill.: Open Court, 1985 / London: Duckworth, 1985), 108.

The first problem about the traditional incarnation doctrine, then, is that Jesus did not teach it and that the suggestion that he implied it is highly debatable. It is precarious to base one's faith on a debatable interpretation of ancient texts. So the question has to be faced: On what ground can we properly claim to know who Jesus was better than he knew himself?

The second problem is that it has not proved possible, after some fifteen centuries of intermittent effort, to give any clear meaning to the idea that Jesus had two complete natures, one human and the other divine. The paradoxical character of the idea is evident. In order to be genuinely and fully human Jesus must have had all the attributes that are definitive of humanity, and in order to be genuinely and fully God he must also have had all the attributes that are definitive of deity. It is relatively easy to say what the essential divine attributes are, according to Christian theology. They include being the eternal, uncreated, self-existent creator of everything other than God; being omnipotent; being omniscient; being omnipresent; being a spirit, without a body; and being infinite in such moral qualities as goodness, love, justice, mercy, and wisdom. A being who lacks any of these attributes is not fully God. The essential human attributes are less easy to list, since we have no orthodox anthropology corresponding to the orthodox theology. But these attributes presumably include being or having a human body with a specific location, and thus not omnipresent; being a creature, and thus not the creator of everything other than God; being limited in power, and thus not omnipotent; being limited in knowledge, and thus not omniscient; and having moral qualities in a finite, not an infinite, degree.

The question, then, that has so vexed theology and that has never been satisfactorily answered, is how a historical individual, Jesus of Nazareth, could have both sets of attributes at once, and indeed, whether we really want to claim that he did. Consider, for example, omniscience. Do we really want to say that the historical Jesus had the infinite knowledge that God has and only pretended ignorance, as in Matthew 24:36? And even if we do want to say this, is it really possible for infinite knowledge to be housed in a finite human brain? The number of human brain cells, although truly vast, is nevertheless finite and therefore can only contain a finite amount of information. How then could the historical Jesus be omniscient?

Again, consider omnipotence. Do we really want to claim that Jesus was literally omnipotent but pretended not to be, as in Mark 6:5? Furthermore, the historical Jesus would clearly seem from the Synoptic Gospels to have been a human creature, not the creator of the universe; to have come into existence at a certain time, rather than being eternally self-existent; and to have been limited to one place at a time, and thus not omnipresent. And while he was good, loving, wise, just, and merciful, there is an obvious problem about how a finite human being could have these qualities in an *infinite* degree.

The Council of Chalcedon (451 A.D.), which first authoritatively defined the orthodox Christology, simply asserted that Jesus Christ was "at once complete in Godhead and in humanity," and as such had two natures, divine and human, which exist "without confusion, without change, without division, without separation; the distinction of natures being in no way annulled by the union, but rather the characteristics of each nature being preserved and coming together to form one person." Thus Jesus had all the divine and all the human attributes, "the characteristics of each nature being preserved." But the Council did not say how this is possible. It insisted that Jesus was both fully human and fully divine and intended to exclude any doctrine that denied either of these, but it did not spell out what it is to be simultaneously fully human and fully divine.

The simplest possible model would be a divine mind in a human body. But this was not acceptable, because a being without a human mind would not count as a genuinely human being. More sophisticated models were attempted. For example, Apollinaris suggested that a human being consists of body, mind, and spirit, and that in the case of Jesus the mind and body were human but the spirit was the eternal Logos. But this too was rejected, because if Jesus had no human spirit he was, once again, not fully human. Many other attempts, some very ingenious, were made during the Christological controversies from about the third to the ninth centuries; but all had to be declared heretical because they failed to do justice either to Jesus' deity or to his humanity. These attempts continue today, perhaps the most interesting contemporary one being the two-minds theory of Thomas Morris and others.[18] I have criticized this elsewhere and am prepared to do so again if any of my coauthors in this book thinks that the two-minds theory is viable.[19]

Cannot all these problems, however, be avoided by the idea of divine *kenosis*, self-emptying? Can we not say, with a whole school of Christological thinking, that in becoming man, God the Son emptied himself of his divine attributes in order to become genuinely and fully human? But this kenotic theory has also been strongly criticized. Is God without the attributes of God still God? In what sense was Jesus God incarnate if he lacked the characteristics in virtue of which God is God? But perhaps we can divide the divine nature—contrary, however, to the Chalcedonian "without division"— and say that Jesus had some of the divine attributes but not others? Perhaps God the Son divested himself of such attributes as self-existence, omnipotence, omniscience, and omnipresence, but retained such other attributes as goodness, love, wisdom, mercy, and justice? It would, of course, need to be explained how a self-existent being can ever cease to be self-existent. But even if that could be made clear, the idea of half-divinity still has major problems. For the divine moral attributes are infinite, and how can infinite qualities be embodied in a finite human being? A finite being *cannot* have infinite attributes. We would have to say instead that Jesus embodied *as much* of the infinite divine moral qualities as could be expressed in a finite human life—rather than that "in him the whole fullness of deity dwells bodily" (Col. 2:9).

A PLURALIST PROPOSAL REGARDING THE INCARNATION AND JESUS

But this reduction of deity is barely distinguishable from the "liberal" understanding of Jesus as a man who was so open to God's presence and so responsive to God's will that God was able to act on earth through him and could thus be said to have been "incarnate" in his actions. Here incarnation is a metaphor, as in "Abraham Lincoln incarnated the spirit of American

---

[18]Thomas V. Morris, *The Logic of God Incarnate* (Ithaca, N.Y.: Cornell Univ. Press, 1986).

[19]John Hick, *The Metaphor of God Incarnate*, ch. 5.

independence" or "Hitler was evil incarnate." And in this metaphorical sense we can say that insofar as any human being does God's will, God is "incarnated," embodied, in a human action. Whenever anyone acts in love on behalf of the sick in body or mind, the weak and oppressed, refugees, vulnerable children, the exploited poor, or the bereaved and grieving, there God's love becomes incarnate on earth.

Thus, on the one hand, the idea of Jesus being God incarnate has no acceptable literal meaning, or at least none that has yet been discovered. On the other hand, it does have a powerful metaphorical meaning, in that Jesus was so open to divine inspiration, so responsive to the divine spirit, so obedient to God's will, that God was able to act on earth in and through him. This, I believe, is the true Christian doctrine of incarnation.

The kind of Trinitarian doctrine that is compatible with such a Christology is one in which the three "Persons" are not persons in our modern sense of three centers of consciousness and will, but in the ancient sense in which a *persona* is a role that someone plays. (On the Roman stage, a *persona* was a mask that an actor used to indicate his role in the play.) Thus the three "persons" are three ways in which the one God is experienced as acting in relation to humankind—as creator, as transformer or redeemer, and as inner spirit. And no Atonement doctrine, in the sense of a theory about how God has been enabled to forgive our sins by the death of Jesus, is required, because Jesus taught us in the Lord's Prayer to approach God directly as our heavenly Father, and to ask for and expect to receive divine forgiveness without any mediator or atoning sacrifice.

Again, in his parable of the prodigal son, Jesus taught us that God freely forgives and accepts those who truly repent. When the erring son returns in deep penitence, his father does not say, "Because I am a just as well as a loving father, I cannot forgive you until your sin has been fully atoned for," but "his father saw him and had compassion, and ran and embraced and kissed him . . . [and said], 'Let us eat and make merry; for this my son was dead, and is alive again; he was lost, and is found'" (Luke 15:20, 23–24). In the story of the Pharisees and the tax collector, the latter "standing far off, would not even lift up his eyes to heaven, but beat his breast, saying, 'God, be merciful to me a sinner.'" Jesus then said, "I tell you, this man went down to his house justified rather than the other" (Luke 18:13–14). And yet again, there is Jesus' insistence that he came to bring sinners to a penitent acceptance of God's mercy: "Go and learn what this means, 'I desire mercy, and not sacrifice'" (Matt. 9:13).

Unlike the traditional doctrines, all this is compatible with religious pluralism. We can see Jesus as the one who has made God real to us, who has shown us how to live as citizens of God's kingdom, who is our revered spiritual leader, inspiration, and model. We can do this without having to deny that other spiritual leaders and other revelatory histories function in the same way and to the same extent (so far as we can tell) for other people within other religious traditions.

RESPONSE TO JOHN HICK

Clark H. Pinnock

John Hick is the scholarly author of many excellent books on various aspects of the philosophy of religion and religious pluralism. All my life I have admired him as an effective communicator of profound theological ideas. This essay does not add anything new in his thinking about religious pluralism but rather reports those ideas in a chatty way to a conservative readership. In his choosing to tell the story of his own pilgrimage, we learn the truth he has discovered through narrative.

I would not be honest if I did not express a little annoyance that I felt by his testimonial about how he successfully escaped the evangelical faith. As an evangelical myself, I ordinarily like testimonies but do not like being talked down to. I received the distinct feeling that the reason he wants us to know he was once an evangelical is to make liberals of us all and that he is using his chapter to this end. I suppose it touched a nerve in me because I too, converted by evangelicals from bland liberalism and genuinely sympathetic with Hick's early concerns about getting serious about the universal salvific will of God, have not found his recent moves so helpful. On the contrary, I look upon his recent direction with sadness as I contemplate the loss to God's kingdom of a theologian who could be commending God's plan to save the world through Jesus effectively but who has decided not to.

The fateful turning point in Hick's life came in Birmingham, where he had positive experiences with people of other faiths that turned him toward an ideology of pluralism, which postulates an unknown God behind all the religions. He has seemingly changed his whole theology on the basis of meeting saintly members of other faiths. Ironically, Hick could just as easily have sustained a high doctrine of Christ by opting for inclusivism on the basis of this experience. An inclusivist can see God's grace at work in other people's religious lives—saintliness is not a sufficient argument for pluralism. The holy pagans of the Old Testament, like Job and Melchizedek, prove that the God of Israel operates in the lives of those outside the covenant with Abraham. I have no difficulty, for example, accepting the fact that there are holy people in other faiths—my inclusivism leads me to expect that. But it does not lead me to radical theological revision. His own telling of the story shows readers where he made his mistake. He had an experience of saintliness and misinterpreted the theological significance of it. He drew radical conclusions that the experience simply did not require.

THE MORAL PARITY OF THE RELIGIONS?

From that point on, Hick tries to turn his discussion into a logical argument. The first argument is that religions seem equally good at producing morally and spiritually good people and must therefore be presumed to operate on the basis of the same sanctifying divine Power. Every religion produces saints, so it doesn't really matter what one believes about God. What about this argument?

First, as Hick says, some will disagree with this estimate. How do we know that other faiths transform sinners as effectively as Jesus Christ? What exactly is saintliness anyway? Is it a life of service to the poor or a life of other-worldly contemplation? Hick can be so vague. I look and see blessings such as universal human rights, the demythologizing of the state, the care of the sick and the poor, the importance of preserving the earth, and the ideal of self-giving service, and I notice that it is mostly the fruit of the Christian gospel and possibly proof of its superior sanctifying power. Eastern religions seem to produce stagnant societies, and Islam, intolerant ones.

Second, even if Hick is right about the equity of transformative power, it would not settle the truth question. Mormons are nice people as a whole, but that does not make Mormon theology and history true. There are other tests for truth we would want to apply. There is no need to rush to rash metaphysical conclusions on the basis of sanctity alone.

Third, Hick says that it doesn't matter what you think as long as you act morally, as if beliefs and behavior were not more closely linked than that. It makes a big difference if one believes salvation is release from the karmic cycle, or if the poor are getting what they deserve for previous lives, or if evil is an illusion, or if the material world is of no importance. Ironically, what Hick as a Western liberal probably wants is the kind of social activism agenda favored by the politically correct. But most world theologies do not give the ground or support for that. Being a liberal Christian sustains Hick's ideal of saintliness best.

THE UNKNOWN REAL

In a second argument, Hick leaps to the conclusion that all religions are human responses to the Ultimate. Since they all produce saints, he assumes that there is an unknowable ultimate Reality behind them. Why not consider God to be an undifferentiated unity beyond any specific designation? This is certainly possible, but questions arise.

First, while claiming to be a view of God that transcends all the culturally generated models of God in the world's religions, it is in fact a truth claim familiar to the Eastern monistic traditions. This means that it is a claim every bit as *particular* as the Christian one, which sounds covertly imperialistic. Second, how does Hick know that the Real exists and that it is unknowable? Has this been revealed to him? Third, even if there exists a Real, we have no idea what it might be like. Does it love us or hate us, or is it sleeping? It strikes me as a bad deal to trade in the God of Jesus for an unknown God. Such a trade would make it impossible to identify as evil religions that are really false and demonic.

A better solution would be to keep the truth question open rather than to fall into agnosticism. In science one does not give up trying to figure out what is out there just because people do not agree about it. Let's keep the truth question in play and share with each other what we have found to be true. This would also allow the Christian mission to go forward.

CHRISTOLOGY

Hick's third argument relates to Christology. He wants Christians to value the metaphor of God incarnate but not suppose there actually is a divine Logos that became flesh. Let them understand Jesus as embodying the ideal of a human life lived in faithful response to God and in which God was active. Let them value this faith as one of a number of human responses to God. He says that this would better serve the cause of world peace and inter-religious dialogue.

Hick wants to leave the impression that his Christology is based primarily upon historical (i.e., Jesus did not teach this doctrine) and theological (i.e., it never did make sense) considerations. It seems more likely that this analysis is a rationalization of the position his system requires. Readers have been told that Hick made his move to pluralism before the problem of Jesus was solved. He had already reached the conviction that there *cannot be* a definitive revelation of salvation if the equality of religions on the basis of an unknown Real is to be maintained. A belief in the Incarnation and Trinity would spoil everything. Therefore, the effort to get rid of the Incarnation has less to do with evidence than with the ideology. Be clear—for Hick, Jesus *cannot be* more than an inspiring example, whatever the evidence is! The bias against the Incarnation is invincible going in.

At the same time, Hick is a good scholar and launches a strong critique that cannot just be dismissed. *The Metaphor of God Incarnate* is a very challenging book. Let me make a few comments. First, did Jesus teach the doctrine of the Incarnation? The answer partly depends on which biblical critics you believe. Skeptics such as those in the "Jesus Seminar" discard all evidence for Jesus' claim and for his bodily resurrection. N. T. Wright and Richard B. Hayes, on the other hand, do not. I would say that the claim of Jesus underlies and authenticates what later came to be known as the doctrine of Incarnation.

Second, does the doctrine possess clear meaning? The answer partly depends on how far one expects human reason to go in explaining the mystery of God incarnate. I would not expect it to be made rational without remainder. For me kenotic Christology comes the closest to explaining it, though it does not eliminate a dimension of mystery. After all, the Incarnation is a gift of the divine freedom.

Third, does the Anselmian soteriology built around the Incarnation in Western theology add up? No, it does not, and Hick himself points to a better way when he refers to early Greek theologians who saw the work of Christ as recapitulation, not appeasement.

There is no question that Hick is an intelligent critic of historic Christology. His unitive pluralism is backed up by impressive attempts to demolish traditional beliefs. The impact on me is to hope for a new generation of evangelical scholars to arise who can defend the Incarnation as effectively as Hick is able to critique it.

In Hick's mind these revisions leave Christianity untouched—he has only winnowed away non-essential beliefs that have fostered superiority. Liberalism typically thinks that way. If we could just discard the element of the gospel that the current culture dislikes, we would ensure a future for it. What actually happens is that the salt loses its savor. There is no future for liberal Christianity because it just listens to culture and has nothing to contribute. It allows itself to be led around by the nose, while ruining the churches and robbing the world of the gospel. If we follow Hick, people will no longer be told about the light of the world. They will not know that, although no one has seen God, the only Son of the Father has made him known (John 1:18). They will not learn of a new creation or of God reconciling the world to himself (2 Cor. 5:17, 19). The Christian faith should not make people feel superior—it should make them feel happiness for the nations because now there is hope and a knowledge of salvation.

RESPONSE TO JOHN HICK

Alister E. McGrath

Professor Hick's essay is lucid and articulate, and I found it easy to interact with. I particularly enjoyed reading the account of his conversion from conservative evangelicalism to liberalism, not least because my own intellectual pilgrimage was in the opposite direction. My own rejection of liberalism was partly based on my perception that it was epistemically and evidentially deficient. That, however, was not a popular thing to say back in the 1970s, when I recall evangelical approaches to Christology being dismissed in a somewhat ungracious manner by many academics at both Oxford and Cambridge Universities. It needs to be made clear that it is unfair to dismiss evangelical Christologies on the basis of a sweeping claim, such as "Jesus did not claim to be God." I think Professor Hick is here falling victim to the tendency to caricature, perhaps through a lack of familiarity with the enormous growth in serious evangelical academic writing since 1980, now so helpfully documented in the field of Christology by Douglas Jacobsen and Frederick Schmidt.[1]

THE DECISIVENESS OF CHRISTOLOGY

Modern evangelical approaches to Christology draw on theological techniques such as those deployed by Wolfhart

---

[1]Douglas Jacobsen and Frederick Schmidt, "Behind Orthodoxy and Beyond It: Recent Developments in Evangelical Christology," *Scottish Journal of Theology* 45 (1993): 515–41.

Pannenberg, Jürgen Moltmann, and Eberhard Jüngel in developing their Christologies. The results may be conservative, in the limited sense of "affirming the traditional doctrines of Christianity." The means by which they are adduced and articulated, however, are often far removed from the simplistic biblicism that Professor Hick appears to attribute to the movement. Perhaps one of the problems here is that evangelicalism has a considerable appeal to ordinary Christians, so that some evangelical theology is phrased, explained, and justified in terms that ordinary Christians can easily grasp.

The transition from biblical affirmations, often stated in the form of narratives, to doctrinal affirmations, often stated in metaphysical language, is complex and highly nuanced, as I point out in my 1990 Bampton Lectures at Oxford University; yet it is certainly legitimate to proceed in this direction.[2] I found myself wondering if Professor Hick's curiously misdirected attack on evangelical Christology at this point might be the symptom of a deep lack of familiarity with the movement, perhaps extrapolating from his boyhood memories to the present day. His hopelessly outdated attempt to pit "biblical fundamentalists" against "mainstream biblical scholars," as if these were two nonoverlapping entities, shows how seriously he is out of touch with the situation in, for example, both British and North American biblical scholarship. I think, for example, of Tom Wright's highly acclaimed study of New Testament Christology.[3] Even Hick's use of the term "fundamentalism" harks back to the certainties of a liberal golden age in the 1960s and 1970s. Things have changed! I found myself wondering if Professor Hick knew that "evangelicalism" and "fundamentalism" are now defined differently; his approach rather suggests that he identifies them.[4]

At any rate, I found his criticism of evangelicalism at this central and crucial point to be tired, uninformed, and weary, and I wondered exactly whom he was criticizing. Professor Hick

---

[2]Alister E. McGrath, *The Genesis of Doctrine* (Oxford: Blackwell, 1990).

[3]Tom Wright, *The New Testament and the People of God* (London: SPCK / Minneapolis: Fortress, 1992).

[4]See Alister McGrath, *Evangelicalism and the Future of Christianity* (Downers Grove, Ill.: InterVarsity / London: Hodder & Stoughton, 1994), for details of the distinction.

does not favor us by naming specific evangelicals who hold the views or approaches he dislikes; theological debate is not advanced by anonymous stereotyped generalizations. If he wants to argue with a named modern evangelical Christology, he can argue with the approach I set out in my Bampton Lectures. This would be of value, both to myself and to a wider audience.

But this criticism must be set alongside an appreciation of Professor Hick's identification of Christology as a major issue. In the end, approaches to religious pluralism are Christologically determined. Who Jesus Christ is has a controlling influence over one's approach to the issue of Christianity and the other religions. The issue is *not* about morality. As it happens, I do not think Christians are automatically morally superior to other people. But any such argument rests on the supposition that there exists a universally valid moral framework, which allows us to judge individual morality in this way. Perhaps one of the most interesting things about living in our postmodern times is that the idea of a universal morality has been abandoned.

The crucial issue concerns the identity of Jesus Christ. If he is just someone like us, then he may fairly be placed in the category of "good religious teachers." But I see no evidence of this categorization in the New Testament or the early Christian tradition. Jesus is different. That does not automatically mean that he is superior—that follows only from another discussion, which must follow in its wake. But we ought to allow orthodox Christianity to be heard at this point: Jesus Christ is seen by Christians to be different to other religious teachers. The question is: On what is that distinctiveness grounded, how is it expressed, and what are its consequences? Any discussion that pretends that Christians think otherwise about Jesus Christ can fairly be criticized as resting on a distorted and inauthentic understanding of Christianity.

I also wonder whether Professor Hick has made some rather ambitious assumptions about the category of "religion." I have been struck by some words of John Cobb, a pioneer of Christian-Buddhist dialogue:

> I see no a priori reason to assume that religion has an essence or that the great religious traditions are well understood as religions, that is, as traditions for which

being religious is the central goal. I certainly see no empirical evidence in favor of this view. I see only scholarly habit and the power of language to mislead. I call for a pluralism that allows each religious tradition to define its own nature and purposes and the role of religious elements within it.[5]

This, it seems to me, is the crucial point: to treat belief systems with integrity.

THE SUPERIORITY OF CHRISTIANITY

My most serious cause for concern relates to Professor Hick's critique of any claim to "superiority" on the part of Christianity. This is a highly loaded and emotive term, one that is potentially misleading. Anyone who argues that a Christian is, by virtue of his or her faith, *morally* superior to a Confucian is open to serious criticism. But that is only one sense of the term. When I was undertaking my doctoral research in molecular biology at Oxford University, I was frequently confronted with a number of theories offering to explain a given observation. In the end, I had to make a judgment concerning which of them possessed the greatest internal consistency, the greatest degree of correspondence to the data of empirical observation, and the greatest degree of predictive ability. Unless I was to abandon any possibility of advance in understanding, I was obliged to make such a judgment. In suggesting that one theory was "superior" to another, I was making no judgment concerning its morality or the morality of those who believed it to be correct. I was simply declaring that it did not fit the empirical data as well as the others, and therefore it seemed a less reliable framework for understanding our experience of the world. I assume that Professor Hick would be prepared to speak of the "superiority" of pluralism in this respect, in that he thinks it makes better sense of the world's religions than other approaches. I would claim the right to speak of the "superiority" of Christianity in this explicative sense. The introduction of a moral dimension at this point merely confuses an important argument.

---

[5]John B. Cobb Jr., "Beyond Pluralism," in G. D'Costa, ed., *Christian Uniqueness Reconsidered: The Myth of a Pluralistic Theology of Religions* (Maryknoll, N.Y.: Orbis, 1990), 84.

Professor Hick argues that it is "not possible to establish the unique moral superiority of any one of the great world religions." That is true, in part because no universal moral framework exists by which such a public and universal judgment can be made; the collapse of the credibility of the Enlightenment worldview has seen to that. But the argument is not about morality. For example, the scientific debate back in the 1950s about the macromolecular structure of DNA did not take place on the basis of which of the various alternatives (e.g., that of the late Linus Pauling) was morally superior, nor which of the investigating teams were nicer people. The simple, relentless, and correct question was this: Which model approximates most closely to what is, and can be, known of the situation?

Professor Hick appears to wish us to avoid making any such judgment, in effect declaring that "religions" (in this curious and undefined sense of the term) stand outside any attempt to verify or falsify them. Much the same applies to his own theory, which seems to me to rest on spurious evidential foundations and is incapable of either verification or falsification. There is clearly a double standard being used here: a severely critical approach to traditional Christian evidential claims, and a much less critical approach to the pluralist hypothesis. Professor Hick himself suggests that the obvious differences between the world "religions" are due to their different perceptions of "the Real." Yet no empirical evidence of any substance has been offered for this assertion. It makes just as much sense to say that the religions are different and should be respected for that—or that some are simply wrong. Lesslie Newbigin, commenting on the views of Wilfred Cantwell Smith, makes much the same point:

> It is clear that in Smith's view "The Transcendent" is a purely formal category. He, she, or it may be conceived in any way that the worshipper may choose. There can therefore be no such thing as false or misdirected worship, since the reality to which it is directed is unknowable. Smith quotes as "one of the theologically most discerning remarks that I know" the words of the *Yogavasistha:* "Thou art formless. Thy only form is our knowledge of Thee." Any claim for uniqueness made for one concept of the Transcendent, for instance the Christian claim that the Transcendent is present in fullness in Jesus

(Colossians 1:19), is to be regarded as wholly unacceptable. There are no criteria by which different concepts of
the Transcendent may be tested. We are shut up to a total
subjectivity: the Transcendent is unknowable.[6]

I do not see, on the basis of the argumentation adduced in Professor Hick's discussion, how he is immune from this criticism.

Professor Hick will probably dismiss this as philosophically
unsophisticated. But philosophy has its limits. As any historian
of the natural sciences will know, the credibility of the physics
of Renaissance Aristotelianism and of the cosmology of Hegel
was shattered by a relentless emphasis on empirical demon-
stration. Well, Professor Hick claims that all religions are different responses to or embodiments of the Real. Can he *show* me
that "Real"? Is it publicly observable, or is it the only conclusion
forced on us by such public observation? And if it is unknown,
why does he make such strong claims on its basis? Nobody can
"show" me a quark; but scientists can show me the experimental and theoretical considerations that lead to it being postulated
and accepted. Can Professor Hick demonstrate that "the Real"
is responded to or embodied in this way? He has often written of
a "Copernican Revolution" in theology. But that Revolution took
place by discrediting the older view by *public empirical observation,* which ultimately forced the rightness (or may I say "superiority"?) of that view on all.

As far as I can see, Professor Hick offers us an unknowable
"Real" as a postulated universal and generic entity behind the
phenomena of the "religions." This is highly convenient for his
evidentially-deficient hypothesis. But for more critical observers,
it confirms that the pluralist hypothesis is simply one among
many explanations of the diversity and divergence of the
world's religions. It is not superior, in any sense, to alternatives,
including any of the three evangelical approaches outlined in
this collection. In our postmodern era, I concede that it is "true
for Professor Hick" and may well have an appeal for my Bahai
friends—who certainly thought it sounded like what they
believed (although they found the terminology confusing). But
Christianity has another set of options open to it, and I happen
to find them superior.

---

[6]See Lesslie Newbigin, *The Gospel in a Pluralist Society* (Grand Rapids: Eerdmans, 1989), 159–61, 168–70.

RESPONSE TO JOHN HICK

R. Douglas Geivett and W. Gary Phillips

Much of Professor Hick's case for religious pluralism depends on his case against Christian orthodoxy. We begin with a response to his several criticisms of orthodoxy and then offer a few direct objections to the pluralistic alternative he favors.

HICK'S CRITIQUE OF ORTHODOXY

Many of Hick's complaints against orthodox Christianity fall into the category of Bible difficulties. These include phenomena reported in the Bible that conflict with our scientific knowledge of the world, biblical affirmations that conflict with our developed moral intuitions, and "numerous contradictions between this biblical text and that." Of course, there are various types of difficulties in the Bible, and a dismissive attitude toward them is unacceptable. One need not, however, ignore these difficulties or dilute the classical doctrine of biblical inerrancy. For on generally accepted principles of rationality the doctrine can be defended against alternative theories of the nature of Scripture.[1] Moreover, creative and plausible hypotheses have been

---

[1]For example, this doctrine better explains the total range of phenomena associated with the production and the content of the Bible than any alternative theory, including Hick's own. In particular, it is the best explanation for Jesus' attitude about the Bible. Also, it is not rational but irrational to abandon an independently plausible theory simply because it has encountered a handful of anomalies—even if those anomalies that Hick calls "awkward questions" are quite persistent. See J. P. Moreland, "The Rationality of Belief in Inerrancy," *Trinity Journal* n.s. (1986): 75–86; Norman L. Geisler, ed., *Inerrancy* (Grand Rapids: Zondervan, 1979).

formulated in response to many alleged errors, dispelling the quaint impression that there are demonstrable errors in the Bible.[2]

Hick's other challenges concern the historicity of the New Testament and the logic of the Incarnation. According to him, it is impossible to identify the historical Jesus with the Jesus presented in the Bible, for the New Testament portrait of Jesus is the result of layers of legendary accretions that evolved during the interval between the events of Jesus' life and the composition of the New Testament. He asserts that Jesus never claimed to be God. If he is right, then the logical status of the Incarnation is moot, for it presupposes that Jesus did regard himself as God.

The fashionable quest for the so-called historical Jesus, however, derives from prior judgments about the nature of God and his possible relation to the world of human history.[3] A complete response to the phenomenon of radical critical scholarship would require a full-dress refutation of naturalism and its baseless intrusion throughout the academy. There are, however, several ways to safeguard the historicity of the New Testament conclusion that Jesus regarded himself as God.

For example, a high Christology is discernible within the minimal core of Jesus' sayings whose authenticity is approved by radical critics themselves. Norman Perrin, a Bultmannian scholar who applied form-critical methods and the so-called criterion of dissimilarity to an analysis of the Gospels, produced a compendium of Jesus' teachings that may confidently be considered authentic.[4] Evangelical scholar Royce Gruenler has

---

[2]See, for example, John W. Haley, *An Examination of the Alleged Discrepancies of the Bible* (Nashville: B. C. Goodpasture, 1951); Gleason L. Archer, *Encyclopedia of Bible Difficulties* (Grand Rapids: Zondervan, 1982); Norman Geisler and Thomas Howe, *When Critics Ask: A Popular Handbook on Bible Difficulties* (Wheaton: Victor Books, 1992). But these problems should not divert our attention. The doctrine of the Incarnation can be supported by New Testament documents that are historically reliable, if not infallible. For the historical credibility of a narrative is not defeated by the presence of a few historical mistakes. See William Lane Craig, *Assessing the New Testament Evidence for the Historicity of the Resurrection* (Lewiston, N.Y. / Queenston, Ont.: Edwin Mellen, 1989), chs. 9–10.

[3]This is demonstrated in the book *Jesus Under Fire: Modern Scholarship Reinvents the Historical Jesus*, ed. Michael J. Wilkins and J. P. Moreland (Grand Rapids: Zondervan, 1995).

[4]See Norman Perrin, *Rediscovering the Teaching of Jesus* (New York: Harper & Row, 1967).

patiently examined each item countenanced by Perrin, paying particular attention to the way Jesus' self-concept is disclosed by his words and deeds. His conclusion is that the Christology implicit in the approved core of sayings is indistinguishable from the high Christology of the more explicit sayings attributed to Jesus throughout the Gospels and repudiated by radical critics.[5]

These critics face a dilemma. The possibility of "reconstructing the historical Jesus," the professed aim of their scholarship, depends upon the availability of a substantial body of knowledge concerning what Jesus said and did. And clearly we are dependent on the New Testament for this. Any scholar approaching these documents with a naturalistic bias will find it difficult to identify anything of historical value—anything that is useful in constructing a plausible portrait of the historical Jesus—that does not also imply a high Christological understanding on the part of Jesus. When the critic has excised all material that implies a high Christology, what remains will hardly support the solid construction of a substantive portrait of the historical Jesus.

To make a convincing case against the historicity of Jesus' claim to be God while also asserting substantive things about his *persona*, Hick must do three things. First, he must identify that core of Jesus' sayings, the authenticity of which he himself is willing to acknowledge. Second, he must rebut specific efforts to demonstrate the implicit presence of a high Christology in the sayings he countenances. It will not do for him simply to assert that any argument that Jesus' words and deeds imply a claim to deity is "highly debatable." He must debate the point.[6] Third, he must show what substantive knowledge of the historical Jesus

---

[5]See Royce Gordon Gruenler, *New Approaches to Jesus and the Gospels: A Phenomenological and Exegetical Study of Synoptic Christology* (Grand Rapids: Baker, 1982); see also David F. Wells, *The Person of Christ: A Biblical and Historical Analysis of the Incarnation* (Westchester, Ill.: Crossway, 1984), 37–43.

[6]Hick himself relies on a similar phenomenology to draw conclusions about the religious significance of Jesus. See his *An Interpretation of Religion: Human Responses to the Transcendent* (London: Macmillan, 1989), 44–46, 156–57, 216–20, 262–63, 299–300, 304, 321, 326, 332–33. Indeed, his entire appeal to the saintliness of other religious figures and the religious significance of their lives depends on just such a phenomenology.

is possible on the slender basis of the sayings he is willing to authorize. Without this it is unreasonable for him to affirm the saintliness of Jesus. But precisely this claim is essential to Hick's conception of the religious significance of Jesus and of the value of Christianity. The trouble is, everything substantive about Jesus is infused with a high Christology. Thus we hold, *pace* Hick, that Jesus did claim to be God, and we reprise the Latin refrain: *aut Deus, aut non bonus*: "Either he was God, or he was not a good man."[7]

Not only do we believe the attribution of divinity to Jesus to be central to the pre-Easter Christology, but we are hopelessly committed to the Chalcedonian formulation as well. Since Hick devotes about a fourth of his chapter to criticizing the traditional doctrine of the Incarnation, some response is in order.

Let us be clear, first, about what Hick claims. He does not say that the orthodox doctrine of the Incarnation harbors a logical contradiction.[8] He holds, rather, that it is completely lacking in religious significance because no explication of the doctrine has successfully demonstrated how Jesus Christ is or can be both genuinely and unambiguously God and genuinely and unambiguously human.[9] As he says, "It is logically permissible to believe anything that is not self-contradictory; nevertheless, not everything that is not self-contradictory makes good religious sense."[10] Since a literal interpretation of the Incarnation fails the

---

[7]That is, if Jesus was not God, he was either morally retrograde or extraordinarily dysfunctional, if not both.

[8]Hick is partially to blame for the confusion he attributes to others in this regard, for he compares the traditional statement, "the historical Jesus of Nazareth was also God," with the locution "this circle drawn with a pencil on paper is also a square," and asserts that the former is "as devoid of meaning" as the latter. See his "Jesus and the World Religions," in *The Myth of God Incarnate*, ed. John Hick (London: SCM, 1977), 178. But the latter is not devoid of meaning. It is, rather, necessarily (that is, as a point of logic) false. If it were meaningless, it would not be false; since it is false, it is not meaningless. But Hick cannot be saying that "Jesus is God" is necessarily (that is, as a point of logic) false. For he explicitly denies this. See Thomas V. Morris, *The Logic of God Incarnate* (Ithaca, N.Y.: Cornell Univ. Press, 1986), 21, n. 4.

[9]See John Hick, *The Metaphor of God Incarnate: Christology in a Pluralistic Age* (Louisville: Westminster/John Knox, 1993), 103–4, 106.

[10]Ibid., 104.

test of religious significance, Hick replaces it with a metaphorical interpretation.[11]

But is Hick's reason for repudiating the orthodox doctrine of the Incarnation plausible? He insists, without argument, that the doctrine is meaningful only if *the relationship between Jesus' humanity and his deity* can be intelligibly spelled out.[12] But why should anyone think that, especially if one of the terms of the relation is God? We remind Hick that much of the meaning of this doctrine is captured by the conjunction of the independent meanings of

(1) Jesus is fully man

and

(2) Jesus is fully God.

The conjunction of (1) and (2) is believable if (a) there are good reasons to believe that (1) and (2) are both true *and* (b) there are no good reasons to think that (1) and (2) cannot both be true. The difficulty (or impossibility, if you like) of being able to "explicate" the conjunction of (1) and (2)—in the sense of explaining *how* two natures are united in one person—is not a good reason to think the conjunction is false. If there are good reasons for affirming both (1) and (2), then the traditional Christian's conviction is both meaningful and believable.

While Hick does not assert the logical incompatibility of (1) and (2), he does believe that the conjunction of (1) and (2) is false. Why? Because (1) and (2) jointly imply

(3) Jesus is the only Savior,

and (3) is contemptible, given the existence of other religious traditions. There can be no doubt that Hick recognizes the import of the traditional doctrine: "If [Jesus of Nazareth] was indeed God incarnate, Christianity is the only religion founded by God in person, and must as such be uniquely superior to all other religions."[13] But a "great and inescapable challenge" has arisen by the

---

[11]"We are not speaking of something that is in principle unique, but of an interaction of the divine and human which occurs in many different ways and degrees in all human openness to God's presence" (ibid., 109).

[12]Ibid., 3.

[13]Ibid., ix; cf. 7.

new knowledge of the human religious world. . . . It is here that the strain is now being felt. For Christianity's implicit or explicit claim to an unique superiority, as the central focus of God's saving activity on earth, has come to seem increasingly implausible within the new global consciousness of our time.[14]

In other words, Hick holds that the conjunction of (1) and (2) must be false, since their conjunction entails the uniqueness of Christianity, and the uniqueness of Christianity is incompatible with our enlightened awareness of other faiths in the world. But this is little more than a shrill accusation that it is bad manners for God to act in a way that we cannot explain or in a way that offends our religious predilections.

If we knew in advance that the Incarnation was the highest form of divine self-disclosure that is metaphysically possible, and if we thought that God's self-revelation might well take its highest form, then the Incarnation would even be *predictable*, though still not necessarily *explained*. If we cannot a priori rule out the possibility of the Incarnation, but we also cannot fully explain it, then this might be a form of divine self-disclosure made to order, its very mysteriousness signaling its plausibility—and all the more so if the doctrine successfully resists the charge of inconsistency.

At any rate, the orthodox position, in addition to being objectively true, is far more *religiously significant* than the metaphorical account Hick invents.[15] His view is not religiously adequate because it is not religiously realistic. According to the richer traditional view, God intervened in human history on a mission of mercy to repair sin's damage to human souls and to restore harmony between himself and human persons. Hick's theology includes no realistic account of the human condition, which orthodoxy diagnoses as alienation from a personal Creator caused by moral failure. We predict that Hick's pluralist interpretation of the Incarnation in terms of myth and metaphor, erected on yet another dubious and ephemeral reconstruction of the historical Jesus, will eventually peter out as a religiously live option.

---

[14]Ibid., 7.

[15]Note that Hick holds that all theology is human construction (see his essay).

HICK'S RELIGIOUS PLURALISM

If we recall Hick's acknowledgment that his hypothesis of religious pluralism is false if the Christian doctrine of the Incarnation is true, and if the evidence for the Incarnation is sufficiently strong, then there is no need for any direct criticism of Hick's pluralistic hypothesis. Still, there are several additional problems worth mentioning.[16]

A Religiously Ambiguous Universe? Hick holds that the universe is "religiously ambiguous," that "the universe, as presently accessible to us, is capable of being interpreted intellectually and experientially in both religious and naturalistic ways."[17] This judgment is basic to his entire pluralist program. It explains his decision to regard competing religious perspectives as equally authentic responses to the same reality and to refer to that reality as "the Real." While Hick repudiates natural theology, we have argued that the universe owes its existence to an identifiable personal Creator who may be expected to address the concerns of human persons.

As Hick conceives of it, the Real is perfectly undifferentiated; that is, it has no properties to which our concepts veridically apply. We demur. If the Real is the ground of our being, then we need not remain completely agnostic about its nature. In the Christian tradition, it is true, God is not fully and finally comprehended by us; but God is partially and veridically apprehended. To the extent that God is known at all, he is known truly. Thus, orthodox Christians are prepared to offer definite and literally true descriptions of God that do not, for all that, exhaust the divine nature.

Furthermore, this notion of the Real as undifferentiated is conceptually implausible. Hick has remarked that "the Buddhist concept of *sunyata* ... provides a good symbol for the Real."[18] But if the Real is as radically undifferentiated as Hick avers, then there is no way even to symbolize it. Symbols are representational objects; they carry the representational content of some

---

[16]These are developed more fully in R. Douglas Geivett, "John Hick's Approach to Religious Pluralism," *Proceedings of the Wheaton Theology Conference* 1 (Spring 1992): 43–53.

[17]Hick, *An Interpretation of Religion*, 129.

[18]Ibid., 246.

object and convey that content to a knowing or perceiving subject. But there is no representational content in the Real as undifferentiated that might be conveyed by a symbol.

Hick's view that the Real is manifested through the various concrete descriptions embodied in differing religious traditions also runs into difficulties. For an entity to be manifested is for some or all of its properties to be revealed. But the Real as undifferentiated has no distinguishable properties. And even if the Real does have objective properties that individuate it as a separate entity, if the Real is strictly inaccessible to us noetically, then we can never know what any of its properties are. Thus, it cannot be *manifested* at all through experience.

The Moral Parity of the Religions? Hick argues for parity between Christianity and many of the world's other religions by comparing the moral lives of their respective devotees. As he says, "I have not found that the people of the other world religions are, in general, on a different moral and spiritual level from Christians." Unfortunately, Hick mistakes one *goal* of true religion for a *criterion of truth* in religion.

Furthermore, while Hick concludes that members of differing traditions are on the average about equally virtuous, the Christian Scriptures teach that all human persons, regardless of religious affiliation, are sinners in need of divine grace (Isa. 64:6; Jer. 17:9–10; Rom. 3:23; 6:23; 1 John 1:9–10). Inter-traditional comparisons of virtue are therefore irrelevant. What matters is the person's standing before God. Christianity holds that all persons are equally helpless before God and that God, who is maximally concerned about the human condition, has arranged for their salvation through Jesus Christ (Rom. 5:6–11).

Finally, the unique moral superiority of Christianity is not founded on the moral character of fallible Christians but is attested by Jesus' own sinless life as the incarnate God-man whose righteousness is imputed to those who believe in him (2 Cor. 5:21; Heb. 4:15; 5:7; 7:26; 12:1–2). Christians have no business trying to establish their own moral superiority, nor should persons be satisfied with merely human speculations about the conditions for salvation when God himself has made these known. Any reason to think that God is interested in the salvation of human persons must be based on a rich conception of the divine nature—a conception of the divine nature that is not available to Hick, given his repudiation of both natural theology and propositional revelation.

Religiously Neutral? Hick's religious neutrality is mythological. While his pluralism initially suggests that he is neutral with respect to particular forms of religious awareness, Hick expresses sentiments about the Transcendent that have a strong affinity with Eastern pantheistic conceptions of reality. Historically, pluralism is antagonistic to the core principles of Christianity. But syncretism and pluralism have been prominent features of Eastern thought for centuries. It appears that Hick is much more at home with Eastern models of religious reality than with the tradition into which he was, as he says, born.

Furthermore, his view does not really encourage genuine dialogue between traditions. One has to wonder what value there is in remaining within a particular religious tradition—or even what it means to "remain in" a particular tradition—if the essential correctness of the pluralistic hypothesis is accepted by the believer. Many religious believers could only accept the pluralistic hypothesis at the cost of drastically reconceiving the nature of their own particular faith tradition. Hick, of course, is prepared to forge a "Christian" theology that is compatible with the pluralistic vision. But traditional Christian theology is not compatible with religious pluralism. Those who embrace a Christianity that is not compatible with religious pluralism will therefore be expected to compromise their own understanding of what is authentic awareness in order to move toward a more pluralistic position. Is it charitable for Hick to demand such a compromise?

CONCLUSION

The reader should keep in mind that the story of Hick's migration from fundamentalism to classical liberalism is not an argument for his position. Other intellectuals who began with traditional Christian beliefs have wandered through the thickets of religious relativism only to return in the end to their orthodox home. In June of 449 A.D., Pope Leo I declared that "our faith will finally be defended to good purpose when the false opinion is condemned even by its adherents."[19] We harbor respectful hope that John Hick may yet conclude that a rich knowledge of God's reality is accessible, that this knowledge of God available through natural theology generates the plausible expectation that God would remedy the human condition, and that God's remedy is indeed embodied in the good news concerning Jesus Christ.

---

[19]"Pope Leo I's Letter to Flavian of Constantinople," in *The Christological Controversy*, ed. Richard A. Norris, Jr. (Philadelphia: Fortress, 1980), 155.

CONCLUSION

John Hick

Let me say first how much I appreciate having been included in this book. I have in recent years been aware of a growing desire among leading evangelical thinkers to face the problems posed by religious diversity and also to engage in dialogue with people located further along on the wide Christian spectrum. I particularly welcome this opportunity to engage in such dialogue if it is true, as Jacobsen and Schmidt say in their survey of recent developments in evangelical Christology, that *The Myth of God Incarnate* (1977) had the regrettable effect of

> snapping evangelicalism in general back to a hunkered-down sense of defensiveness—especially with regard to christology. Hick was [they say] especially problematic in this case because he was himself an apostate evangelical. Hick's shadow over evangelical christology has been long.[1]

I was unaware of this fact—assuming that it *is* indeed a fact—and should, of course, have preferred the book to have prompted further reflection rather than a defensive reaction. Hopefully the new approach in *The Metaphor of God Incarnate* and in my contribution to the present book may be more helpful to some.[2] I continue to be thankful for my own evangelical

---

[1]Douglas Jacobsen and Frederick Schmidt, "Behind Orthodoxy and Beyond It: Recent Developments in Evangelical Christology," *Scottish Journal of Theology* 45 (1992): 519.

[2]John Hick, *The Metaphor of God Incarnate* (Louisville: Westminster/John Knox, 1994 / London: SCM, 1994).

conversion as a student and have always held that the evangelical wing of Christianity can fulfill a valuable function in jolting secularized young people out of their apathy—providing that as they continue in the Christian life, they can grow in wisdom and sort out the acceptable and unacceptable aspects of the evangelical theological package, gradually discarding the latter.

THE INSTABILITY OF INCLUSIVISM

I am, however, sorry to have irritated Clark Pinnock by sharing that evangelical conversion with readers and letting them know that for a number of years I believed something similar to his own strongly conservative theology. But, his feelings apart, I do not think that I need to apologize either for the facts that I related or for referring to them when presenting a pluralist understanding of religion to a conservative readership. I am, incidentally, by no means the only "liberal" theologian who began as an evangelical. On the contrary, among those whom I know, this pattern is the rule rather than the exception.

Clark Pinnock is to be saluted for having done much to lead the evangelical wing of Christianity away from the old exclusivism, which believes that only Christians are saved, to an inclusivism that recognizes that non-Christians also may ultimately be saved and that Judaism, Islam, Hinduism, Buddhism, and so on have value, even if only as preparations for the Christian gospel.

In taking this step, Pinnock inevitably exposes himself to criticism both from those who think that he has gone too far and from those who think that he has not gone far enough. I am one of the latter. I see inclusivism as an inherently unstable position, comparable with the epicycles that were added to the old Ptolemaic astronomy to preserve it a little longer as new observations were increasingly beginning to threaten it. The theological analogy of the Ptolemaic picture of the universe, which placed our earth at the center, is the claim that our own religion is central to the salvific process and thus uniquely superior to all others.

The Copernican Revolution in astronomy recognized that the sun is at the center of the solar system and that our earth is only one of the planets revolving around it. A comparable revolution in theology acknowledges that the ultimate reality we call God is central, with Christianity as one of the worlds of faith revolving around that divine center. The halfway position that Pinnock shares with most Roman Catholic theologians today, and with Vatican II and the Pope, grants that the religions all revolve around God, but it adds that God's saving grace nevertheless shines directly only in Christ and is then reflected from the church to the people of the other worlds of faith. But from the premise, for which I argued in my chapter, that we find more or less equal evidence of saved lives within the other great world religions, it seems to me more realistic to conclude that the divine grace shines directly on us all—Christians, Jews, Muslims, Hindus, Buddhists, and others alike. For if Christianity is indeed the only religion to have been founded by God in person, so that we alone know the full truth, and if in the church we have unrivaled means of grace, why is this not evident from the lives of Christians? Does our traditional belief-system match the observable facts of human life?

EVANGELICALS AND CHRISTOLOGY

Alister McGrath feels that I have not taken recent evangelical writers seriously enough. Perhaps this seems so to him because he is a theologian, widely read in current as well as classical theology (as his recent *Christian Theology: An Introduction* shows[3]), while I am primarily a philosopher of religion. As such I have been mainly interested in dialoguing with evangelicals in their attempts to grapple with the problem of the coherence and intelligibility of the traditional doctrine of the Incarnation. The most recent philosophically impressive attempt is, in my view, that of Thomas Morris in *The Logic of God Incarnate*.[4] And I have offered a detailed critique of this both in *The Metaphor of God Incarnate* and, more fully, in a journal article.[5] I have also engaged in published (as well as private) dialogue with another leading evangelical philosopher, Stephen Davis (who is a friend and a

---

[3]Alister McGrath, *Christian Theology: An Introduction* (Oxford: Blackwell, 1994).

[4]Thomas V. Morris, *The Logic of God Incarnate* (Ithaca, N.Y. / London: Cornell Univ. Press, 1986).

[5]John Hick, "The Logic of God Incarnate," *Religious Studies* 25 (December, 1989): 409–23.

former colleague at Claremont), in his valuable edited book *Encountering Jesus* and in two conference volumes, and on another issue with Douglas Geivett in a contribution to his book *Evil and the Evidence for God*.[6] In terms of the Jacobsen/Schmidt typology, these count, I presume, as "custodial" evangelicals.[7]

Among "penumbral" evangelicals and independent scholars who largely agree with them, I have engaged in published (as well as private) dialogue with another friend, Canon Brian Hebblethwaite, and with Bishop Lesslie Newbigin and Professor Charles Moule in *Incarnation and Myth: The Debate Continued*, and in public debate (Birmingham, 1994) with David Brown.[8] So I have not been altogether out of touch with the evangelical and near-evangelical world.

I do not think, however, that I dismissed "evangelical Christologies on the basis of a sweeping claim like 'Jesus didn't claim to be God,'" as McGrath claims, so that my "criticism of evangelicalism [is] tired, uninformed, and weary." I focused on the central issue posed by the standard orthodoxy of Nicaea and Chalcedon. And it is extremely relevant to this that the historical Jesus did not claim to be God—as is acknowledged today even by conservative New Testament scholarship. Wolfhart Pannenberg, who holds firmly to the traditional orthodoxy and whom Professor McGrath mentions as one of those whose methods evangelicals follow, says, "Today it must be taken as all but certain that the pre-Easter Jesus neither designated himself as Messiah or Son of God nor accepted such a confession to him from others."[9] Indeed, Jesus would probably have regarded the

---

[6]Stephen T. Davis, ed., *Encountering Jesus* (Atlanta: John Knox, 1988); Linda J. Tessier, ed., *Concepts of the Ultimate* (London: Macmillan, 1989 / New York: St. Martin's, 1989); Harold Hewitt, ed., *Problems in the Philosophy of Religion: Critical Studies of the Work of John Hick* (London: Macmillan, 1991 / New York: St. Martin's, 1991); R. Douglas Geivett, *Evil and the Evidence for God: The Challenge of John Hick's Theodicy* (Philadelphia: Temple Univ. Press, 1993).

[7]See note 1.

[8]See Brian Hebblethwaite, *The Incarnation* (Cambridge Univ. Press, 1987), and "John Hick and the Question of Truth in Religion," in Arvind Sharma, ed., *God, Truth and Reality: Essays in Honour of John Hick* (London: Macmillan, 1993 / New York: St. Martin's, 1993); Michael Goulder, ed., *Incarnation and Myth: The Debate Continued* (London: SCM / Grand Rapids: Eerdmans, 1979).

[9]Wolfhart Pannenberg, *Jesus, God and Man*, trans. Lewis Wilkins & Duane Priebe (London: SCM, 1968), 327.

idea that he was God incarnate as blasphemous! So this is surely a legitimate point to make when considering the plausibility or otherwise of a Christology that assumed that Jesus did in fact teach his own deity; for the Chalcedonian definition supports its Christology by affirming that it is "as the Lord Jesus Christ taught us."

Thus I agree with Douglas Geivett and Gary Phillips that if Jesus did not claim to be God, "then the logical status of the Incarnation is moot, for it presupposes that Jesus did regard himself as God." At this point they are more forthright than their colleagues in this book. It is impossible to discuss the relevant New Testament texts here, but I have already quoted in my chapter a number of leading conservative (not liberal) New Testament scholars who, after examination of the texts, are agreed that Jesus did not claim to be God; and this indeed represents a general consensus today within mainline scholarship, whether Catholic or Protestant, conservative or liberal. It is true that until comparatively recently, such Fourth Gospel sayings as "I and the Father are one" and "He who has seen me has seen the Father" were believed to have been uttered by the historical Jesus, so that one could argue that he must have been either mad, or bad, or God. In my own evangelical student days, I certainly believed this and used that argument; and Geivett/ Phillips use it when they say that "if Jesus was not God, he was either morally retrograde or extraordinarily dysfunctional, or both." But I presume that more moderate evangelicals would not be found using this discredited argument today.

THE MORAL SUPERIORITY OF CHRISTIANITY?

Clark Pinnock takes up the question of a possible Christian moral superiority and seems to agree that, as regards individual men and women, no such superiority is evident. He says that he has no difficulty in "accepting the fact that there are holy people in other faiths." He resists, however, any inference from the fact of saintly Jews, Muslims, Hindus, and Buddhists to the validity of these faiths, independently of Christian influence. And if there were only a few such non-Christian saints—in the sense of men and women through whom there shines the transforming presence of the divine—these might perhaps be regarded as "flukes," having no great significance. But in reality, they seem to be as numerous in proportion to population and as spiritually impressive as within Christianity. Moreover, ordinary men and women of the other great traditions seem, on average, to be no less loving and compassionate, no less honest and truthful, and no less concerned for others than are Christians on average.

In other words, the other world religions do not seem to be less genuine contexts than is Christianity of the salvific transformation from natural self-centeredness to a new orientation, centered in the divine. I say "seem to be" because we are dealing here with aspects of human life that cannot be precisely measured or quantified. But the onus of proof, or at least of evidence and argument, lies inescapably on anyone who wishes to claim that Christians in general are morally and spiritually better human beings than Jews, Muslims, Hindus, and Buddhists.

Alister McGrath also agrees that "anyone who argues that a Christian is, by virtue of his or her faith, morally superior to a Confucian is open to serious criticism," and he endorses my own statement that it is "not possible to establish the unique superiority of any one of the great world religions." He adds that this is because there are no universal moral standards by which to make such judgments. But I pointed out in my chapter that the basic ideal of love and concern for others, and of treating them as you would wish them to treat you, is taught by all the great traditions, and I offered supporting quotations from their scriptures. I will add here some further words of the same kind:

> Do you love your Creator? Love your fellow-beings first.
>
> Kindness is a mark of faith: and whoever has not kindness has not faith.
>
> All God's creatures are His family; and he is the most beloved of God who does most good to God's creatures.
>
> What actions are most excellent? To gladden the heart of a human being, to feed the hungry, to help the afflicted, to lighten the sorrows of the sorrowful, to remove the wrongs of the injured.
>
> Assist any person oppressed, whether Muslim or non-Muslim.

These all come from the *Hadith*, containing Muhammad's teachings to the early Islamic community.[10]

Neither Clark Pinnock nor Alister McGrath apparently expect Christians generally to be morally better human beings than Jews, Muslims, Hindus, and Buddhists. But given their theologies, this strikes me as extremely odd. If Jesus was God (i.e., the second person of a divine Trinity) incarnate, so that Christianity is the only religion to have been directly founded by God in person, embodying a new relationship and access to God through incorporation into Christ and benefiting from unrivaled means of grace, should not all this make at least some observable difference in the quality of Christian lives? It would not, of course, be fair to expect any randomly chosen Christian to be morally superior to any randomly chosen non-Christian. But surely the *average* level of what Paul calls in Galatians 5:22–23 "the fruit of the Spirit"—"love, joy, peace, patience, kindness, goodness, faithfulness, gentleness, self-control"—should be more evident in the lives of Christians than of those outside the sphere of Christian salvation. Yet this does not seem to be the case!

Is it sufficient to respond that just as the truth of a scientific theory does not depend on the moral quality of the scientist who propounds it, so the truth of the Christian gospel does not depend upon the moral quality of those who live by it? Surely the cases are very different. The gospel cannot be compared with a scientific hypothesis; rather, it is a saving truth whose truthfulness *does* consist in its power to bring people to the ultimate reality that we call God, and thereby to change their lives and produce in them the kind of fruit listed by Paul. The same requirement applies to the Torah, and to the message of the Qur'an, and to the Bhagavad Gita, and to the teachings of the Buddha. But if the saving power of the traditional Christian message seems to be on a par with the messages of the other great world faiths, are we justified in claiming for it a unique superiority that puts all the others in the shade?

As well as the question of individuals, there is the question of societies. Here Clark Pinnock shares a Western superiority

[10]These sayings of Muhammad in the *Hadith* are taken from Allama Sir Abdullah and Al-Mamum Al-Surhrawady, eds., *The Sayings of Muhammad* (New York: Citadel, 1990), 82, 89, 90, 112.

complex that has today worn extremely thin. He rightly condemns various reprehensible features of non-Christian cultures. But he seems blind to the different but equally reprehensible features of Christian cultures. Our Western, supposedly Christian, civilization has more than its full share of drug abuse, divorce, abortion, suicide, and pornography—as, indeed, is regularly emphasized in evangelical sermons! Moreover, the Christian West is mainly responsible for the destruction of the ecosphere and the greedy over-consumption of the earth's nonrenewable resources, in order to support the privileged lifestyle of the well-to-do of the first and second worlds. For example, if every country used paper at the same rate as the United States, within two years there would be no trees left on earth. And the present century has seen in Christian societies the rise of Nazi and Fascist dictatorships, the appalling attempt to exterminate the Jewish people, and the two most destructive wars in history in which, apart from the extension of World War II into the Far East, Christians were slaughtering one another by the millions. Only a strongly a priori conviction, impervious to observation, could even suggest that the world situation is "possibly proof of [Christianity's] superior sanctifying power," as Pinnock writes.

Surely the reality is that, unhappily, evil is much more readily built into social and political structures than is good, and that Christianity has been no more successful in countering this than have the other great world faiths. Therefore, when we look at the complex mass of different and often incommensurable goods and evils in the histories of the different world religions, it is in my view impossible to conclude that any one of them has proved itself to be morally superior to all the others.

Geivett/Phillips also take up the question of Christian moral superiority. On the one hand, they seem to agree that no such superiority is evident. The people of all religions, including Christianity, are sinners, so that "inter-traditional comparisons of virtue are therefore irrelevant." But on the other hand, they still affirm "the unique moral superiority of Christianity," which, they say, "is not founded on the moral character of fallible Christians but is attested by Jesus' own sinless life as the incarnate God-man, whose righteousness is imputed to those who believe in him." This seems to mean that Christians are morally superior to non-Christians, not, however, in humanly detectable ways but in the sight of God, who imputes Jesus' righteousness to them. But much the greater part of Jesus' teaching was about how to live in God's presence now, in this world, in ways that make an earthly difference and are humanly observable.

There is a challenge here to evangelical theology that has to be met. If it cannot be met, however, this does not mean that we must, in Clark Pinnock's words, "trade in the God of Jesus for an unknown God." It means that we stay with our own Christian encounter with the Divine but do not deny the reality of other different such encounters. For religious pluralism, the different epoch-making human awarenesses of the Real that lie at the root of the great religious traditions—the experiences of the Hindu *rishis* and *acharyias*; Gautama the Buddha's consciousness of the transforming Dharma; Moses', the prophets', and the rabbis' consciousness of the God of Israel; Jesus' consciousness of that God as the heavenly Father; Muhammad's consciousness of Allah *rahman rahim*, God gracious and merciful—constitute authentic human awarenesses of the Ultimate, which have developed historically into the complex streams of religious thought, experience, and life that we call the great religions.

We ourselves have been born into and formed by one of these, the one that was initiated by Jesus. Because we have been formed by it, it fits us and we fit it, and it constitutes our natural spiritual home. But millions of others, who have been born into Muslim, Hindu, or Buddhist families, have been formed by those other traditions that constitute *their* natural spiritual homes. And the practical outcome is that normally (there are individual exceptions) we should live fully within the tradition into which we have been born; for each has shown itself to be a genuine, though far from perfect, context of the salvific transformation that is the purpose of human life.

THE DECISIVE ISSUE OF CHRISTOLOGY

Turning to the "crunch" question of Christology, Clark Pinnock speaks of my wanting to "get rid of the Incarnation." In fact, I hold that Christianity began with and centers on a moment of divine incarnation in human life. But I go on to ask what "divine incarnation" means; and I have tried to show that it has no religiously acceptable literal meaning, but that it does have a religiously powerful metaphorical meaning. This suggestion, Professor Pinnock claims, "has less to do with evidence than with ideology." But evidence is given in my chapter in this book and more fully in my *The Metaphor of God Incarnate*, and these reasons stand on their own feet and invite a response.

Geivett/Phillips represent a much more "hard-line" custodial form of evangelicalism than either McGrath or Pinnock. Comment is made difficult by the fact that I have already answered their critical points in my initial chapter, so that we are left simply asserting different positions! It does not seem to me tenable to say, with Geivett/Phillips, that "everything substantive about Jesus is infused with a high Christology." What, for example, about the Lord's Prayer? This contains none of the later church doctrines of Incarnation, Trinity, or Atonement.

They hold to "the classical doctrine of biblical inerrancy," which forbids them to allow for any inconsistencies or contradictions, any historical distortions, or any mistaken prescientific assumptions in either the Old or the New Testaments. Geivett/Phillips are free to believe this, but I hope they do not impose such a sacrifice of the intellect on their students.

Geivett/Phillips accept the "difficulty (or impossibility, if you like) of being able to 'explicate' the conjunction of ['Jesus is fully man'] and ['Jesus is fully God']—in the sense of explaining *how* two natures are united in one person." They apparently regard the Chalcedonian formula as a mystery that we must believe without understanding it. But it is in fact a human (and nonbiblical) theory adopted by the church, after long and sometimes acrimonious debates, at the Council of Chalcedon in 451. As a humanly constructed doctrine, it must be open to critical examination, and this reveals that no one has yet been able to assign an acceptable literal meaning to the formula. On the other hand, the metaphor of divine incarnation—human beings freely doing God's will, so that God is acting through them and becomes "incarnate" in their actions—is both powerful and intelligible.

Geivett/Phillips' criticisms of the concept of the Real or the Divine in itself as lying beyond the range of human thought and imagination have already been answered in my initial chapter. The Real is not a blank but the infinitely rich reality whose nature cannot be captured by our human concepts, other than purely formal ones. Geivett/Phillips quote my statement that "the Buddhist concept of *sunyata* ... provides a good symbol for the Real." In the full sentence I wrote, "*sunyata* in one of its developments, namely as an anti-concept excluding all concepts, provides a good symbol for the Real."[11] I interpret the concept of *sunyata* as indicating that the Ultimate (in Buddhist terms, the Dharmakaya) is empty of everything that the human mind projects in the activity of awareness. It thus lies outside our human concept-structured field of experience but is at the same time the transcendent ground of its various personal and non-personal manifestations to human consciousness.

Geivett/Phillips conclude with the "respectful hope" that I will return to their kind of theology. I, in return, cherish a respectful hope that they, and our readers, will open their minds to the glorious reality of God's presence throughout the entire world and recognize that different faith communities see and respond to different "faces" of the infinite transcendent Reality.

---

[11]John Hick, *An Interpretation of Religion: Human Responses to the Transcendent* (London: Macmillan, 1989/ New Haven: Yale Univ. Press, 1989), 246.

Chapter Two

AN INCLUSIVIST VIEW

Clark H. Pinnock

AN INCLUSIVIST VIEW

Clark H. Pinnock

A psalmist declares: "O God our Savior, [you are] the hope of all the ends of the earth and of the farthest seas" (Ps. 65:5). Central to the Bible is belief in the comprehensive and all-embracing character of divine sovereignty and grace. God's love for the world is both broad and inclusive (1 Tim. 2:4). One should not begrudge God's generosity (Matt. 20:15)—Christ did not die for our sins only but for the sins of the whole world (1 John 2:2). The rainbow of divine mercy encircles the throne of God (Rev. 4:2), and there is a tree of life in the midst of the new Jerusalem for the healing of the nations (22:2). Christian theology must speak of universality and of inclusion.[1]

TIMELINESS IN THEOLOGY

One of the most challenging issues facing contemporary theology is how to relate God's salvific will to religious pluralism. How can a particular, historical person (Jesus of Nazareth) have universal saving significance? Does it not appear that those in close touch with Jesus would be privileged over others? Though the saving benefit of Christ is said to accrue to all humanity, would it not in reality have a more limited scope?

The Bible claims, for example, that the nations will worship the Lord at the end of history (Ps. 22:27) and will bring the glory

---

[1]Hence the title chosen for my book on religious pluralism: *A Wideness in God's Mercy: The Finality of Jesus Christ in a World of Religions* (Grand Rapids: Zondervan, 1992).

and honor of their cultures into the new Jerusalem (Rev. 21:26). But how intelligible is a plan to bring salvation to the nations at the end of history if most people get left out because they died too soon? If God cares for the whole world, is it not fair to ask what he is doing in advance of the mission among those who have not had the good news preached to them? This is a question of coherence in our message, not a skeptical inquiry.

Theological interpretation ought to be both faithful and *timely*: true to divine revelation and discerning the ways of the Spirit. The awareness of religious pluralism is a characteristic of the present moment, and we must ponder what the Spirit is saying to us about it. It is not enough to get the information of past revelation right if, at the same time, we are not discerning as to what God is doing right now (Luke 12:56).

This book is designed to introduce readers to some of the models used in theology for relating Christian faith to other religions. It inquires into our theology of religions.[2] Inclusivism is one of these models, which explores the possibility that the Spirit is operative in the sphere of human religion to prepare people for the gospel of Christ. It believes that God, who is gracious and omnipresent, is redemptively at work in the religious dimension of human culture, just as he is in all the other spheres of creation.[3]

Several factors have made religious pluralism an urgent challenge for us. One factor is cultural. Although there has always been a plurality of religious beliefs, close interaction between people of different faiths is much more commonly experienced today than formerly. Religious pluralism has come home to people's consciousness, making the question a live one for large numbers. It is no longer, as it once was, an exotic question for foreign missionaries. We are aware of our inhabiting a small and fragile planet and of our belonging to a single human

---

[2]Compare Glyn Richards, *Towards a Theology of Religions* (London: Routledge, 1989); Gavin D'Costa, *Theology and Religious Pluralism: The Challenge of Other Religions* (Oxford: Blackwell, 1986); Alan Race, *Christians and Religious Pluralism: Patterns in the Christian Theology of Religions* (Maryknoll, N.Y.: Orbis Books, 1982).

[3]Paul F. Knitter refers to inclusivism as the "Catholic" model because it was formulated most impressively by the Second Vatican Council: *No Other Name? A Critical Survey of Christian Attitudes Toward World Religions* (Maryknoll, N.Y.: Orbis Books, 1985), ch. 7.

race. The awareness of a single planetary culture is rather new and drives the modern debate. It was the sense of our being one humanity that led Pope John XXIII to call the Second Vatican Council, as is plain in his opening speech and in virtually all of the subsequent documents.[4]

Another factor is ecclesial. Theology has always claimed that God loves the whole world but has found it difficult to speak coherently about it. Alongside a general hope for the salvation of humanity, many have beliefs that create doubt about the sincerity of God's love for the world. For example, Western theology has been reluctant to acknowledge that grace operates outside the church, and there is the abhorrent notion of a secret election to salvation of a specific number of sinners, not of people at large. Such beliefs are deep in the Western tradition and place the genuineness of God's universal salvific will in considerable doubt. My sense is that Christians today are less willing than before to accept such a hard and pessimistic theology.[5]

The conjunction of cultural change with an uneasiness regarding certain inherited traditions has pressured theologians today to develop a better model for handling the doctrine of salvation as it pertains to the multitudes who have lived their lives outside the church and apart from the gospel. The willingness of Christians to tolerate equivocation about God's salvific will has diminished, and more and more it is being taken for granted that God's boundless mercy is a primary truth that cannot be compromised. There has been a shift in attitude among the churches and a more positive outlook in regard to other religions. Inclusivism, though a new proposal in certain ways, has been developed as a reinterpretation of historic theology in what we hope is a timely and faithful manner. But let readers be aware from the outset that this is a complex, not a simple question. They must be prepared for the host of challenging issues that it stirs up.

---

[4] I will be referring often to these writings, which are so significant to all the churches: *The Documents of Vatican II*, Walter M. Abott, ed. (New York: Guild Press, 1966). I make no apology as an evangelical in admitting an enormous debt of gratitude to the Council for its guidance on this topic.

[5] So Francis A. Sullivan, *Salvation Outside the Church? Tracing the History of the Catholic Response* (New York: Paulist, 1992), 199–204.

DEFINING INCLUSIVISM

Inclusivism believes that, because God is present in the whole world (premise), God's grace is also at work in some way among all people, possibly even in the sphere of religious life (inference). It entertains the possibility that religion may play a role in the salvation of the human race, a role preparatory to the gospel of Christ, in whom alone fullness of salvation is found.

The premise seems theologically well founded. God is present as the triune Creator and Redeemer everywhere—in the far reaches of space, in every culture, and in every human heart. Therefore, divine grace is also prevenient everywhere—since God has created the whole world, since Jesus Christ died for all humanity, and since the Spirit gives life to creation. Most specifically and crucially, inclusivists believe that the Spirit is everywhere at work in advance of the mission to prepare the way for Jesus Christ. We refuse to allow the disjunction between nature and grace or between common and saving grace, on the supposition that, if the triune God is present, grace must be present too.

The inference is more controversial, though I think it only draws out what is inherent in the premise. Hitherto it has only seldom been proposed that the Spirit might be present in the religious sphere of human life. Theologians may have been willing to say that God's grace operates outside the church—but not to say that grace may be encountered in the context of the non-Christian religions. Inclusivism runs a risk of suspicion in suggesting that non-Christian religions may be not only the means of a natural knowledge of God, but also the locale of God's grace given to the world because of Christ.

Like the other models, inclusivism is not a single, tightly defined position. Just as not every pluralist is happy with John Hick's version of pluralism or every exclusivist pleased with Ronald Nash's version of exclusivism,[6] so there is also a spectrum of opinion within inclusivism about the activity of the Spirit in other religions and their precise salvific status. A cautious attitude is exemplified by Vatican II and by the present essayist.[7] This approach is open to seeing God at work in non-

---

[6] I refer to Ronald H. Nash, *Is Jesus the Only Savior?* (Grand Rapids: Zondervan, 1994).

[7] An important analysis of the Council is Miikka Ruokanen, *The Catholic Doctrine of Non-Christian Religions* (Leiden: E. J. Brill, 1992).

Christian persons and in non-Christian religious institutions but with important qualifiers.

First, cautious inclusivism does not glorify religions, as though there were not depths of darkness, deception, and bondage in them. It avoids being rosy-eyed about religions that can be wicked as well as noble. Vatican II itself downplays criticism of religion because of its overall desire to be positive about the world and modern developments. A closer reading, however, still reveals a critical judgment. For example, the famous passage in which it is said that atheists can be saved goes on as well to speak of deceptions of the Evil One.[8]

Second, cautious inclusivism stops short of stating that the religions themselves as such are vehicles of salvation. The Council, for example, does not recognize the salvific reality of non-Christian religions, though it does recognize this reality in Protestant churches. It does not say that other religions as such mediate God's grace, though some theologians have imputed more liberal ideas to the Council or found them implicit there.

A less cautious attitude is exemplified by the most famous inclusivist, Karl Rahner, who is very positive about other faiths and considers them to possess a salvific status. Other religions for him are like training schools of divine mercy. Rahner calls them "lawful" in his famous essay, because grace is mediated through them.[9] I believe that Rahner's approach to this issue arises out of the sacramental orientation of his Catholic theology, which reasons in this manner: If grace is communicated to people outside the church, the sacramental means by which it is mediated must be the religions available to them. The fact that Vatican II itself did not register this point caused Rahner some disappointment.[10]

I believe the Council was wise in not making this move, which would involve an unwarrantedly positive judgment about religion. Religion is not the only social bearer of meaning in this world—there are the family, guilds, governments, and

---

[8]*The Documents of Vatican II*, "Dogmatic Constitution on the Church," art. 16.

[9]Karl Rahner, "Christianity and the Non-Christian Religions," *Theological Investigations* 5 (London: Darton, Longman & Todd, 1966): 121–31.

[10]Many Catholic scholars, like Rahner, go further than the Council, and some go even further than him: for example, Arnulfs Camps, *Partners in Dialogue: Christianity and Other World Religions* (Maryknoll, N.Y.: Orbis Books, 1983).

the like. That God's dealings with the soul are not restricted to the religious sphere is plain when the Council mentions the salvation of atheists for whom religion is not involved at all. Did Jesus, for example, not encounter more piety outside formal religion than inside it, among outsiders who found faith in the course of ordinary human interaction?[11]

I call the cautious approach of the spectrum "modal" inclusivism.[12] It does not claim that God *must* or always *does* make positive use of religion in drawing people. It would be surprising if all religions were equally salvific, given the contingencies and diversities involved. It would be comparable to assuming that all current theories in science or philosophy are equally illuminating—a strange assumption. Furthermore, we are not in a position anyway to say what God *must* do or conclude what God has done before testing the given instance. Surely a given religion might be unusable, owing to the depth of darkness or the severity of bondage in it. It seems wiser to say that God *may* use religion as a way of gracing people's lives and that it is *one* of God's options for evoking faith and communicating grace. This avoids a priori judgments concerning God's use of or nonuse of religion. Whether God makes use of religion is a contingent matter to be explored case by case with discernment.

Modal inclusivism then holds that grace operates outside the church and *may be* encountered in the context of other religions. My version of it is oriented to the Spirit as graciously present in the world among all peoples, even in non-Christian religious contexts. I believe that the Spirit is present in advance of missions, preparing the way of the Lord. One could call it a pneumatological approach. Such inclusivism offers the reader an alternative to exclusivism, which is pessimistic about such possibilities, and to pluralism, which posits an unknown Reality everywhere present in religion.[13]

---

[11]Lesslie Newbigin makes this point against Rahner in "The Christian Faith and the World Religions," in *Keeping the Faith*, Geoffrey Wainwright, ed. (Philadelphia: Fortress, 1988), 323–37.

[12]Paul J. Griffiths, "Modalizing the Theology of Religions," *Journal of Religion* 73 (1993): 382–89. Schubert M. Ogden also advises this caution *Is There Only One True Religion Or Are There Many?* (Dallas: Southern Methodist Univ. Press, 1992).

[13]Some readers may note that my way of referring to pluralism in this essay has Hick's version of it in mind more than, say, Gordon Kaufman's. I am aware of

THE APPEAL OF INCLUSIVISM

Though relatively new, inclusivism has become widely accepted and may even be called the mainline model. "It probably represents," John Hick writes, "the nearest approach to a consensus among Christian thinkers today."[14] It has achieved success so quickly because of a number of positive features. First, hope attracts and inclusivism engenders hope. Christians want to believe that grace will prove stronger than sin in the flow of history. In view of Easter, we do not want to think that most human beings will perish. Rather, our biblical faith encourages us to want them to be saved. If inclusivism can be shown to be congruent with Scripture, it holds a great appeal.

Second, inclusivism relieves us of those dark features of the tradition that suggest that (at worst) God plays favorites or (at best) inexplicably restricts his grace, so that whole groups are excluded from any possibility of salvation. More and more Christians are refusing to believe these notions. The problem of evil is large enough without adding to it the idea that most of the race is beyond the possibility of salvation through no fault of their own. Fewer and fewer are willing to tolerate a doctrine of salvation that favors a few over all the others.[15] It is not always easy to interpret theologians from earlier times about this issue, however. Irenaeus, for example, was unaware of the existence of a large number of unevangelized people and thus of our entire problem. We cannot say what he might have thought had he lived in our day.[16]

---

differences here, but the set-up of this book establishes the priority of Hick's views for our discussion.

[14]John Hick, *The Metaphor of God Incarnate: Christology in a Pluralistic Age* (Louisville: Westminster/John Knox, 1993), 88. Paul Knitter calls it "the mainline model" in *No Other Name?* 135, and Richard H. Drummond shows it to be such in *Toward a New Age in Christian Theology* (Maryknoll, N.Y.: Orbis Books, 1985).

[15]Carl Henry is much admired by evangelicals, but many of them (I think) would be shocked to hear him say that God is perfectly within his rights to save some and not others if he chooses. See his essay "Is It Fair?" in William V. Crockett and James G. Sigountos, eds., *Through No Fault of Their Own? The Fate of Those Who Have Never Heard* (Grand Rapids: Baker, 1991), 253. Henry is, of course, only restating John Calvin's view, and the general skepticism about it among evangelicals today indicates how much things are changing in the movement that Henry spearheaded.

[16]See Terrance L. Tiessen, *Irenaeus on the Salvation of the Unevangelised* (London: Scarecrow, 1993), 261, 281.

Third, inclusivism appeals because of its honest willingness to acknowledge sanctity in persons and religions other than Christian. Too many of us have encountered saintly persons of other faiths to deny that the religious communities behind them are in a state of some openness to God.

A fourth source of attraction lies in the way inclusivism offers a more coherent version of orthodoxy. It affirms the universality of God's salvific will more coherently than exclusivism because of its acknowledgment of the universal prevenience of divine grace. And it achieves universality without reducing "God" to a vague Kantian Reality in certain forms of pluralism, a Reality that none can define and that replaces the historic confession of the triune God. Inclusivism offers the reader a middle ground between exclusivism and pluralism, holding both to the particularity of salvation through Christ and to the universal scope of God's plan to save sinners. Catholics and mainline Protestants have heard the argument more than evangelicals— therefore, my chief concern is to get through to the latter.

TRINITARIAN FOUNDATIONS

Beginning with the theological axioms, the centerpiece of modal inclusivism is belief in the Spirit as everywhere active, even in the context of the religious life, in advance of mission, preparing the way of the Lord. This belief is based on the doctrine of the omnipresence of one loving and personal God, whose Spirit is present everywhere in the world as the Spirit of the Father and the Son. Logically, if the breath of the gracious God is present, it follows that the Spirit is striving for life and wholeness in every sphere, including the religious. To affirm that the Spirit is prevenient and then deny that he wants to minister grace is tantamount to saying there are two Spirits—analogous to Marcion's notion of two Gods, a God of creation and a God of redemption. If there is only *one* Spirit and if he is omnipresent in the world, that Spirit works for good everywhere, even in the sphere of religions if circumstances permit, because that is his nature and vocation. Since all created life is a gift of God's Spirit, we look for evidence of the Life-giver everywhere and on every level.

Our inclusivism is grounded in a relational ontology—in the being of the triune God. When we speak of Father, Son, and Spirit, we confess God's triune identity. This insight into the divine nature, disclosed in Christian revelation, captures a vivid image of the love of God, incarnate in Jesus Christ, and experienced through participation in the Spirit. This ontology points to relationality, liveliness, and openness in the nature of God. It sees God as an event of loving communion, poured out in creation and reaching out to the world in redemption. Out of the fullness of shared life, God calls forth a world to mirror his own loving mutuality, inviting everyone to participate in the fullness of triune life, in a community of love that constitutes tripersonal being. Inclusivism responds to the boundless love that God is by nature and brings its model forward to respond to the challenge of religious pluralism.[17]

When in the creed Christians confess faith in God the Father Almighty, maker of heaven and earth, we are referring to the creative ground of being, understood as interpersonal love in the light of revelation in Jesus Christ. We refer to the God whom Jesus called *Abba* (Father) and whom he taught us to think of as boundlessly generous.[18] Creation itself is an act of love and an expression of grace. God *is* love and invites sinners to a festive meal. First in the hierarchy of Christian truths is that God, the mystery of love, streams forth in Son and Spirit toward the human race, toward those whom we call Muslims, Hindus, and others, who are undeserving sinners like ourselves. Regardless how they see things religiously, we believe that God has shown his love for them in Jesus Christ, not because they deserve it, but because of his grace. A Christian cannot view any human being as other than loved by God.

We also confess in the creed our faith in Jesus Christ, God's only Son, our Lord, full of grace and truth. The Incarnation is the means by which we have come to know the primordial mystery of the world. In this event that mystery is disclosed, and we know God to be the loving friend of sinners. Belief in God as

---

[17]On our relational ontology, see Catherine M. LaCugna, *God For Us: The Trinity and Christian Life* (San Francisco: HarperSanFrancisco, 1991), ch. 8 ("Persons in Communion").

[18]Joachim Jeremias, *New Testament Theology: The Proclamation of Jesus* (New York: Charles Scribner's Sons, 1971), 108–21.

personal love is grounded in the Incarnation, which is not viewed as a problem as it is in pluralism, but as the foundation for believing that God cares for humanity.[19]

The Word became flesh and God-for-us in the death and resurrection of Jesus. In Christ, God was uniquely and definitively present and at work decisively for the salvation of humanity. Jesus is the incarnation of the wisdom of God and the revelation of God's love for humankind. Being historical does not prevent Jesus from being the Savior of the world, because the light that was in him is the same light that enlightens every one entering the world (John 1:9, 14). And now that he has been lifted up on the cross, having finished the work God sent him to do, he is drawing all men and women to himself by the Spirit (John 12:32). Since God is for sinners, it follows we must be for them too in a positive way. We cannot act as if these "not-yet" Christians are rivals or enemies, if our God has made them his friends. If God loves them and Christ died for them, we must love them too and always foster the homecoming of believers from the other flocks of Christ (John 10:16). As Barth says: "If [Christians] are aware and sure of the fact that God loves them, they must also be aware and sure of this fact in respect of others also."[20]

We also confess and believe in the Holy Spirit, the Lord and Giver of life, the dynamic and free presence of God in the world, which blows where it wills (John 3:8). In the economy of God, the Spirit is under nobody's control but free to grace any person or any sphere, however remote from the church's present boundaries. The Spirit embodies the prevenient grace of God and puts into effect that universal drawing action of Jesus Christ. The world is the arena of God's presence, and the Spirit knocks on every human heart, preparing people for the coming of Christ; the Spirit is ever working to realize the saving thrust of God's promise for the world. From the Spirit flows that universal gracing that seeks to lead all people into fuller light and love. No people is totally devoid of inspiration as God works to bring the prodigal home. As Irenaeus said: "There is but one and the

---

[19]On this issue in relation to John Hick, see Gavin D'Costa, *John Hick's Theology of Religions: A Critical Evaluation* (New York: Univ. Press of America, 1987), 103–4.

[20]Karl Barth, *Church Dogmatics: The Doctrine of Creation* III/4 (Edinburgh: T. & T. Clark, 1961), 503.

same God who, from the beginning to the end by various dispensations, comes to the rescue of humankind."[21]

A real weakness in the traditional theology of the Spirit, however, has been an almost exclusively ecclesial understanding of his work, as if God's breath were confined within the walls of the church. There has been too little openness to the salvific presence of the Spirit in other religions and too little recognition of his role in bringing God to people everywhere in the world. We have stressed so strongly the Spirit's role in bringing people to faith in Christ that we have neglected the salvific presence of the Spirit in humanity's search for meaning generally.[22]

Christ, then, is the Savior of all people, but they do not all come to him at once historically. God's people, as even the Westminster Confession (8.6) notes, exist everywhere in the world, not just in churches. People have to be given time to find their way home. Not all of those who will eventually come have yet found Jesus or entered into the communion of Christ's church. The Spirit is working on the inside *and* on the outside of the churches, pursuing his assignment from the Father to make all things new. Christians do not have a monopoly on the Spirit, and the Spirit is not tied to our apron strings. Moltmann even says:

> The Spirit is not concerned about the church as such. He is concerned with the church, as he is with Israel, for the sake of the kingdom of God, the rebirth of life and the new creation of all things.[23]

The life-giving power of the holy breath is everywhere at work in creation furthering the saving work of God. The Spirit works in advance of mission beyond the confines of the Christian community. As a result, we may hope that wherever we go as ambassadors of Christ, the Spirit has gone there first. What an encouragement this is for mission!

---

[21]Irenaeus, *Against Heresies* 3.12.13.

[22]Philip J. Rosato, *The Spirit as Lord: The Pneumatology of Karl Barth* (Edinburgh: T. & T. Clark, 1981), 160–66. Not seeing this kept Barth in the confines of exclusivism, if not restrictivism.

[23]Jürgen Moltmann, *The Spirit of Life: A Universal Affirmation* (Minneapolis: Fortress, 1992), 230.

In viewing the Spirit's work abroad in the world, we refuse to drive a wedge between what God does in creation and in redemption, because the Spirit is Lord and Life-giver in both spheres. Creation is a gift of grace and capable of mediating grace, which is present not only in the church but outside as well, calling all persons to share in the life of God. Grace flows through both sets of divine activities and is not an add-on to nature. The saving grace of God can be effective through a person's relationship to God as creature in advance of conversion to Christ.

The Holy Spirit plays a prominent role in my understanding of inclusivism. I rejoice in Pope John Paul II's decision to speak in these terms also. In his first encyclical ("Redemptor Hominis" 1979), he spoke about the presence and activity of the Spirit in non-Christian religions, and he has continued to do so in various addresses since, especially in his encyclical on the Holy Spirit ("Dominum et Vivificantem" 1986). The Spirit is central to this model—not general revelation or the religions themselves, but the ubiquitous inspiration of the Spirit. Through the Spirit, God offers every person the mystery of his grace, because in their hearts, as the Council says, he works in unseen ways.[24]

While acknowledging the gracious presence of the Spirit in human life and culture, I am not dogmatic about how that hidden grace is present exactly. Whether a religion serves as a means of grace remains an open question, needing more study and always careful discernment. We do not know exactly what role, if any, a given religion plays in the divine economy. We are simply confident that the Spirit is operating in every sphere to draw people to God, using religion when and where it is possible and appropriate.

GOD'S PRESENCE IN RELIGION

Having set forth theological considerations, I turn now to religious realities on the ground. I am critical of scholars who try to settle their theories without consulting the actual situation. A

---

[24]The economy of the Spirit is central for Jacques Dupuis, *Jesus Christ at the Encounter of World Religions* (Maryknoll, N.Y.: Orbis Books, 1991), ch. 7; also for John V. Taylor, *The Go-Between God: The Holy Spirit and the Christian Mission* (London: SCM, 1972), ch. 9.

famous story is told about Karl Barth in this regard. When asked if he knew a Hindu, he replied that he did not need to know one in order to be sure about the status of his religion. Rahner also stays somewhat distant from the actual phenomena of religion when stating his thesis. This is partly due to his sense of a proper division of labor—he also stays away from biblical exegesis, seeing it as the work of others. Nevertheless, one ought to say something about the actual religious situation. How does inclusivism see God making positive uses of religion, bestowing grace and mercy on people? Where does it see prevenient grace operating among those of other faiths?

Formed as I was in the context of North American conservative-evangelicalism with its strongly exclusivist temper, there were not many lines of inclusivist thinking coming my way as a young Christian. There were, however, a few important exceptions to the rule.

When I was a young believer in the 1950s, C. S. Lewis helped me understand the relationship between Christianity and other religions in an inclusivist way. Because I trusted him as an orthodox thinker, I was open to hear him say that he could detect God's presence among other faiths and that he believed people could be saved in other religions because God was at work among them. His view was wonderfully summed up for me in that incident in *The Last Battle*, the last volume of the Narnia cycle, where the pagan soldier Emeth learns to his surprise that Aslan regards his worship of Tash as directed to himself. Anyone who appreciates that incident is on his or her way to inclusivist thinking.

The other influence was Sir Norman Anderson, a scholar of Islamic law and a longtime leader in the InterVarsity Fellowship in Great Britain. In 1970, he wrote a book called *Christianity and Comparative Religion*, which in 1984 was revised and retitled *Christianity and World Religions*. Anderson taught that people could be saved while being members of other faiths, much the way people were saved in Old Testament times apart from any Christian confession. Both these scholars helped me as a young student avoid the narrow outlook toward other faiths that was otherwise characteristic of evangelicalism.

Being part of conservative Christianity in North America, I was also aware of dispensational theology, which is influential in these circles. I noticed in this position a view of God's dealing with people in more than one way, depending on historical circumstances. Charles Ryrie spoke of a dispensation where God accepted pagans like Job on the basis of faith but without knowledge of either Moses or Christ. I felt this was biblical and found it appealing. I remember thinking how helpful it would be if this arrangement were still true for today for people in the same situation. I keep hoping dispensational theology will progress in this direction too and that a dispensational inclusivist will come forward to help people burdened by restrictivism in his or her camp. It hasn't happened yet, and I'm not holding my breath.[25]

Moving from the parochial and personal to the world stage, the key historical influence for inclusivism is undoubtedly the work of the Second Vatican Council in its articulation of this teaching. The spirit of the whole Council was one of openness to the world and a seeking after the unity of humanity. Its new thinking about religious pluralism originated in the church's own vexed relationship with the Jews, and from that point the bishops decided to speak about other world religions as well. Its standpoint was to view religions as arising from the spiritual dimension of created life and to seek the hidden presence of God in that sphere.

Exclusivism and pluralism do not enjoy the visibility that the Council gave inclusivism—a visibility that has continued in papal teachings since the Council. This sanction gives the model the feeling of official status that may help to explain why inclusivism enjoys such widespread success among many denominations. To me, the model appears to have supplanted exclusivism as the reigning ideology in the ecumenical churches and is now engaged in a debate with pluralism, which wishes to take things farther. Strategically, however, a strong reason for its popularity is the hope that inclusivism will make the more radical option of pluralism unnecessary and save the structure of historic doctrine.

---

[25]Ramesh P. Richard does not encourage me much in this hope: see his *The Population of Heaven* (Chicago: Moody, 1994), ch. 5. Nevertheless, changes going on in dispensationalism are considerable enough to cause me to continue to hope: see Craig A. Blaising and Darrell L. Bock, *Dispensationalism, Israel and the Church: The Search for Definition* (Grand Rapids: Zondervan, 1992).

As an inclusivist, I acknowledge my debt to the Catholic Church for its leadership in this regard, and, as an evangelical, I am concerned that the model be shown to be congruent with the Scriptures. In agreement with the Council, I want the model to be not only theologically coherent, but also exegetically well founded.

Let me sketch the way in which I see inclusivism to be congruent with the Scriptures. In the Old Testament, Melchizedek is an important symbol (Gen. 14:17–24). The story of his encounter with Abram shows that God was at work in the religious sphere of Canaanite culture. Abram accepts the blessing of this pagan priest and pays tithes to him. He is satisfied that the king of Salem worships the true God under the name *El Elyon*. God seems to be teaching Abram that his election does not mean that he is in exclusive possession of God, but rather that God is calling him to be a means of grace to all nations among whom God is also and already at work.[26] Melchizedek represents for me the larger group of pagan saints in Scripture among whom God worked.[27] For too long we have stared at the corrupt forms of religion mentioned in the Bible as if they represented the fullness of what religion can be according to the Scriptures, when there is more to it than that.

In the New Testament, Cornelius is a key symbol (Acts 10:1–48). God used this godly Gentile to teach the apostle Peter that there is no partiality in God's dealings with humanity. Though a non-Christian and a Gentile, Cornelius was devout and God-fearing—evidently God was present in the religious sphere of his life. He represents the wider hope of the book of Acts and the New Testament generally that affirms that God never leaves himself without witness among all peoples (Acts 14:17).

More exposition can be found in my book *A Wideness in God's Mercy*. I believe that the Bible supports inclusivism. It declares Jesus to be the fundamental way to salvation as God's eternal Son and sacrifice but does not confine the saving impact

---

[26]Two evangelicals point to Melchizedek. Don Richardson lifts up "The Melchizedek Factor" and Harry Boer speaks about "The Primacy of Melchizedek." See Richardson, *Eternity in Their Hearts* (Ventura, Calif.: Regal Books, 1981), part 1; Boer, *An Ember Still Glowing* (Grand Rapids: Eerdmans, 1990), ch. 2.

[27]I derived this expression from Jean Daniélou, *Holy Pagans of the Old Testament* (London: Longmans, Green, 1957).

of God's saving work to one segment of history. God has been at work saving human beings before Jesus was born and does so where Jesus has not been named. The patriarch Abraham was justified by faith without knowing Jesus, and Paul holds him up as a model believer for us all, even though he never heard the gospel (Rom. 4:1–25). Faith in Jesus as the Savior of the world leaves room for us to be open and generous to other religious traditions. Scripture encourages us to see the church not so much as the ark, outside of which there is no hope of salvation, but as the vanguard of those who have experienced the fullness of God's grace made available to all people in Jesus Christ. The Spirit is universally present in the world as well as uniquely present in the fellowship of the church.

This motif I find in the Scriptures rings true to modern experience, which confirms God's sometimes making use of religion in visiting grace upon humans. In the "Constitution on the Church," the bishops mention Judaism and Islam (article 16), and in the "Declaration on the Relationship of the Church to Non-Christian Religions," they refer to Hinduism and Buddhism. They speak of God's hidden presence among religions and refer, without naming them, to other religions that strive to satisfy the restless searchings of the human heart. In a memorable line they say:

> The Catholic Church rejects nothing which is true and holy in these religions. She looks with sincere respect upon those ways of conduct and of life, those rules and teachings which, though differing in many particulars from what she holds and sets forth, nevertheless reflect a ray of that Truth which enlightens all men.[28]

Not a scholar of comparative religions, I welcome the Saiva Siddhanta literature of Hinduism, which celebrates a personal God of love, and the emphasis on grace that I see in the Japanese Shin-Shu Amida sect. I also respect the Buddha as a righteous man (Matt. 10:41) and Mohammed as a prophet figure in the style of the Old Testament.[29] Similarly, Don Richardson in *Eter-*

---

[28]"Declaration on the Relationship of the Church to Non-Christian Religions," par. 2.

[29]See Pinnock, *A Wideness in God's Mercy*, ch. 3. John Hick is right to observe, citing Sarah Coakley, that the term *incarnation* has several meanings. One can use it

nity in their Hearts describes a world in many ways prepared for
the gospel by means of redemptive bridges. I delight in the testimony of Sacred Feathers, a Mississauga Indian of my vicinity,
who found in Jesus the golden chain that fulfilled what God had
already taught him in native traditions.[30] I am conscious of the
need for more missionaries to report on their experiences of how
the Spirit has been working in pagan contexts in advance of the
mission. They have more authority to speak about such matters
than I do.

John Hick calls attention to the same sort of data for reasons
of his own model. He traces a rising hope for human transformation in what he calls the axial religions.[31] From an inclusivist
perspective, I would say that people are sensing the coming of
God's kingdom declared in the gospel and are hoping for a
transformation that is surely coming. On a personal basis, we
encounter saints from other religions in daily experience. We are
like Abraham in his encounter with Abimelech. He was afraid
at first but discovered later that the fear of God was indeed in
the man's house. In fact, in the story the pagan behaved more
like a believer than the patriarch did (Gen. 20:1–18). There is testimony in human experience that God is redemptively at work
in other religious communities, which confirms what inclusivists
expect.

Of course, religions do not teach the same things and do not
even have the same goals.[32] There is much that distinguishes and
separates them. But this is not news, and evangelicals have
emphasized the point enough. It is time to speak of what is common and connecting among us.

---

in a weaker sense than Christian orthodoxy in reference to those saintly persons in
whom people see God acting and in whom they sense the divine presence, without
denying, as Hick does, the unique incarnation of God the Son in Jesus of Nazareth.
See Hick, *The Metaphor of God Incarnate: Christology in a Pluralistic Age* (Louisville:
Westminster/John Knox, 1993), 9–10.

[30]Donald B. Smith, *Sacred Feathers: The Reverend Peter Jones and the Mississauga
Indians* (Toronto: Univ. of Toronto Press, 1987), ch. 5.

[31]John Hick, *An Interpretation of Religion: Human Responses to the Transcendent*
(New Haven: Yale Univ. Press, 1989), chs. 3–4, 17–18.

[32]This is an emphasis of J. A. DiNoia, *The Diversity of Religions: A Christian Perspective* (Washington, D.C.: Catholic Univ. of America Press, 1992).

A NEW RELATIONSHIP TO OTHER RELIGIONS

Inclusivism implies a new relationship between Christianity and other religions, if God is preveniently at work among the peoples. It calls for a generous openness to the possibility of God's gracious presence there. We must not continue to walk the path of superiority and chauvinism that has too often sadly characterized the old relationship. I deplore, for example, Calvin's wretched comment that God revealed a little truth to non-Christians to increase their condemnation.[33]

Inclusivism calls for a more dialogical relationship among religions. As is stated in the "Declaration on the Relationship of the Church to Non-Christian Religions":

> The Church urges her sons to enter with prudence and charity into discussion and collaboration with members of other religions. Let Christians, while witnessing to their own faith and way of life, acknowledge, preserve, and encourage the spiritual and moral truths found among non-Christians.[34]

The bishops clearly have in mind not only discussion and cooperation, but also testimony to the grace of God in Jesus Christ. The missionary dimension is always integral to their thinking, as it should be. The hope is that, in the process of dialogue, the Spirit will use this testimony as a catalyst to bring about change, both in individuals and even in society.[35]

There are various types of dialogue. One kind discusses how to live together in peace, another shares religious experiences mutually, yet another might try to assess truth claims. All such forms of dialogue are important. Dialogue arises out of our caring for other people and involves a willingness to listen respectfully to one another.[36]

---

[33]John Calvin, *Institutes* 2.2.18. See Kenneth Cracknell, *Towards a New Relationship: Christians and People of Other Faith* (London: Epworth, 1986), ch. 1.

[34]"Declaration," par. 2.

[35]Similarly see Jürgen Moltmann, *The Church in the Power of the Spirit* (London: SCM, 1977), 158–59; Thomas Finger, *Christian Theology: An Eschatological Approach* II (Scottdale, Pa.: Herald, 1989), ch. 12.

[36]David K. Clark speaks in terms of a dialogical approach: *Dialogical Apologetics: A Person Centered Approach to Christian Defense* (Grand Rapids: Baker, 1993).

In dialogue we respect other persons as fellow human beings and seekers after truth. We need to honor the truth in other religions and be willing to learn from them. It is not acceptable to preach *at* people. We must learn about their doctrines, take them seriously, and watch for bridges and points of contact. We should expect to find evidence of God's grace at work in the lives of those who do not know Jesus. Truth is agonistic—we make progress when we speak and respond, when we struggle with ideas and try to overcome misconceptions. We dialogue, not because we are indifferent to truth, but because we care so much for it.[37]

There should also be a willingness to be seriously global in our work—to do theology in public not in a ghetto. For the gospel to penetrate culture, it is necessary for the Christian position to engage other sets of convictions (which are by no means the same) and strive after a maximal illumination of reality.

Furthermore, we ought to testify, argue, and offer reasoned arguments for our faith. There are important questions to ask and be asked as we probe for truth together. History is the sphere of a contest of the gods and a competition between religions for human loyalty. We do not assume that truth is equally present among all parties or that it lies exclusively with only one religion. Religions die when their light fails, when their interpretation no longer illuminates reality. Dialogue is prominent in the New Testament—we must continue with the practice.[38]

At the same time, inclusivism should not be rosy-eyed about religion, which can contain noble truths as well as terrible errors and commend virtuous deeds as well as horrible atrocities. This is because not only the Spirit of God, but the angel of darkness as well hovers over them. The apostle John warns us not to believe every spirit, but to test the spirits to see whether they are from God (1 John 4:1). Religions contain truth and error, the Spirit and the fallen powers of this age. It is therefore essential to have a criterion of differentiation, without which one can be lost at sea. Witchcraft and Nazism are not valid responses to the divine, according to the gospel. Religions can be pathways to damnation, and history is the graveyard of

---

[37]Paul J. Griffiths, "Why We Need Interreligious Polemics," *First Things* 44 (June/July 1994): 31–37.

[38]For more about dialogue, see Pinnock, *A Wideness in God's Mercy*, ch, 4, and Cracknell, *Towards a New Relationship*, ch. 2.

the gods. Relativism in regard to such matters is not safe in religion or anywhere else where truth and justice matter.

We need an interpretive lens to bring things into focus and to sort things out. Christians find this criterion in Jesus Christ, the Savior of the world, in whom God has been revealed decisively. Some forms of pluralism are relativist and signal the collapse of truth and values. Ironically, this undermines even the pluralist belief itself, namely, that all faiths arise from the same source and tend toward the same goal. How do we know that they do? Without a criterion, there is no way to make necessary judgments about truth and error, goodness and corruption in religion. If God is unknown and all paths are thought to be equally valid, one cannot tell whether a belief or practice is true or false, right or wrong, healing or destructive. Error and vileness go unchallenged, and there is no reliable way to differentiate wholesome from poisonous spiritual food. Despite political correctness, tolerance is not always a virtue.[39]

Christians must not believe every prophet or go with every flow, because not every spirit has a valid claim to be heard. As omnipresent, the Spirit is *in* everything but not *as* everything. Certainly God is present outside the symbolic world of Christianity, and his life-giving activity is not restricted to one segment of history. Nevertheless, not everything in the world, not everything in religion, can be attributed to the Spirit. The Paraclete is the Spirit of Jesus, and we orient ourselves by this insight. When we see Jesus' path, we know that the Spirit is near. As Lord of all, Jesus is the criterion of truth in religion, including the Christian religion.[40]

Admittedly, this criterion is a contested one. Any criterion is. The purpose of dialogue is in part testing such truth claims. We enter into dialogue from a Christian commitment, accepting that all claims, including our own, are provisional, and we seek to show that the revelation of God in Jesus Christ is best able to illumine human life and pass the other tests for truth.[41]

---

[39]S. D. Gaede, *When Tolerance Is No Virtue* (Downers Grove, Ill.: InterVarsity, 1994).

[40]Christopher Morse, *Not Every Spirit: A Dogmatics of Christian Disbelief* (Valley Forge, Pa.: Trinity Press International, 1994).

[41]We agree with Pannenberg, who advances this understanding of dialogue; see Stanley J. Grenz, "Commitment and Dialogue: Pannenberg on Christianity and the Religions," *Journal of Ecumenical Studies* 26 (1989): 196–210.

OTHER ISSUES ARISING IN INCLUSIVISM

Religion in culture. Inclusivists view religion as lying at the heart of created human life. We were made for fellowship with God, and our hearts are restless until we find it. God is the goal of our life, and we were made to participate in divine life. Pursuing this goal, most people look to religion for answers to their deep questions. The basic function of religion in culture is to supply people with truth and meaning.

The conviction of inclusivism is that the Christian message is the fulfillment, not only of Old Testament religion, but in some way of all religious aspiration and of the human quest itself. The aspirations of the ancient world, the messianic hope of Israel, the quest of the Greek people, and the longings of the Orient can find fulfillment in Jesus Christ. They are among the many and varied ways by which God has spoken to nations.

All good elements in life and culture are gifts of God (James 1:17) and prepare us for the coming of the truth proclaimed in the gospel. Salvation through Christ perfects the natural goodness of created life and brings humanity to its goal. Positive values of non-Christian religions prepare for and are perfected by the light and power of God's revelation in Jesus Christ. Reading the New Testament one is often surprised by the way in which the Old Testament is sometimes said to be fulfilled there, as when the fulfillment goes beyond the promise. Jesus, for example, was more than the prophets said he would be.[42] Similarly I think, other anticipations of Christ may be fulfilled in surprising but satisfying ways, owing to the freedom of God, who knows in his wisdom how to fulfill every intimation of Christ in the best way.

The author to the Hebrews, after speaking about those who had faith before Christ came, that is, about those pagans and Jews who had pleased God by faith (all of them as non-Christians), observes that they did not receive what was promised (the Messiah) because God had a better plan, according to which they would not suffer loss (Heb. 11:39–40). Are we not all burdened by the apparent unfairness of a message that we say has

---

[42]On this phenomenon, see Stephen Travis, *I Believe in the Second Coming of Christ* (Grand Rapids: Eerdmans, 1992), 139–41.

universal saving significance, but which has not actually been available to a sizable percentage of the race hitherto? Hebrews wants to tell us that all these people had access to God, even though they longed for a fuller gift that in God's sovereignty was not yet given historically—namely, the better covenant, the better sacrifice, the better hope, and so on. Jesus also said that the eyes of his disciples were blessed, for prophets and righteous ones had longed to see their day but did not see it (Matt. 13:16–17). But Hebrews assures us that those who went before are not penalized or prevented from enjoying the saving reality of the gospel. It was not their fault to have lived too soon; it was God's idea to move from historically small beginnings to a large consummation. God's plan was not to make salvation universal at the beginning but at the end of history. But he takes care not to make that a penalty for those who live too soon.

Other religions. What is the status of other religions, according to inclusivism? First, religion is a central part of human culture and embodies the human search for meaning. At the very least, religions are expressions of human life created by God and for God. Religions flow out of built-in human aspirations.

More than that, religions provide a window of opportunity for the Spirit to engage people, because—in spite of a measure of deceptive activity, the mystery of evil—God is also mysteriously present and working. The Spirit is not limited to the boundaries of churches but gives life to the whole creation. The Spirit is ever at work setting in motion the plan of redemption revealed in the gospel.

This does not make religions salvific as such, however. The Spirit is the power of God unto salvation, not to religion. God *may* use elements in them as a means of grace, even as God may use the moral dimension, the celestial bodies, or social interaction to lead people to himself. We must be alert to the possibility that God is effectively at work in the religious dimension in a given instance, but there are no guarantees of it. Religions as such do not mediate salvation. Modal inclusivism acknowledges the presence of God in this sphere but does not endorse the salvific character of religion per se. Present in every sphere, God is drawing people to himself in a variety of ways, which can include the religious sphere. But often the resistance is of such a magnitude that pursuing this avenue is futile even for God, who does not always get his way.[43]

If a non-Christian believes (as in Heb. 11), it is faith and not membership (or non-membership) in a religious community that counts. By faith, one receives the prevenient grace of God on the basis of an honest search for God and obedience to God's word as heard in the heart and conscience. A premessianic believer is, one might say, latently a member of Christ's body and destined to receive the grace of conversion and explicit knowledge of Jesus Christ at a later date, whether in this life or after death.

Faith cannot be identified with adherence to Christianity or any other religion. God saves through faith, through a heart response not confined to a religious framework. God can relate to the human soul inside or outside these structures. It is not under our control where the Spirit breathes. There is no time or space where he is not free to move or where a person cannot call on God for mercy. God is free to speak his word at any time and in any way. God's word is not bound or confined (2 Tim. 2:9).

General revelation. Inclusivism believes that God can use both general and special revelation in salvific ways. Western theology since Augustine has been pessimistic about admitting God's grace outside the church and salvific divine revelation outside of Christ. This tradition has said that general revelation provides a rudimentary knowledge of God and creates significant points of contact for missionaries, but it does not create the possibility of redemption. This implies that God reveals himself to all people, not to help them, but to make their condemnation more severe. It is easy to understand why Barth took the logical step of denying that general revelation even exists. What kind of God is it who would reveal himself in order to worsen the condition of sinners and make their plight more hopeless?[44]

Preferable is the view of the early church fathers. Though their assessment of other religions was negative, they viewed

---

[43]My view of divine providence is that it involves risks for God. This reveals my Arminian tendency over against the Calvinistic view. In contrast, see Paul Helm, *The Providence of God* (Downers Grove, Ill.: InterVarsity, 1994), ch. 2.

[44]This is a question for Bruce Demarest, *General Revelation: Historical Views and Contemporary Issues* (Grand Rapids: Zondervan, 1982), and "General and Special Revelation: Epistemological Foundations of Religious Pluralism," in *One God, One Lord: Christianity in a World of Religious Pluralism*, ed. by Andrew D. Clarke and Bruce W. Winter (Grand Rapids: Baker, 1993), 189–206.

God's providence and general revelation as graciously intended and did not recognize the later distinction that negated their salvific value. They saw creation itself as a gift of God's bountiful love, which could be accepted as such by sinners through faith. Inclusivism approves of their view of the salvific possibility of each type of revelation and does not adopt the later view that prejudices God's good intentions in revealing himself to all persons. The triune God is present in the whole world and can be encountered by anyone. We recognize God's grace as operative in both modes of revelation.[45]

There is a witness in creation and providence that God uses for human good. God reveals himself to all peoples and never leaves himself without witness (Acts 14:17). Revelation is embodied in other religions. The revelation in creation is capable of mediating a knowledge of God. God, the compassionate Father of our Lord Jesus Christ, is always and everywhere seeking lost sheep. What we call general revelation and common grace contains not merely natural but supernatural and gracious elements.[46]

False beliefs. How can God use positive elements in other religions and work within them when they espouse false beliefs alongside the true, and when as systems they do not commend a salvation of the Christian sort? Hendrick Kraemer refers to the totalitarian character of religions, which seems to make this impossible.[47]

While it is true that incorrect beliefs do not lead people to faith, that is not the whole story about religion. There are other levels to faith than the intellectual. The act of faith is more than cognitive. Authentic faith and holy action may flow from persons inhabiting an unpromising religious and doctrinal culture. Someone might be an atheist because he or she does not understand who God is, and still have faith. They called Socrates an atheist because he did not believe in the unworthy gods of

---

[45]Irenaeus, for example, in opposition to the Gnostics, emphasized that God gives the Spirit both in creation and in new creation in a continuous manner (*Against Heresies* 5.18.2). This issue is basic to the theology of the Vatican Council on religious pluralism, and I agree with it; see Ruokanen, *The Catholic Doctrine of Non-Christian Religions*, 11–12, 18, 25–26, 29, 115, 119.

[46]Walbert Buhlmann, *God's Chosen Peoples* (Maryknoll, N.Y.: Orbis Books, 1982).

[47]A point discussed by Gavin D'Costa, *Theology and Religious Pluralism*, 92–96.

Athens, but we assume that he had more faith than the general populace of that city. Did Jesus not tell us that giving the thirsty a drink of cold water is an act of participation in the selfless love of God revealed in the gospel and makes one his sheep (Matt. 25:31–40)? Created in God's image, a person can decide to accept the mystery of one's being, which is the goal of his or her life. Concerning the unevangelized, John Wesley wrote: "We have great reason to hope, although they lived among the heathen, yet (many of them) were quite of another spirit, being taught of God, by his inward voice, all the essentials of true religion."[48] Inclusivism has roots in the evangelical tradition.

At the same time, more positively, there are often truths that can be seized upon in other religions. C. S. Lewis writes,

> There are people in other religions who are being led by God's secret influence to concentrate on those parts of their religion which are in agreement with Christianity, and who thus belong to Christ without knowing it.[49]

Everyone must eventually pass through Jesus to reach the Father, but there is more than one path for arriving at this place. Is this not the stuff of Christian testimony—how one came to know him? One can get to that place from many points on the compass. All the paths that lead to God end up at Jesus, but they do not all start with him.[50]

Pagan saints. All inclusivists recognize that there are pagan saints in other religions, but not all would call them "anonymous Christians" as Rahner does. I myself think it would be better and more biblical to speak of them as believers awaiting messianic salvation. The Bible itself speaks of such people as believers (e.g., Job), a usage that has the advantage of being more acceptable terminology. People like Abel were justified by faith and experienced God truly, though they lived prior to the outpoured Spirit of Pentecost. Paul himself speaks of believers prior to Christ as servants destined to become sons (Gal. 3:23; 4:1). To speak of "anonymous Christians" might minimize the newness

---

[48]John Wesley, "On Faith," *The Works of John Wesley*, 3d ed. (Peabody, Mass.: Hendrickson, 1986), 7:197.

[49]C. S. Lewis, *Mere Christianity* (New York: Macmillan, 1967), 176.

[50]Mark Heim, *Is Christ the Only Way? Christian Faith in a Pluralistic World* (Valley Forge, Pa.: Judson, 1985), 129–30.

of what Christ has brought into the world.[51] Not using this terminology also avoids the practical embarrassment of calling a Buddhist an anonymous Christian, a point always raised against Rahner.

Motivation for missions. How does inclusivism affect the motivation for world mission? If we think the unevangelized can be saved by faith, the motive would have to transcend fire insurance. It would be conceptualized more broadly, in terms of proclaiming the good news of the kingdom of God, spreading the news about Jesus, and summoning people into the historically new people of God. Everyone needs to hear about this, whether they have responded to premessianic light or not. God is presently drawing the nations toward his kingdom, and participating in mission joins in that process. The Christian mission calls people to the fullness of salvation in the fellowship of the body of Christ until it reaches maturity. Inclusivism does not reduce the motivation for missions but understands it in a larger framework and in terms of more factors. It removes the feeling of panic created by restrictivism.

Inclusivism can improve our motivation and enhance our hope as we go forth to testify to Christ, since we are entitled to believe that God has gone before us, preparing the way for the gospel. It can help us bear witness to Christ, knowing that the Spirit is the initiator and true witness, not us. To the one who has already reached out to God in the premessianic situation, we call them to come higher up and deeper in, to know God better and love God more.[52]

An issue needing more attention by inclusivists is the question: What about those who, when presented with the gospel, still choose to remain within their own faith—a Muslim, for example, who is drawn to Jesus but cannot break with his people? Perhaps he is afraid. My instinct is to leave this matter with the grace of God, who knows the factors that go into such a decision and makes valid judgments. Living in a country where there is no danger in becoming Christian, I am in no position to judge such a case. At the same time, it is no small matter to turn away from the grace of God (Heb. 2:1–3).

---

[51]On this point, see Sullivan, *Salvation Outside the Church: Tracing the History of the Catholic Response*, 175.

[52]"The Decree on Missionary Activity" of the Council discusses this issue.

Chauvinism. One of the features of religion that people today tolerate least is a sense of superiority and chauvinism. They know it is only fairly recently that Christians have been willing to recognize grace outside the church, truth outside Christian theology, and abiding values outside Western civilization. And they remember what this has meant for the Jewish people over the centuries and for relations with the people of other faiths. They have not forgotten this doubtful heritage and will not let us forget it.[53]

Among other things, inclusivism is an attempt to overcome this painful legacy and shares this concern with pluralists like Hick. By recognizing noble features in other religions and by positing the prevenience of the Spirit among nations, we hope to avoid an attitude of superiority and dispel the criticism. Nevertheless, critics wonder whether inclusivism can dispel it. By continuing to say with exclusivists that Jesus Christ is uniquely the Savior of the world, it seems to foster the same superiority in a more polite sounding way. Does it not still imply that other religions operate on a lower level, both salvifically and theologically? In order to be truly egalitarian, should we not stop insisting on the uniqueness of Jesus Christ as the Savior of the world because it inevitably fosters superiority?[54]

First, we would not normally consider someone acting "superior" if they reported on a wonderful discovery they had made, let us say in medicine or science. On the contrary, we would listen with interest. We should not call such a discovery "superior." Yet this is precisely what is going on in sharing faith. Christians are reporting the belief that God entered time in Jesus Christ, whose resurrection signals new creation. All religions testify to crucial insights. All of them make truth claims of this sort and cannot be forbidden. Of course, in doing so one *might* testify in a superior manner, but that would not be necessary and, in the case of the Christian faith, would be inappropriate. Let us not forget that it is possible for even a pluralist to behave in a superior manner, if he or she believes an insight to be crucial.

[53]See, for example, David Pailin, *Attitudes to Other Religions: Comparative Religion in Seventeenth and Eighteenth Century Britain* (Manchester: Manchester Univ. Press, 1984).

[54]Hick and Knitter feel this strongly; see Hick, *The Metaphor of God Incarnate*, 87–88; Paul Knitter, *No Other Name?* ch. 9.

Second, one gets the impression from critics that one can freely adapt the faith and drop out central elements in it, such as belief in the Incarnation, in order to achieve the desirable social goal of peace and harmony. This minimizes the element in religious experience of not being able *not* to speak of one's central convictions (Acts 4:20). Christians cannot, even in order to create more amicable interreligious relationships, *not* speak of the triune God and the resurrection of Jesus Christ. They cannot agree to give up testifying to a God who loves humanity passionately and to limit themselves to speaking about ineffable Reality (assuming there is one) or a Transcendence, which (we are told) can be described in differing and even contradictory ways. Other religions are unlikely to respond to the suggestion positively either. Imagine asking a Muslim to stop talking about Mohammed as the final prophet because others do not endorse it. Academics in an atmosphere of political correctness are drawn to this strategy for religious harmony, but not people with strong religious convictions.

Third, holding beliefs not universally shared is unavoidable, and pluralists are not immune from it. Religions make truth claims and therefore run the risk of sounding or acting superior, since they herald a unique insight. Pluralists do the same thing when they claim there is a Reality differently responded to by various faiths. They get attention because it is an interesting possibility, but it remains one claim alongside the others. Like myself, they believe something unique about God, but unlike me they are reluctant to admit it. But my belief in the Incarnation and their belief in an unknowable God, validly interpreted by everybody, are on the same plane—both are contestable truth claims, sincerely held. Ineffable Reality may exist or the triune God may exist—there is a choice to be made and a truth question to sort out.[55] Superiority is a red herring kind of charge that conceals this fact. Superiority has little to do with it. A pluralist, an inclusivist, or an exclusivist may behave in a superior or in a humble way.

Some pluralists (not Hick) like the fable about five blind men and an elephant to explain how religious pluralism works.

---

[55]Mortimer J. Adler emphasizes the centrality of the truth question in *Truth in Religion: The Plurality of Religions and the Unity of Truth* (New York: Macmillan, 1990).

It describes how five blind men try to describe the beast from various points of view—one handling the tail, one stroking the trunk, another feeling the legs, etc. Each religion, they say, describes God from a limited vantage point but each in a valid way. What they do not mention is that the king who brought the animal into the room knows very well what the animal looks like from his privileged position. Pluralists are a little like the king who is not blind and knows the animal is in fact an elephant. Those who dogmatize about God's ineffability and tell us to get into line with their view should not speak too loudly about superiority because they face the temptation confronting us all.[56] Has conversion to Kant replaced conversion to Christ in liberalism?

Inclusivism is a timely and appealing model, and I offer it for consideration. It interprets faith in Jesus Christ as not entailing narrowness or pessimism in our understanding of God's redemptive purposes. I think that if we were to reform theology in the direction of inclusivism, we might enhance the credibility of our faith and render more radical options unnecessary.

---

[56]Lesslie Newbigin, *The Gospel in a Pluralist Society* (Grand Rapids: Eerdmans, 1989), 9–10.

RESPONSE TO CLARK H. PINNOCK

John Hick

From a pluralist point of view, Clark Pinnock's inclusivism represents an enormous advance on Christian exclusivism. The latter holds that only those who in this life explicitly accept Jesus as their Lord and Savior are saved, so that Jews, Muslims, Hindus, and Buddhists are not. In contrast to this, Pinnock suggests that the Holy Spirit is operative not only within the church but also within the other great world religions, working to prepare their members for the gospel of Christ. According to Pinnock, all salvation is exclusively Christian salvation, bought by the blood of Jesus; but while "everyone must pass through Jesus to reach the Father," nevertheless "there is more than one path for arriving at this place." A sincere and devout Jew, Muslim, or Buddhist may thus be a "premessianic believer," who is "latently a member of Christ's body and destined to receive the grace of conversion and explicit knowledge of Jesus Christ at a later date, whether in this life or after death." This shows a positive appreciation of Hindus, Muslims, Jews, and Buddhists, which is more realistic in relation both to God's love and to the human situation than the old exclusivism. But is it realistic enough?

AGREEMENTS WITH PINNOCK

Before suggesting why I believe that we have to go further along the road that led from exclusivism to inclusivism and leads on to pluralism, let me register points of agreement with Pinnock. First, I reject with him the morally repugnant idea of God's condemning to eternal perdition the majority of the human race who have not heard or accepted the Christian gospel.

I also agree with him that religion is not always good; it is a mixture of good and evil. Each of the great traditions, including Christianity, has brought both immense benefit but also immense harm to humanity. On the one hand, they have provided a framework of meaning for life; they have elevated the morality of whole civilizations, teaching mutual love and a commitment to justice; they have sponsored education and healing, produced great saints and great thinkers, and inspired great literature and great works of art. On the other hand, however, they have validated every war that has ever been fought, validated the subordination of women, and validated social injustices such as slavery, caste and class, imperialism and colonialism, racism and anti-Semitism. A critical as well as appreciative stance towards the world religions, including Christianity, is thus always in order.

Finally, I welcome Pinnock's readiness to "acknowledge sanctity in persons and religions other than Christian," though I question whether he has sufficiently considered the implications of the reality of saintliness, goodness, and piety outside the borders of Christianity.

THE RELOCATION OF INCLUSIVISM'S OPTIMISM TO THE ESCHATON

We must first, however, note that any idea that the non-Christian majority of humankind will be converted to Christianity in this life is a fantasy. Already the majority of human beings who have lived and died on this earth have done so outside Christianity. And while the number of Christians is increasing, the proportion of Christians in the world population is decreasing and has shrunk during the present century from about a third to about a quarter. This is due to the continuing global population explosion, which is occurring much more within the mainly non-Christian third world than in the mainly Christian first and second worlds. It is likely, for example, that within a generation the largest religious community on earth will be Islam. Thus any realistic hope of a universal conversion to Christianity must now be transferred from this life to the next.

This is increasingly accepted today by Christian inclusivists, of whom Pinnock is a main proponent.[1] The Catholic variation of an encounter with Christ in the moment of death is advocated by J. A. DiNoia in his *The Diversity of Religions*.[2]

This shifting of the salvation of the majority of human beings into a postmortem sphere involves a major departure from the traditional orthodoxy, which has held that death forecloses our options and that after death it is too late to repent or to be converted. Thus within Catholicism, the first Vatican Council declared that "after this mortal life there is no place for repentance for justification," and that "if anyone says that a man can be justified even after death ... let him be anathema."[3] Among evangelical Protestants it has been a widespread conviction, supported by such texts as the parable of the rich man and Lazarus (Luke 16:19–31) and Hebrews 9:27, that there is no second chance after death.

The idea of a second chance has been regarded as a liberal heresy, and its adoption now is significant as an implicit acceptance of the principle that we may, and indeed must, develop our theology to meet new, or newly perceived, problems. As a result of greatly increased travel, the information explosion, and massive east to west immigration, we have today a much greater awareness of the other great world faiths and of the moral goodness and spiritual sanctity that is to be found as much within them. This new awareness calls for important developments in Christian thinking. The question is not whether change is needed, but whether it is sufficient simply to shift the problem into the unknown realm beyond the grave.

INCLUSIVISM'S FAILURE TO ACKNOWLEDGE THE DISTINCTIVE RELIGIOUS LIVES OF NON-CHRISTIANS

The reason why this is not sufficient is, in my view, that it is an a priori dogma that does not do justice to the actual reli-

---

[1]See John Sanders, *No Other Name* (Grand Rapids: Eerdmans, 1992), for information about other discussions of "eschatological evangelization."

[2]J. A. DiNoia, *The Diversity of Religions* (Washington, D.C.: Catholic Univ. of America Press, 1992).

[3]*The Church Teaches: Documents of the Church in English Translation*, tr. John F. Clarkson et al. (St. Louis: Herder, 1961), 353.

gious life of Jews, Muslims, Hindus, and Buddhists now, in this life. I have suggested in my own chapter that the spiritual and moral fruits that reflect a right relationship to the ultimate transcendent reality we call God are as evident in Jewish, Muslim, Hindu, and Buddhist lives as in Christian lives. And I have suggested that the real substance of salvation is this change in men and women. In its most fundamental sense, salvation is not a juridical transaction between the Father and the Son, or a future postmortem possibility, but a human transformation that begins in this life from natural self-centeredness to a new orientation centered in the Divine, the Ultimate, the Real—that for which our distinctively Christian concept is the Holy Trinity. If salvation consisted in being forgiven and accepted by God because of Jesus' death on the cross, then it would be a tautology that only the church knows and teaches the possibility of salvation. But if salvation—or, better, salvation/liberation—consists in an actual human change from self-centeredness to Reality-centeredness or God-centeredness, then it is manifestly not confined in this life to Christians. It is the goal of all the great religions, including Christianity, and I have suggested that so far as we can tell, it occurs to a more or less equal extent within all of them.

This salvific transformation is seen to varying extents in men and women of all races, cultures, and faiths, to the extent that they respond creatively during their lives to the challenges and opportunities of human existence. We see it most clearly in the saints, or paradigm figures, of all traditions—whether we think of St. Francis or Nelson Mandela, of Gautama or the Dalai Lama, of Muhammad or Rumi, of Ramakrishna or Gandhi. Of course, there are also all too many men and women living in such harsh conditions that they can do no more than survive; and there are others who regress into evil rather than progress towards the full humanity of children of God. Clearly, therefore, the salvific process must continue beyond this life. But it is equally clear that it has begun for many people, of whatever religious tradition or none, during this life. Furthermore, each of the great world faiths seems to constitute a more or less equally effective context for this salvific transformation. It therefore seems to me more realistic to accept them, as I have argued in my own chapter, as different but apparently equally authentic human responses to the Divine, the Ultimate, the Real.

THE DIVINE CREATIVE PROCESS AMONG HUMANS

On this understanding of the cosmic situation, the whole of humankind is involved in a divine creative process that begins in this present life and continues to its completion beyond it. The great world religions, including Christianity, have grown out of particular powerful world-changing awarenesses or "revelations" of the Real—in the life and teaching of Jesus the Christ, in the life and teaching of Gautama the Buddha, in the religious experience of the Vedic sages and their successors, in the experiences of Moses, the Hebrew prophets, and the Jewish rabbis, in the experience of Muhammad in receiving the Qur'an. And the traditions that have developed from these revelatory occasions have all proved to be contexts of salvation/liberation—and apparently more or less equally so—enabling men and women to begin to undergo the salvific transformation from animal self-centeredness to Reality-centeredness. Thus, the non-Christian world religions are more than "premessianic" preparations for Christian conversion. They are different but, so far as we can tell, equally authentic spheres of salvation/liberation, through which the universal presence of the Real, the Ultimate, the Divine is mediated to human beings.

This is not an a priori dogma but a hypothesis that accounts for the observable salvific response, as well as lack of response, to the Divine within all the major religious communities. It does not have to downgrade the religious life of Jews, Muslims, Hindus, and Buddhists in order to maintain the dogma of Christian superiority. Jews, Muslims, Christians, and other religious practitioners are all alike part of the same worldwide salvific process.

In contrast to this, is there not something arbitrary, lop-sided, and even parochial in the idea that human beings can only fully respond to God through the person of Jesus of Nazareth, who lived so comparatively recently in human history, after great civilizations and great religious traditions had long existed in China and India; and that the function of the world faiths, despite the great saints whom they have produced, is only to prepare the majority of humankind for the Christian gospel?

RESPONSE TO CLARK H. PINNOCK

Alister E. McGrath

Professor Pinnock has been the catalyst for much rethinking within the evangelical movement, not least on account of his Arminian approach to issues of salvation and grace. While this Wesleyanism may be a minority presence within American evangelicalism, it has served to catalyze a reexamination of many aspects of the traditional evangelical heritage.[1] I read his chapter with particular interest for two reasons. First, it allows its readers to explore whether the Arminian position has anything significant to contribute to the debate on religious pluralism, especially when compared with its Reformed alternatives. Second, it allows its readers to consider whether the Logos-Christology Pinnock adopts casts light on any of the issues we are confronted with in this volume.

PINNOCK'S INCLUSIVISM

The style of approach Pinnock adopts has clear parallels with that found in the Second Vatican Council, especially the writings of Karl Rahner.[2] Thus his inference that grace may be encountered in the context of the non-Christian religions can be

---

[1] See Robert Brow, "Evangelical Megashift," *Christianity Today* 34 (February 19, 1990):12–14; see also Pinnock's response in the same issue, p. 15.

[2] Vatican II, "Nostra Aetate" (October 28, 1965), in *Vatican II: Conciliar and Postconciliar Documents*, ed. Austin Flannery, OP (Northport, N.Y.: Costello, 1975 / Dublin: Dominican Publications, 1975), 738–42; Karl Rahner, *Theological Investigations*, vol. 5 (London: DLT, 1966), 115–34.

discerned in Rahner's approach and gives rise to the same objection that he himself correctly anticipates: Does this mean that non-Christian religions are also vehicles of God's grace, and even of the presence of Christ, though in an anonymous manner? This criticism has certainly been directed against Rahner; I was therefore relieved to note Pinnock's acknowledgment of this point and his deliberate distancing of himself from this approach. There are parallels between the approach offered by Pinnock and that of Norman Anderson in his *Christianity and World Religions* (1984). The latter's work can be thought of as an evangelical counterpart of Rahner's approach, but one that avoids its weaker features—a point particularly clear in his studious and judicious consideration of the relation between Israel and the church as a case study for the broader discussion.

Pinnock has clearly made a significant case for his approach to the issue. As he points out, there can be no doubt that at least some form of knowledge of the Lord existed outside Israel during the period of the Old Testament. The theme of the "holy pagans," such as Melchizedek and Job, must be reflected in any Christian approach to natural theology or to the broader issue of religious pluralism. For Pinnock, other religions may well have "a role preparatory to the gospel of Christ, in whom alone fullness of salvation is found." Karl Rahner allowed other religions salvific status until the coming of Christ. Pinnock, following the Second Vatican Council, declines to follow this approach, wisely regarding it as flawed and possibly being based on a form of sacramental theology that evangelicals feel no particular need to accept.

If I have understood Professor Pinnock correctly, he is suggesting that other religious traditions may be functioning as ways of preparing the way for the coming of the Christian gospel, in much the same way as Judaism prepared that way. This is certainly a way in which some of my Indian Christian colleagues regard Hinduism, seeing it—perhaps even to the point of displacing the Old Testament—as representing God's gracious preparation for Christ in their cultural situation. Similarly, many Chinese Christian converts see the gospel as bringing to fulfillment the great religious and philosophical traditions of their own culture. In the Mandarin version of John's gospel, for example, we find the following translation of John 1:1: "In the beginning was the *Tao*, and the *Tao* was with God, and the *Tao* was God." In other words, the fundamental principle of Taoism is thus declared to be none other than Jesus Christ, to whom Taoism ultimately pointed. Similarly, Jesus later reveals himself to his disciples with the phrase: "I am the true and living *Tao*." Here we can see a clear statement of the conviction that Jesus Christ brings to fulfillment all that is good and noble in native Chinese culture, while at the same time providing a criterion by which it may be judged.

I have much sympathy with this approach. It maintains the notion of prevenient grace, in that God is recognized to be at work in other cultures. I see no difficulty in extending this approach to include secular philosophy, as well as to those who do not count themselves as religious but are nevertheless passionate seekers after truth. In all these contexts, God is seeking to make himself known. It is, however, only through the coming of Christ that God makes himself known most fully, and it is only in Christ that salvation is fully available.

I think, however, that there are assumptions behind Pinnock's approach that are perhaps unstated and need identification and comment. Of these, I have space to examine only two. Professor Pinnock states that religions may contain "noble truths" and "terrible errors." This is an important statement, which serves as a highly necessary correction to the bland endorsement of all religious beliefs and practices that has been so distressing a feature of some liberal accounts of the matter. But how do we know which beliefs are "truths" and which are "errors"? There is a need for an evaluative framework, an interpretative grid, that allows us to criticize the religions. From a Christian perspective, this is provided through Scripture. Although I do not think that Pinnock ever allows the possibility, we must ensure that we do not import a set of criteria from outside the Christian revelation and allow that to become of normative importance in evaluating the religions. We must develop a Christian response on the basis of a Christian set of criteria.

IS THIS SALVATION CHRISTIAN?

Second, I think Pinnock avoids an issue raised by his discussion—indeed, one raised by all four chapters. Are all religions salvific, in the Christian sense of that term? I am not sure he really answers this question. I think that, in the end, his answer, like mine, would be: We must trust that God will do what is right. For example, consider his statement: "God's plan was not to make salvation universal at the beginning but at the end of history. But he takes care not to make that a penalty for those who live too soon." This can only really be taken to mean that those who, for historical reasons, did not hear the gospel proclamation will be judged on the basis of whatever values and norms they accepted as good. I am sure that Pinnock is affirming that whoever is saved, is saved through Christ. But I wonder if he is drawing back from stating explicitly the implications of the statement I have just noted. I also found myself wondering the same in relation to his musings about whether a "premessianic believer" receives "the grace of conversion and explicit knowledge of Jesus Christ at a later date, whether in this life *or after death*" (my emphasis). The idea of such a postmortem encounter raises serious questions for Protestants, and it is clear that the implications of this approach—as well as the reliability of its biblical foundations—will need to be carefully examined within the evangelical community.

Although I am much more particularist in my outlook than Pinnock, I gladly concede that he has made many important points and raised many questions that will require our attention and discussion in the future. He has established a reputation as someone who makes evangelicals rethink issues; his chapter confirms this reputation and issues a firm challenge to evangelicalism to reconsider the biblical basis of its approaches to pluralism.

The Reformers of the sixteenth century urged us to constantly reexamine beliefs and practices on the basis of their biblical foundations. The historical circumstances faced by the Reformers meant that neither evangelism nor religious pluralism found their way onto the theological agendas of the Reformation. Those of us who regard ourselves as their successors need to forge approaches to evangelism and religious pluralism that are firmly grounded in the Reformation tradition. Perhaps this volume will stimulate further discussion and debate towards that end.

RESPONSE TO CLARK H. PINNOCK

W. Gary Phillips and R. Douglas Geivett

Professor Pinnock presents inclusivism as a "timely and appealing model" of salvation that he considers a more coherent form of orthodoxy than particularism and that may even "save the structure of historic doctrine." While he notes with pleasure the predominance of inclusivism within mainline denominations, his "chief concern" is to persuade *particularist evangelicals* to accept inclusivism.[1] We offer one type of particularist response to the arguments he develops in his chapter.

THE ARGUMENT FROM GOD'S PRESENCE IN THE WORLD

Pinnock's definition of inclusivism includes an argument for inclusivism. He reasons from God's presence in the whole world to the operation of God's grace among all people, and from the operation of God's grace among all people to the operation of his grace within the context of non-Christian religions. The vagueness of his avowal that "God is present in the whole world" makes it difficult to evaluate this argument.

Perhaps Pinnock's position is that, because God is omnipresent, every people group and every human individual has *cognitive access* to the reality of God (cf. Acts 17:27). But it certainly does not follow from this teaching that God is accurately

---

[1]See also Clark H. Pinnock, *A Wideness in God's Mercy: The Finality of Jesus Christ in a World of Religions* (Grand Rapids: Zondervan, 1992), 87.

represented in all or any of the ideas and practices of human persons, individually or collectively. Persons with cognitive access to God's actual nature might exchange the truth of God for a lie (Rom. 1:25); that is, they might embrace wrong ideas about religious reality. Their doing so may even be reprehensible and blameworthy, as Romans 1:20 indicates. "Idolatry" is the term the Bible uses to label any system of ideas or practices that trades divine truth for a false alternative (see 1:22–25; 1 Cor. 8:4–7; 1 John 5:19–21). To our minds, this is what each of the non-Christian religions does. Even Judaism's zeal for God is not sufficient for salvation if it holds a false view of Jesus Christ (Rom. 10:1–4). Faith in Jesus is needed to deliver both Jews and Gentiles from darkness and the dominion of Satan (Acts 26:15–18).[2]

Can we say that wherever God is grace is? Yes. We may even say that God's grace is, in all cases, efficacious—it accomplishes what it intends. But we must also say what we mean. Saving grace is not a *property* of God's nature, but an *activity* of his person. The operation of grace on the human heart produces results that may fall into one of two general categories, repentance (Rom. 2:4) and rebellion (v. 5). When grace is met with repentance, an individual enters into the salvation of the Lord; when it is met with resistance, the individual stores up wrath for himself or herself and is set apart for righteous judgment. The offer of salvation is itself grace in action, quite apart from the response of the individual (see 1 Cor. 1:18). While God desires that all persons everywhere should repent, his grace produces what it must when persons do not repent, namely, judgment (Acts 17:30–31). So even the pervasiveness of God's grace does not entail that God is somehow soteriologically present within alternative religious traditions.

THE ARGUMENT FROM DIVINE SOVEREIGNTY

Pinnock reasons that since "the Spirit is under nobody's control" and, like the wind, "blows wherever it pleases" (John 3:8), the particularist position needlessly limits the scope of

---

[2]Pinnock's treatment of these and similar texts is woefully inadequate, for he considers false religions to be only a proper subset of non-Christian religions (see *A Wideness in God's Mercy*, 85–110). Where does Judaism stand on Pinnock's "valuational spectrum" (ibid., p. 85) in relation to the best strains of Buddhism, Hinduism,

God's sovereignty. Of course, we do not wish to limit the activity of the Spirit in any way. We can agree that, if there were not strong biblical evidence to the contrary, God's salvation arrangement might well be more inclusive. In this regard, however, we are utterly dependent on what God has revealed. To the extent that God reveals a particular method for saving individuals, his veracity limits his flexibility.

The point is more than academic, for the Christian's motivation for world evangelism is at stake. When it is suspected that God will arrange for the salvation of others without our cooperation, there will be an understandable tendency for believers to doubt the necessity of obeying the Great Commission (Matt. 28:18–20).[3] We think that particularism constitutes the best explanation for the character and the urgency of the Great Commission. But even if it does not, it surely is salutary for evangelicals to be sure of themselves before recommending a theology that tends to erode evangelistic zeal.

Furthermore—and this is perhaps most disquieting of all—Pinnock's outlook must inevitably generate confusion about whether the evangelist or missionary should even insist on conversion to Jesus Christ if a sincere adherent to another faith might be persuaded to convert only upon hearing adequate reasons to do so. This concern, about which Pinnock is most taciturn, may be the Achilles' heel of his position. He opens his book with this vital question: "How will we communicate the gospel in a pluralist setting?"[4] But in his comments, he is remarkably unresolved about the fate of the individual "who is drawn to Jesus but cannot break with his people." There is a problem here not only of what God will do with such a person, but also of how the Christian should advise him or her (see Matt. 10:24–39). While Pinnock's writings present a kind of theology of religions, they do not address the specific practical questions that inevitably arise concerning the actual communication of the gospel.

---

or Islam (cf. p. 100)? If the devotees of Judaism—arguably the most exemplary of non-Christian faiths—are consigned to darkness and are under the dominion of Satan, there is little chance that those of other faiths will fare much better apart from faith in Jesus Christ.

[3]For a discussion of documented evidence of this effect of inclusivism, see Ronald H. Nash, *Is Jesus the Only Savior?* (Grand Rapids: Zondervan, 1994), 165–69.

[4]Pinnock, *A Wideness in God's Mercy*, p. 7.

THE PNEUMATOLOGICAL ARGUMENT

Not only is Pinnock pleased with the emerging inclusivist consensus, but he explains this consensus in terms of the activity of the Holy Spirit. He believes that the Spirit is moving theologians of the present generation to express discomfort with the more traditional particularist theology of religions and to formulate a more "merciful" inclusivist position.[5] This is a surprising rendition of the Holy Spirit's *modus operandi*, for it links the Spirit's activity with the current cultural drift toward openness at all levels of inquiry. Christian theologians living in a generation for which feeling and the popularity of a position is the measure of truth must be especially cautious in their response to the lure of the bandwagon. Pinnock is more confident than cautious in his judgment that the current shifting of theological paradigms is sponsored by God.

Indeed, his position implies a theory of special revelation that owes more to Thomas Kuhn's analysis of paradigm shifts in the academy than to the biblical teaching about inspiration.[6] In this respect he resembles John Hick, except that Hick does not tag the Holy Spirit with responsibility for this type of theological development but attributes it to the strictly human character of all theologizing.

There may be better explanations for the perceived popularity of inclusivism—explanations that have less to do with the impulse of the Holy Spirit or with biblical exegesis and more to do with the sociological aspects of a pluralistic culture. Pinnock assumes that if orthodox theologians of previous generations had known of the existence of large numbers of unevangelized people, this knowledge would have been reflected in their exegesis and hermeneutics so that particularism would not have become such an entrenched position among evangelicals.[7] But

---

[5]Ibid., 41–42.

[6]See Thomas Kuhn, *The Structure of Scientific Revolutions* (Chicago: Univ. of Chicago Press, 1962; 2d ed., 1970); also Imre Lakatos and Alan Musgrave, ed., *Criticism and the Growth of Knowledge* (London: Cambridge Univ. Press, 1970).

[7]We might with equal confidence suppose that had the early church fathers adopted a more inclusivist position, they would not have been so resolute about preserving an orthodox position concerning the nature of Jesus Christ during the conciliar period of the fourth and fifth centuries, for correct belief about Jesus would be soteriologically dispensable no matter what the truth is.

as it happens, Christian thinkers have traditionally been aware of the presence of other faiths in the world, and many have thought long and hard about whether the saved will be few or many. At any rate, while Christian theologians have not ignored the task of developing a theology of religions, the present social context has pushed this issue to the front of the theological agenda *and, at the same time, invited an attitude of leniency.*

Premature announcements about the emergence of some new "consensus" is a feature of paradigm shifting that can precipitate broad acceptance of a novel theory. When Pinnock opines that inclusivism has "supplanted exclusivism as the reigning ideology in the ecumenical church" and that it "has become widely accepted and may even be called the mainline model," he perpetuates a mythology that the old orthodoxy is on the brink of disaster. While this sort of language may embolden some to fall in step with the inclusivists, it is unrealistic about the resolve of many particularist detractors. It will be some time before any sort of inclusivist consensus among evangelicals can be unequivocally documented.

THE ARGUMENT FROM THE SAINTLINESS
OF NON-CHRISTIANS

Pinnock argues that inclusivism best explains the manifest saintliness of persons of non-Christian faith. But there are problems with this suggestion. First, it subordinates the rationality of specific truth-claims to the moral effectiveness of the lives of religious figures. In other words, the significance of a person's behavior is tied to one's worldview. But the measure of a person's life cannot be given in terms of external behavior alone. Also, it trivializes the value these saints themselves place on their own truth-claims. Ethical Muslims do not suppose that they are on the path toward Christianity, and they can be expected to resent the suggestion that they are.

Second, religious pluralists of John Hick's type also rely heavily on the moral criterion that Pinnock uses in assessing religions. But Pinnock's pluralistic cousins are motivated by their conviction that no other criteria are available for adjudicating between religions. Their disdain for natural theology and for the divine authority of Scripture compels them to compare religious traditions in terms of their effectiveness in producing morally exemplary persons. For them, apparent saintliness is the mark of religious reality because it is the only possible criterion left.

Someone like Pinnock, who affirms both the value of natural theology and the authority of the Bible, should recognize that a moral criterion cannot be so decisive in the evaluation of religious traditions. For true saintliness is revealed in Scripture to be a consequence of reconciliation with God on the terms that he has stipulated. Reconciliation between God and human beings is mediated by Jesus Christ, and righteousness accrues only to those who are "in Christ" by virtue of their response to "the word of reconciliation." It is incumbent on any "ambassador for Christ," as a good steward of "the ministry of reconciliation," to urge men and women to be reconciled to God *through Christ* (see 2 Cor. 5:17–21, NASB).

THE ARGUMENT FROM GOD'S LOVE

The intrapersonal love shared among the members of the Trinity, according to Pinnock, overflows onto all of God's creation. "Out of the fullness of shared life, God calls forth a world to mirror his own loving mutuality, inviting everyone to participate in the fullness of triune life, in a community of love that constitutes tripersonal being." The idea seems to be that withholding salvation from the sincere of other faiths represents a failure of love among the members of the Godhead.

There are two problems with this suggestion. First, Pinnock subordinates God's holiness to his love. But why should God's love rather than his truth or his holiness "overflow" in the way suggested? Second, from the fact that God loves it does not follow that his love is manifested apart from the incarnation and atonement of Jesus Christ (John 3:16–17; Rom. 5:7–11), or that it is not attended by certain conditions (1 Thess. 2:13; Heb. 4:2). Pinnock confuses God's love for all persons with their being friends with God. But God has many enemies whom he loves; that is, some whom God loves are not his friends.

THE ARGUMENT FROM SCRIPTURE

Pinnock insists on the congruence of his position with the data of the Bible. This means that he considers his inclusivism to be compatible with Scripture, regardless of whether it explicitly teaches inclusivism. But there are moments when he also suggests that a case for inclusivism can be made directly from the Bible.

Our response is twofold. First, Pinnock does not show how his view is exegetically derived. He cites few texts in his chapter, and the exegesis he provides in his other publications is strained (see our chapter). After appealing to the need for exegesis, he simply *mentions* Old Testament and New Testament passages that he claims support his point and then remarks, "though it needs more exposition, I believe that the Bible supports inclusivism." So obvious is the need for further exposition, however, that it is surprising that Pinnock does not provide more exposition himself.

Second, Pinnock's theological method is not executed with enough deference to the prima facie evidence for particularism in the Bible. While there certainly is scope for the play of our intuitions in making sense of the Bible, we must be careful not to impose a strained interpretation on the Bible simply in order to preserve our most cherished feelings for the unsaved. Propositional revelation is given partly in order to correct many of our intuitions and to illuminate deep fissures within the body of human theological knowledge and awareness. While we know that the Judge of all the earth will do right, we cannot always be sure what form his righteous action will take (Gen. 18:25). Whenever we think we are sure what form it will take, that is because we believe it has been clearly revealed. "It is dangerous to be more generous than God has revealed himself to be."[8]

CONCLUSION

Professor Pinnock's essay soars with a polemic that is frequently vague. He argues that the analogies of Abraham, Melchizedek, Job, Jethro, and others allow us to be "open and generous" to other religious traditions. Yet he has not established

---

[8]Roger Nicole, "Universalism: Will Everyone Be Saved?" *Christianity Today* 30 (March 20, 1987): 38.

that these figures were without special revelation, nor is he precise about what it means for us to be "open and generous." To say that God's grace may be encountered through other religions is vague. Which other religions? And what elements?

Many of Pinnock's assertions assume a knowledge of God's ways that most other evangelicals do not presume to have. For example, he exudes confidence about the operation of the Spirit within other religions and the final destiny of "saintly persons of other faiths." Furthermore, by innuendo and nuance, he betrays an insensitivity to the actual dynamics of particularist theological reflection and misrepresents the underlying reasons for the particularist point of view.[9] Kathleen Boone, who is not an evangelical, has correctly observed that particularists generally hold their position because of their commitment to the authority of the Bible and a certain understanding of what the Bible teaches.[10]

Evangelicals agree that we should not "walk the path of superiority and chauvinism." But when particularists conclude that their view is better supported by the biblical data, they do not "begrudge God's generosity," as Pinnock suggests. Certainly, God's "boundless mercy is a primary truth that cannot be compromised." But how does particularism compromise God's mercy? Indeed, particularists often express a personal preference for the inclusivist position without allowing this preference to dictate for them the contours of the biblical picture of God's arrangement for human salvation. We invite Pinnock to declare unequivocally that it is *not possible* that God himself is a particularist.

---

[9]For example, he implies that particularists (a) compromise God's salvific will, (b) fail to discern what "God is doing" in our current pluralistic context, (c) inexplicably restrict the scope of God's grace, (d) bifurcate the Spirit, (e) oppose God's plan for redeeming sinners, and (f) arrogate to themselves a monopoly on the Spirit. Such thinly veiled charges betray a dogmatic tendency unbecoming for a theologian who claims simply to be exploring *possibilities* and offering a model "for consideration" (note those places where Pinnock uses the phrase "cautious inclusivism" to describe his view). His tone ignores the reality that many particularists respect people of other faiths and acknowledge the presence of truths within other religions.

[10]See Kathleen Boone, *The Bible Tells Them So: The Discourse of Protestant Fundamentalism* (Albany, N.Y.: SUNY Press, 1989).

CONCLUSION

Clark H. Pinnock

INCLUSIVISM'S TWO CENTRAL THESES

Inclusivism celebrates two central theological truths. The first is a particularity axiom that says God has revealed himself definitively and has acted redemptively on behalf of the whole human race through the Incarnation. The second is a universality axiom that says God loves sinners and wants to save them all. The challenge to theology is to do justice to both these truths and not allow one to cancel out the other. Conservative theology tends to deny universality and liberalism rejects particularity.

But both axioms are well established scripturally. On the one hand, the church is a community that confesses Jesus as Lord and anticipates sharing in his resurrection. We acknowledge no other name than this to have universal significance and to offer life and hope to all nations. We know no other Savior; Jesus is the source and ground of salvation. If non-Christians are saved in any dispensation, as they were in the Old Testament, it is through the event of Jesus Christ. We do not believe that other religious traditions equal Christianity in salvific significance. Three of the authors in this book—Geivett/Phillips, McGrath, and I—all affirm God's reconciliation of sinners through Christ alone.

On the other hand, God, who is love in his trinitarian essence, is always seeking to communicate his presence and grace. This love is at the heart of the universe, and God desires the salvation of all persons. Jesus is the only way to salvation, but this does not imply God has a narrow strategy. Our creator and sustainer is present in love to the whole of humankind by the Spirit, ever blessing and gracing us. Through the prevenience of grace, God is at work among all people, making the offer of grace a universal one. As Amos said, God is at work not only among Israelites, but among Cushites too (Amos 9:7). We must say the same thing to ourselves: God is at work outside the churches as well as inside them. Jesus symbolizes particularity, and the Spirit symbolizes universality. The Spirit's universal drawing and gathering in the whole of history reaches its goal in One who is the light of the world.

Inclusivism permits us to hold both particularity and universality at the same time. I am delighted by McGrath's proposal to see him also embracing these two truths, thus creating an alliance between us in this discussion. Not only do McGrath and I uphold particularity and universality in unison, we are also joined by one of the other two authors on each axiom, thus creating a double majority of three against one in our favor.

The reader will notice that three out of the four proposals support particularity—that Christ is the only Savior of sinners. Geivett/Phillips join McGrath and me in support of this axiom, and only Hick declines. Three out of four also support universality—that God wants all to be saved. Hick joins McGrath and me in support of this axiom, and only Geivett/Phillips decline. This means that when it comes to particularity, three direct criticisms against Hick who denies it; and when it comes to universality, three direct criticisms against Geivett/Phillips. This puts McGrath's and my proposal in a strong position in the debate, because we enjoy a three-quarters majority in regard to both axioms when taken separately. I hope that readers, when they realize that each axiom enjoys the support of three authors out of four, will conclude that the best proposal is probably the one that contains them both.

MCGRATH'S POSITION

There is only a small choice, if any, to be made between my proposal and McGrath's, making this nearly a three-views book. While he stresses the uniqueness of different religions, I put emphasis on the possibility of God's working in them to help the unevangelized. Neither of us really denies what the other affirms, and the result seems complementary.

I detect a slight difference in sensibility perhaps. Though we both claim that God is working among the unevangelized to save them, I am less reluctant to look for God's working in the realm of the religious dimension of culture. We both agree that the Spirit works in the circumstances of ordinary life, but I am more willing to speak of the presence of God through the Spirit in other religions. I entertain the hope more than McGrath that God's boundless love revealed in Jesus Christ may be offered to them in the context of their faith. I did not hear McGrath say that, and if so, he is closer to tradition than I am. One might say that he is closer to Lesslie Newbigin and I am closer to Karl Rahner. However, since I am only claiming that God *may* work in the religious sphere, not that he must or always does work there (modal inclusivism), and since McGrath does not actually declare this to be impossible, we are not far apart.

In their response to McGrath, Geivett/Phillips sense that too, and I found nothing in McGrath's response to me that was negatively critical. A slight complaint would be his allusion to my being Arminian, which I suppose is an attempt to attribute my remarks as coming from a supposedly rare breed of evangelicals and to limit their more general relevance. In the same offending paragraph, he also suggests that I am promoting a Logos Christology when, if anything, I am promoting a pneumatology of universality. However, I am hard to offend, and I am delighted with McGrath's contribution.

GEIVETT/PHILLIPS' PARTICULARISM

This leaves two other proposals—one on the right and the other on the left of the spectrum. Beginning with Geivett/Phillips on the right side, McGrath, Hick, and I all find unconvincing their denial of the universal salvific will of God. They present God as if he did not care that most people perish through no fault of their own. It is not so much the fact that their position leaves the strong impression of unfairness, which it does. More serious is the fact that it distorts the nature of God and the heart of the good news. They are asking the reader to believe in a God who deliberately sets in place a plan of salvation that denies access to salvation for the majority of human beings. Geivett/Phillips present a God significantly lacking in mercy, and although they say that perspective is not their fault since it is due to the way God has established the rules, the impression is pretty awful.

A way around this is found in my proposal. One can hold both axioms, reading the Bible in ways that preserve the uniqueness of Christ and the universality of God's saving love. Hebrews 11, for example, documents the salvation of a whole variety of people who were saved by faith in God but who never heard or invoked the name of Jesus. It is unfortunate that Geivett/Phillips used up so much of their space on natural theology, which lacks clear relevance to this discussion, and found themselves in a position where they are unable to take the biblical evidence to which I point seriously. They sweep it away with a minimum of consideration. They give the appearance of not allowing the restrictivist paradigm to undergo challenge and of refusing alternative biblical renderings without due consideration.

For a moment I thought I saw a glimmer of hope in Geivett/Phillips' bleak proposal when they endorsed middle knowledge in a response to McGrath. Middle knowledge is not an easy theory to prove philosophically, but it is relevant to issues of grace and fairness. Think of it—if God knows what sinners would do with an opportunity of salvation if they had one, and if God took that into account in judging them, then presumably a similar percentage of people who respond to the gospel, say, in North America might be expected to respond in some unevangelized region. This might seem to suggest that a large number of the unevangelized will be saved. I do not hold the theory of middle knowledge myself because I do not find it to be philosophically sound, and therefore I do not make use of it. I ask myself how God could possibly know what truly free agents would choose in hypothetical situations. But putting my beliefs aside, if the reader is able to accept middle knowledge, they can escape soteriological restrictivism, and I consider that a positive thing. I see its value in this context, because it might mean that the unevangelized can be saved through hypothetical faith, and their not having heard the gospel would not prevent God's grace from flowing to them.

But alas, middle knowledge does not work that way for Geivett/Phillips. It does not help any unevangelized person to be saved. The hypothetical response in their view of it would have to be followed, I surmise, by an actual missionary arriving on the scene and by a response to the preaching of the gospel. How this might have happened in Outer Mongolia in the tenth century B.C., I do not know. If no missionary arrived, that would mean that there was no one who deserved to hear. It almost comes down to a rationalization of the Christian failure to take the gospel to the unevangelized. The tenor of this use of middle knowledge is that people who do not hear the gospel do not hear it because they would not have received it anyhow. Geivett/Phillips write, "Anyone who dies without hearing the good news is a person who would not have believed had he or she heard." I take it that we need not worry about the lack of opportunity for salvation for huge numbers of people because their nonopportunity is proof of their nonopenness. Certainly Geivett/Phillips' appeal to middle knowledge has no positive implication and offers no hope.

The Achilles' heel of this position is its soteriological restrictivism. It does not enjoy epistemic parity, as they claim, because the Bible, though Christ-centered, is not soteriologically restrictive. The reason many believers today are abandoning this model is not because it is culturally driven, as they allege, but in order to get back to a Bible that speaks of Christ who died for the sins of the whole world because God wants all persons to be saved. More and more Christians are beginning to realize that God does not leave millions without an opportunity to be saved and are looking for a better answer than this form of particularity. Theologians have laid heavy burdens on their shoulders, and they are starting to feel the weight. They are weary of being told that the Bible teaches such an unbiblical position and of being warned against hoping for multitudes who through no fault of their own have no chance to be saved.

In the closing lines of their response to my chapter, Geivett/Phillips challenge me to declare whether I thought God could be such as they describe. My reply is that the God and Father of our Lord Jesus Christ is not a merciless God, as they suggest in their model, and therefore will not behave in the severe way they propose. In theory there could be a God like that—but not in the light of the gospel of Jesus Christ.

Let me comment on a few other aspects of Geivett/Phillips' proposal. First, it reads more like an apologetic program for Christianity than a proposal about religious pluralism. They prove there is a God and a Christ, and, when they finally get around to religious pluralism, what they have to say is brief and perfunctory. Second, the epistemology of this apologetic program is rational in approach—that is, it expects to demonstrate things beyond reasonable doubt. But this gets them into trouble with John Hick over natural theology; they were not able in the space available, and probably never would be able, to establish the existence of a theistic God to a skeptic. Third, they grant that there is a general revelation that creates the expectation of a divine saving initiative. What, I ask, if people put their faith in that expectation as the Jews did in the Old Testament? In this proposal, God gives a powerful general revelation but sends no grace along with it. What a strange thing for the God and Father of Jesus to do! Fourth, I like their effort at defending the Incarnation; McGrath and I attempt to do the same thing.

The proposal of Geivett/Phillips is important for the evangelical community because it articulates the standard position that is normally assumed but not spelled out. My hope is that when people see it explained and defended, they will notice how vulnerable it is to criticism and begin to consider alternatives.

HICK'S PLURALISM

On the left side of the spectrum, John Hick denies the particularity axiom. He contends that Christians need not continue to confess belief in the Incarnation as a metaphysical singularity and that it suffices to regard it as a metaphor. On this point Geivett/Phillips, McGrath, and I join in finding his position unacceptable, and we all mount arguments against it. It seems to me and to the others that Hick plays fast and loose with the central truth claim of the New Testament and appears motivated in his denial by the requirements of religious pluralism itself. Even the Synoptic Gospels, not to mention the other strata of the New Testament, present a strong claim to deity on the part of Jesus, if only implicitly: he will be the judge of humankind, he forgives sins, his presence is God's presence, one's attitude to him decides one's destiny, his actions are God's actions, he teaches with divine authority, he receives worship, he is the model human being, and he applies to himself Old Testament texts that describe God. The synoptic witness is often undersold, and neglecting it simplifies Hick's task of denying a high Christology before Easter in order also to negate the post-Easter witness. In my opinion, he cannot effectively dispense with the uniqueness of Jesus at the heart of Christianity.

I commend Hick in affirming the universality axiom in a qualified way. This is because, although he used to affirm it, according to his more recent Kantian view of the Real or God, one cannot claim to know that the Real is a loving Person. That is one of many constructions placed upon the Real by human beings and cannot be made a dogma. The universality axiom, then, is in jeopardy because it was rooted in the higher Christology of Hick's earlier period. One needs a high Christology to sustain it, namely, the kind of position found in my own and in the other two proposals of the book. Hick thinks that removing the strong version of the Incarnation from the Christian message is a positive step because it removes barriers to mutual understanding between peoples, but I am more impressed by the loss that would be incurred by removing it. Without the Incarnation, we are not in a position to say that God is love with any confidence—only that God is unknown. This does not feel like a step forward in the history of religion but like turning the clock back many millennia.

In another area, I am happy to hear Hick insist against McGrath that religions are not all the same and that the differences between them really matter. They do matter, as all four of us concede. But if they matter, the door is open to dialogue among religions, not only in areas of practical cooperation, but in areas of theological and historical conviction as well. The differences among religions make interreligious apologetics necessary, in which claims like the Incarnation or the cogency of Buddhist anthropology can be profitably discussed. Although Hick seems pessimistic about making progress in dialogue in cognitive areas that lie outside the area of ethics, owing to the Kantian restriction, that pessimism too can be a topic for the dialogue. Others are not as agnostic about issues metaphysical and theological as Hick is. As a student of Hick's, I think Geivett/Phillips are particularly adept in dealing with his ideology of pluralism.

Hick is a little off target in his remarks about postmortem evangelization in my case. I do not hold to evangelism for the unevangelized after death, as Fackre and Bloesch do. Rather, I contend that those who have had faith in God during their earthly lives, as Hebrews 11:6 indicates, are "believers," even if they are not Christians; and I hold that after death, these people encounter the reality of God's grace in Christ for which they had longed. The analogy is Abraham, whom Paul calls the father of believers, because he trusted God even though he did not know Christ (Rom. 4:16). After death, Abraham presumably encountered the triune God who saved him, just as he saves the rest of those who believe.

Hick also issues a challenge to me in his remarks, and I would like to respond to it. He likes the general tenor of my proposal, and I fear that my evangelical friends will not let me hear the last of that! He suggests I need to go farther down the road away from exclusivism, beyond inclusivism, and all the way to pluralism. I have no objection to going farther if the evidence warrants. Better to change one's mind than to remain in the wrong. But I question the assumption that pluralism *is* farther down the road that inclusivists are following. Pluralists seem to me to be traveling down a different road altogether. Having crossed the Rubicon when they deny the finality of Jesus Christ, they are committed to blazing a new trail, one that is not a continuation of the old road from restrictiveness to wider hope. To get to Hick's position, I would need to deny one of the two axioms of inclusivism, the Christological, and would need to move outside the paradigm. I appreciate his concern for my future pilgrimage, but I plan to remain where I am now until I see better reasons to move farther than Hick offers.

Chapter Three

A PARTICULARIST VIEW: A POST-ENLIGHTENMENT APPROACH

Alister E. McGrath

A PARTICULARIST VIEW: A POST-ENLIGHTENMENT APPROACH

Alister E. McGrath

Religious pluralism is as much a fact of life today as it was in the context in which Paul first preached the gospel in Europe. It is, however, an issue of greater importance today because of a strongly rights-oriented Western culture, linked with a political polity that does not wish to disadvantage anyone on account of his or her religious beliefs. It is important to appreciate the cultural issue often linked with this debate: To defend Christianity is seen as belittling non-Christian religions, which is unacceptable in a multicultural society.

Especially to people of liberal political convictions, the multicultural agenda demands that religions not be permitted to make truth claims, in order to avoid triumphalism or imperialism. Indeed, there seems to be a widespread perception that the rejection of religious pluralism entails intolerance or unacceptable claims to exclusivity. In effect, the liberal political agenda dictates that all religions should be treated on an equal footing. It is, however, a small step from this essentially *political* judgment concerning toleration to the *theological* declaration that all religions are the same. But is there any reason for progressing from the acceptable demand that we should respect religions other than our own, to the more radical demand that we regard them all as the same or as equally valid routes to a common salvation?

My task in this essay is to explore a cluster of issues involving the theme of religious pluralism, especially as it focuses on the issue of salvation. This is a vast field, which is becoming more and more important as Western society becomes increasingly multicultural and as Christianity continues its expansion into hitherto non-Christian cultures, especially in the Pacific Rim. To do justice to this topic, it is necessary to consider several major themes relating to religious pluralism before exploring the more specific issue of salvation.

Let me make it clear from the outset: I regard the concerns raised by pluralists as legitimate and important. In no way can they be dismissed lightly or cheaply. I must stress that my criticisms of pluralism are rooted in a respect for the questions it has raised and the integrity of those who have raised them. In particular, I honor the moral issues that pluralist writers have addressed, especially their anxieties about the morality of a particularist approach to salvation. Christian theology in the West, especially evangelicalism, has thus far failed to address many of the issues raised by pluralists. I regard the rise of pluralism as an important stimulus to begin the task of exploration of these issues. These issues are so complex that I can only hope to touch on them in this chapter, laying the groundwork for something more substantial in the future.

THE NATURE OF PLURALISM

Commenting on the theme of "the gospel in a pluralist society," Lesslie Newbigin remarks:

> It has become a commonplace to say that we live in a pluralist society—not merely a society which is in fact plural in the variety of cultures, religions and lifestyles which it embraces, but pluralist in the sense that this plurality is celebrated as things to be approved and cherished.[1]

Newbigin here makes a distinction between pluralism as a fact of life and pluralism as an ideology—that is, the belief that pluralism is to be encouraged and desired and the belief that normative claims to truth should be censured as imperialist and divisive.

---

[1]Lesslie Newbigin, *The Gospel in a Pluralist Society* (Grand Rapids: Eerdmans, 1989), 1.

With the former, there can be no arguing. The Christian proclamation has always taken place in a pluralist world, in competition with rival religious and intellectual convictions. The gospel emerged within the matrix of Judaism and expanded in a Hellenistic milieu. The rise of pluralism poses no fundamental objection to the theory or practice of Christian evangelism; indeed, if anything, it brings us closer to the world of the New Testament itself. Commenting on the situation confronted by the early church as described in the book of Acts, the leading Anglo-Canadian evangelist Michael Green remarks:

> I find it ironic that people object to the proclamation of the Christian gospel these days because so many other faiths jostle on the doorstep of our global village. What's new? The variety of faiths in antiquity was even greater than it is today. And the early Christians, making as they did ultimate claims for Jesus, met the problem of other faiths head-on from the very outset. Their approach was interesting. . . . They did not denounce other faiths. They simply proclaimed Jesus with all the power and persuasiveness at their disposal.[2]

The proclamation and consolidation of the gospel within a religiously pluralistic setting continued throughout the early Christian expansion, as can be seen from the expansion of the church in pagan Rome, the establishment of the *Mar Thoma* church in southern India, or the uneasy coexistence of Christianity and Islam during the period of the Islamic Caliphate. These are examples of situations in which Christian apologists and theologians, as well as ordinary Christian believers, were aware that there were religious alternatives to Christianity.[3]

This insight may have been lost to English or American writers of the late nineteenth or early twentieth centuries. For such writers, pluralism seems to have meant little more than a variety of forms of Protestantism, while "different religions"

---

[2]Michael Green, *Acts for Today: First-Century Christianity for Twentieth-Century Christians* (London: Hodder & Stoughton, 1993), 38.

[3]The literature is huge. On the Arab context, see Robert B. Betts, *Christians in the Arab East* (Atlanta: John Knox, 1989). The situation in India has been surveyed masterly by Stephen Neill, *A History of Christianity in India*, 2 vols. (Cambridge: Cambridge Univ. Press, 1984–85).

were understood as the age-old tension between Protestantism and Roman Catholicism. But immigration from the Indian sub-continent changed things in England, with Hinduism and Islam becoming foci of identity for ethnic minorities, just as France was shaken by the new presence of Islam through emigration from its former North African colonies. As a result, Western theologians—who still seem to dominate global discussion of such issues—have at long last become aware of and begun to address issues that are routine facts of everyday life for Christians in many parts of the world.

Yet the theological approaches to other religions developed within these Christian communities have had no impact on Western theology. The approaches adopted are based on Western assumptions, either explicitly stated on the part of Western theologians or passively accepted by people from such regions of the world who have been educated in an allegedly more advanced Western context. We can explore this by looking at that elusive word *religion* in a little more depth.

WHAT IS RELIGION?

An example of excessive reliance on Western categories can be seen in relation to the term *religion* itself. In his classic, but highly problematic work, *The Golden Bough* (1890), Sir James Frazer made this fundamental point: "There is probably no subject in the world about which opinions differ so much as the nature of religion, and to frame a definition of it which would satisfy everyone must obviously be impossible." Yet there has recently been a determined effort to reduce all religions to the same basic phenomenon.

There is a question of intellectual power here. Who makes the rules that determine what is a religion and what is not? The rules of this game determine the outcome. Who decides them? Underlying much recent Western liberal discussion of "the religions" is the assumption that "religion" is a genus, an agreed-on category. But it is nothing of the sort. John Milbank, in an important recent study, notes that the "assumption about a religious genus" is central to

the more recent mode of encounter as dialogue, but it would be a mistake to imagine that it arose simultaneously among all the participants as the recognition of an evident truth. On the contrary, it is clear that the other religions were taken by Christian thinkers to be species of the genus "religion," because these thinkers systematically subsumed alien cultural phenomena under categories which comprise western notions of what constitutes religious thought and practice. These false categorizations have often been accepted by western-educated representatives of the other religions themselves, who are unable to resist the politically imbued rhetorical force of western discourse.[4]

We must therefore be intensely suspicious of the naive assumption that *religion* is a well-defined category that can be sharply and surgically distinguished from *culture* as a whole. The fact that classical Greek mythology, Confucianism, Taoism, the various and diverse religions of India that have been misleadingly brought together under the generic term "Hinduism," Christianity, totemism, and animism can all be called "religions" points to this being an alarmingly broad and diffuse category without any real distinguishing features.

The first step in addressing religious pluralism is to eliminate notions of religion that reflect Western cultural bias. There is no place in global theology for an ethnocentric notion of religion, so clearly reflecting Western assumptions and misunderstandings of non-Western cultural phenomena. Western theology has singularly failed to do this. Sociology has been much more open to respecting the astonishing variety of beliefs within the religions. As Anthony Giddens, professor of sociology at the University of Cambridge, points out, "religion" cannot be defined in Western terms:

> First, religion should not be identified with monotheism. ... Most religions involve several deities. ... In certain religions there are no gods at all. Second, religion should not be identified with moral prescriptions controlling the behavior of believers. ... Third, religion is not necessarily concerned with explaining how the world

---

[4]John Milbank, "The End of Dialogue," in G. D'Costa, ed., *Christian Uniqueness Reconsidered: The Myth of a Pluralistic Theology of Religions* (Maryknoll, N.Y.: Orbis, 1990), 174–91 (quote on p. 176). This essay merits detailed reading.

came to be as it is. . . . Fourth, religion cannot be identified with the supernatural, as intrinsically involving
belief in a universe "beyond the realm of the senses."[5]

In short, there is a need to respect the individuality of what we
still insist on referring to as religions, instead of constructing artificial and reductionist definitions of what *religion* is.

Generalizations may be helpful in allowing us to understand religions; yet such generalizations are only descriptions
and can never be permitted to become prescriptions of what
religion can and cannot be. The whole issue of religious pluralism has been fatally flawed by a mentality that demands that all
shall be reduced to the same mold. Perhaps most arrogant of all
is the (happily increasingly rare) use of the term *higher religions*
to refer to those religions that are regarded as superior to others
on the basis of Western sensibilities. The use of such terms is
insulting and degrading to the religions of sub-Saharan Africa
in particular and ought to be abandoned. At best, they are meaningless and have value only to those with reductionist agendas;
at worst, they are imperialist and offensive.

RESPECTING OTHER RELIGIONS

A discussion about the place of Christianity among the
world religions must be conducted on the basis of mutual
respect, both on the part of Christians for those who are not
Christians, and on the part of those who are not Christians for
those who are. This respect can be expressed in dialogue, which
is to be understood as an attempt on the part of people with different beliefs to gain a better understanding of each other. But
this dialogue cannot be conducted on the basis of the deeply
patronizing assumption that "everyone is saying the same
thing." Dialogue implies respect, but it does not presuppose
agreement.

The distinctive emphasis placed on dialogue within pluralism seems to rest on a Socratic model of dialogue.[6] Such an

---

[5]Anthony Giddens, *Sociology* (Oxford: Polity Press, 1989), 452.

[6]On this, see Michael C. Stokes, *Plato's Socratic Conversations: Drama and Dialec-
tic in Three Dialogues* (London: Athlone Press, 1986). For the application of the method
in therapy, see Tullio Maranhao, *Therapeutic Discourse and Socratic Dialogue* (Madi-
son: Univ. of Wisconsin Press, 1986).

approach assumes that the participants in the dialogue are all speaking of substantially the same entity, which they happen to see from different perspectives. Dialogue thus provides a style of approach that allows these perspectives to be pooled, generating a cumulative perception transcending the particularities of each and thus allowing each participant to go away enriched and informed. In the context of interreligious dialogue, the approach is often compared to a king and his courtiers who amuse themselves by arranging for blind people to fondle different parts of an elephant. Their different reports on what they felt, though superficially irreconcilable, can easily be harmonized as different perspectives on the same greater reality. Each perspective is genuine and valid; but on its own, each one is inadequate to describe the greater reality of which it is but part.

But how appropriate is this mode of discourse in relation to understanding the relation between the religions of the world? Lesslie Newbigin makes a vitally important observation that needs to be weighed carefully.

> In the famous story of the blind men and the elephant . . . the real point of the story is constantly overlooked. The story is told from the point of view of the king and his courtiers, who are not blind but can see that the blind men are unable to grasp the full reality of the elephant and are only able to get hold of part of it. The story is constantly told in order to neutralize the affirmations of the great religions, to suggest that they learn humility and recognize that none of them can have more than one aspect of the truth. But, of course, the real point of the story is exactly the opposite. If the king were also blind, there would be no story. The story is told by the king, and it is the immensely arrogant claim of one who sees the full truth, which all the world's religions are only groping after. It embodies the claim to know the full reality which relativizes all the claims of the religions.[7]

Newbigin brings out the potential arrogance of any claim to be able to see all the religions from the standpoint of one who sees the *full* truth. For people to claim that they see the big picture while Christians and others see only part is tantamount to

---

[7]Newbigin, *The Gospel in a Pluralist Society*, 9–10.

imperialism, unless it can be demonstrated that there is a universally available public knowledge open to general scrutiny and critical evaluation.

Claiming privileged access to a total and comprehensive knowledge of reality is generally treated with intense skepticism, not least on account of its clear lack of empirical foundations and its resistance to verification or falsification. Scholars generally agree that there is no privileged position from which the "big picture" can be seen. Until and unless the "full reality that relativizes all the claims of the religion" is made publicly available and subjected to intense empirical analysis, the claim that all the religions somehow instantiate its various aspects is little more than an unverified claim without legitimate basis. Indeed, it represents an unverifiable and unfalsifiable claim, an intrusion into the world of speculation rather than solid empirical research.

DIALOGUE AND DISAGREEMENT

It is perfectly possible for the Christian to engage in dialogue with non-Christians, whether of a religious persuasion or not, without in any way being committed to the intellectually shallow and paternalist view that "we're all saying the same thing."[8] As Paul Griffiths and Delmas Lewis put it so aptly,

It is both logically and practically possible for us, as Christians, to respect and revere worthy representatives of other traditions while still believing—on rational grounds—that some aspects of their world-view are simply mistaken.[9]

Contrary to John Hick's more homogenizing approach, John V. Taylor remarked that dialogue is "a sustained conversation between parties who are not saying the same thing and who recognize and respect the differences, the contradictions, and the mutual exclusions between their various ways of thinking."[10]

---

[8]See Arnulf Camps, *Partners in Dialogue* (Maryknoll, N.Y.: Orbis, 1983), 30.

[9]Paul Griffiths and Delmas Lewis, "On Grading Religions, Seeking Truth, and Being Nice to People: A Reply to Professor Hick," *Religious Studies* 19 (1983):78.

[10]John V. Taylor, "The Theological Basis of Interfaith Dialogue," in J. Hick and B. Hebblethwaite, eds., *Christianity and Other Religions* (Philadelphia: Fortress, 1981), 212.

Dialogue thus implies respect, not agreement, between parties—and is, at best, a willingness to take the profound risk that the other person may be right and that recognition of this fact may lead to the changing of positions. There is, for example, a real possibility that a disillusioned Muslim will find a Christian understanding of salvation considerably more attractive and meaningful than his or her own and will decide to convert to Christianity. This phenomenon, which occurs regularly (and in many different directions) in the real world, must be incorporated in any attempt to understand and come to terms with religious pluralism.

Dialogue is important, partly because it enhances our understanding of other religions and partly because it acts as a gadfly, inviting us to reassess our understanding of our own faith by forcing us to reexamine its various aspects in the light of its foundational sources. One of my interests concerns the development of Christian doctrine.[11] I have often noticed how significant doctrinal developments are in response to dialogue with those outside the Christian faith. I am not for one moment suggesting that this means that some Christian doctrines are a response to non-Christian pressures; rather, I am stating, as a matter of observable fact, that dialogue with non-Christians can provide a stimulus to Christians to reexamine long-held views that turn out to rest on inadequate scriptural foundations.

Dialogue is a pressure forcing Christians to reexamine their doctrinal formulations, with a view to ensuring that they are as faithful as possible to what they purport to represent or embody. Evangelicalism must be committed to the principle that the *ecclesia reformata* is an *ecclesia semper reformanda*; dialogue is one pressure to ensure that this process of continual self-examination and reformation continues. It is a bulwark against complacency and laziness and a stimulus to return to the sources of faith, rather than resting content in some currently acceptable interpretation of them.

Discussions about religious pluralism have been seriously hindered by some folk with a well-meaning but ultimately spurious mindset that is locked into the "we're really all saying the

---

[11]See my 1990 Brampton Lectures at Oxford University, published as Alister E. McGrath, *The Genesis of Doctrine* (Oxford: Blackwell, 1990).

same thing" worldview, which suppresses or evades the differences between faiths in order to construct some artificial theory to account for commonalities. The deliberate suppression of differences is academically unacceptable. Their evasion cannot be tolerated by any who are concerned about doing justice to the religions of the world as they are viewed by their own adherents, rather than in the artificially reconstructed versions of these faiths that emerge from the homogenizing tendencies of scholars of religion.

In an important recent study, Yale theologian Kathryn Tanner argues that liberal pluralist theology has succumbed to "colonialist discourse."[12] Any attempt to reduce the religions to manifestations of the same transcendental impulses or to minimize their differences for the sake of theoretical neatness is unacceptable:

> Pluralist generalizations about what all religions have in common conflict with genuine dialogue, in that they prejudge its results. Commonalities, which should be established in and through a process of dialogue, are constructed ahead of time by pluralists to serve as presuppositions of dialogue. Pluralists therefore close themselves to what people of other religions might have to say about their account of these commonalities. Moreover, ... a pluralist focus on commonalities slights differences among the religions of the world. The pluralists' insistence on commonalities as a condition of dialogue shows an unwillingness to recognize the depth and degree of diversity among religions, or the positive importance of them.[13]

In addition, Tanner makes the point that pluralists conceal the "particularities of their own perspectives by claiming to form generalizations about the religions of the world." Apart from being untrue, Tanner remarks, this approach "brings pluralist theorists of religion close to the kind of absolutism that it is part of their own project to avoid."[14]

---

[12]Kathryn Tanner, "Respect for Other Religions: A Christian Antidote to Colonialist Discourse," *Modern Theology* 9 (1993): 1–18.

[13]Ibid., 2.

[14]Ibid., 2. See also John Apczynski, "John Hick's Theocentrism: Revolution or Implicitly Exclusive?" *Modern Theology* 8 (1992): 39–52.

It is obvious that differences exist among the religions of the world, whether one looks at matters of historical interpretation or of doctrinal exposition. The New Testament is emphatic that Jesus died on a cross. The Qur'an is equally emphatic that he did not. Here is a simple case of disagreement on a matter—an *important* matter—of history. Equally, some believe in the transmigration of souls; others deny this doctrine. This would also seem a clear case of conflicting truth claims. To deny that such is the case amounts to replacing reasoned argumentation with special pleading and petulant assertion.[15] Honest disagreement is no sin. Furthermore, a willingness to recognize differences removes the most fundamental criticism directed against interfaith dialogue—that it is not prepared to acknowledge genuine differences.

Consider the dialogue between Jews and Christians, with which I have been involved personally. In an important recent study, the distinguished Jewish writer Jacob Neusner has argued that, as a matter of fact, there has been *no* Jewish-Christian dialogue, in that the central belief of each faith—the doctrine of the Incarnation in the case of Christianity and of the divine vocation of Israel in the case of Judaism—has been evaded by those engaged in such discussions.[16] Can this be real dialogue, he asks, if there has been a failure to face up to such clear and overt differences? Why is it that such interfaith discussions seek to establish points of agreement and pass over such major differences?

In part, the answer to his question is simple: The point of such dialogue is usually to establish commonalities in order to enhance mutual understanding and respect in a highly polarized modern world in which religious differences are of substantial political importance.[17] Yet this praiseworthy goal has its

---

[15]See the remarkable essay of Wilfred Cantwell Smith, "Conflicting Truth Claims: A Rejoinder," in J. Hick, ed., *Truth and Dialogue: The Relationship between the World's Religions* (London: Sheldon, 1974), 156–62, which interprets "truth" in such an experimental and elastic manner that contradiction is virtually excluded as a matter of principle.

[16]Jacob Neusner, *Telling Tales: The Urgency and Basis for Judeo-Christian Dialogue* (Louisville: Westminster/John Knox, 1993).

[17]Gilles Kepel, of the Institute of Political Studies in Paris, stresses this point. See his *La revanche de Dieu: chrétiens, juifs et musulmans à la reconquete du monde* (Paris: Seuil, 1991).

more negative side. It can all too easily lead to the deliberate suppression of differences in the interests of harmony. It is proper that the religions of the world should be recognized as disagreeing with each other in matters of their beliefs. The Christian tradition regards God's final self-revelation as having taken place in Jesus Christ; Islam regards it as having taken place through Mohammed. Although agreed on the idea of a final revelation of God, the two religions happen to differ on its mode of revelation and its content. Christians insist Jesus was crucified; Muslims insist he was not. Well, let us respect these differences. They remind us that Muslims are not Christians, and vice versa. If the religious believer actually believes *something*, then disagreement is inevitable—and proper. As the distinguished American philosopher Richard Rorty remarked, nobody "except the occasional cooperative freshman" really believes that "two incompatible opinions on an important topic are equally good."[18]

It is no crime to disagree with someone. It is, however, improper to suppress or evade such differences on account of an a priori belief that no such differences can exist. George Lindbeck has written of the liberal tendency to "homogenize" everything; my approach is to honor and welcome genuine differences and to seek to explore their implications. There is no place for an intellectual dishonesty that refuses to acknowledge, for example, that Christians worship and adore Jesus Christ as Lord and Savior, whereas Muslims regard the Qur'an as the authoritative word of God and Mohammed as his prophet. Both religions are committed to evangelism and conversion (to use two Christian terms that have no exact parallels within Islam) in the belief that they are correct; neither regards their mutual differences as a threat to their distinctiveness.[19] For Islam, Christianity is different—and wrong.

---

[18]Richard Rorty, *The Consequences of Pragmatism* (Minneapolis: Univ. of Minnesota Press, 1982), 166.

[19]Islam, like Christianity, is a missionary religion, which is actively seeking to expand its influence in the West through conversion (*da'wah*) and territorial expansion (*dâr al-islâm*): see Larry Poston, *Islamic Da'wah in the West: Muslim Missionary Activity and the Dynamics of Conversion to Islam* (New York: Oxford Univ. Press, 1992).

A PARTICULARIST APPROACH TO RELIGIONS AND SALVATION

So what approach may be adopted to the religions and to the salvific place of Christianity within the world religious situation? The most helpful starting point is to consider the notion of *salvation* itself. The Christian notion of salvation is complex and highly nuanced. The controlling images used in the New Testament to articulate its various aspects include terms and concepts drawn from personal relationships, physical healing, legal transactions, and ethical transformation. Yet amidst this rich diversity of understandings of the nature of salvation, one factor remains constant: However salvation is to be understood, it is grounded in the life, death, and resurrection of Jesus Christ.[20] Salvation is a possibility only on account of Jesus Christ. The early Christians had no hesitation in using the term "Savior" (Gk. *soter*) to refer to Jesus Christ, despite the fact that this term was already widely used within the complex and diverse religious context in which the gospel first emerged. For the New Testament writers, Jesus was the *only* Savior of humanity. On the basis of the evidence available to the New Testament writers, this conclusion seemed entirely proper and necessary. The evidence concerning Jesus needed to be interpreted in this direction, and it was thus interpreted.

This does not, however, mean that the first Christians thought that Jesus as *soter* offered the same *soteria* as others who bore this title before him. In classical Greek religion, Poseidon and the Dioskouroi were all acclaimed as *soteres*.[21] Yet the "salvation" in question appears to have been conceived in terms of temporal deliverance from a present threat rather than any notion of eternal salvation.

The New Testament thus affirms the *particularity* of the redemptive act of God in Jesus Christ.[22] The early Christian

---

[20]See Alister E. McGrath, "Christology and Soteriology: A Response to Wolfhart Pannenberg's Critique of the Soteriological Approach to Christology," *Theologische Zeitschrift* 42 (1986): 222–36.

[21]See Walter Burkert, *Greek Religion* (Oxford: Blackwell, 1975), 137, 213, and references there.

[22]See Lesslie Newbigin, *The Finality of Christ* (Richmond, Va.: John Knox, 1969); more recently, Clark H. Pinnock, *A Wideness in God's Mercy: The Finality of Jesus Christ in a World of Religions* (Grand Rapids: Zondervan, 1992), 49–80.

tradition, basing itself on the New Testament, reaffirmed this particularity. Although the early Christians acknowledged that God's revelation went far beyond Jesus Christ, insofar as God made himself known to various extents through such means as the natural order of creation, human conscience, and civilization, this general knowledge of God was not understood to entail universal salvation. John Calvin stated the various styles of knowledge of God available to humanity when he drew his celebrated distinction between a "knowledge of God the Creator" and a "knowledge of God the Redeemer."[23] The former was universally available, mediated through nature and in a fuller and more coherent manner through Scripture; the latter, which alone constituted a distinctively Christian knowledge of God, was known only through Jesus Christ as he is revealed in Scripture. Thus Calvin would have had no problem in allowing that both Jews and Muslims have access to a knowledge of God as Creator; while the particular and distinctive aspect of a Christian understanding of God related to knowing him as Redeemer rather than as Creator alone.

Calvin here expresses a long-standing consensus within the Christian theology that knowledge of God may be had outside the Christian tradition. Within the Reformed tradition, the general position of Calvin has been maintained, despite the vigorous challenge of Karl Barth, who insisted that no knowledge of God was available or possible outside Christ, thus shifting from a Christocentric to a Christomonist position. The strong tradition of natural theology within the Reformed tradition points to a belief, grounded in Scripture, that God has not left himself without witnesses in the world, whether in nature itself, classical philosophy, or other religions. For example, Romans 1:18–32 clearly implies divine revelation as taking place in human culture and experience prior to the coming of Jesus Christ and indicates that this may be regarded as a preparation for the gospel (*praeparatio evangelica*) itself.

The same general principle is maintained in Lutheran dogmatics, often expressed in terms of the distinction between *Deus absconditus* and *Deus revelatus*. As Carl Braaten expresses this, "Lutheran theology typically affirms a twofold revelation of

---

[23]See Edward A. Dowey, *The Knowledge of God in Calvin's Theology* (New York: Columbia Univ. Press, 1952).

God: through the hidden God of creation and law (*Deus abscon-ditus*) and through the revealed God of covenant and gospel (*Deus revelatus*)."[24] A similar approach is also associated with the Second Vatican Council.[25] Allowing for knowledge of God outside the specifically Christian community is nothing new or controversial; it is merely reiterating a long-standing consensus.

Nevertheless, some correctives must immediately be added.

(1) The Christian tradition bears witness to a particular understanding of God and cannot be merged into the various concepts of divinity found in other religions. To allow that something may be known of God in non-Christian religions is not to say that every aspect of their understandings of God are consistent with Christianity, nor that every aspect of the Christian understanding of God is found in other religions. We are talking about "points of contact" and occasional convergences, not identity nor even fundamentally consistent agreement.

(2) In the Christian understanding, factual or cognitive knowledge of God is not regarded as saving in itself. As Søren Kierkegaard pointed out in his *Concluding Unscientific Postscript*, it is perfectly possible to know about the Christian understanding of God without being a Christian.[26] Knowledge of God is one thing; salvation is another. To allow that something may be known of God in non-Christian religions is not to imply that salvation, in the Christian understanding of that term, is available through them.

(3) Furthermore, the notion of salvation varies considerably from one religion to another. In the native religions of West Africa, for example, there is often no discernible transcendent element associated with their notions of salvation. A certain laziness in dealing with English translations of the religious writings of other faiths, especially those originating from India and China, has allowed the rise of the assumption that all religions share common ideas of salvation. In fact, the English term

---

[24]Carl E. Braaten, "Christ Is God's Final, Not the Only, Revelation," in Carl E. Braaten, *No Other Gospel! Christianity among the World's Religions* (Minneapolis: Fortress, 1992), 65–82 (quote on p. 68).

[25]Miikka Ruokanen, *The Catholic Doctrine of Non-Christian Religions According to the Second Vatican Council* (Leiden: Brill, 1992).

[26]Søren Kierkegaard, *Concluding Unscientific Postscript* (London: Oxford Univ. Press, 1941), 169–224. Cf. Paul L. Holmer, "Kierkegaard and Religious Propositions," *Journal of Religion* 35 (1955): 135–46.

salvation is often used to translate Sanskrit or Chinese terms with connotations and associations quite distinct from the Christian concept. These divergences are masked by the process of translation, which often suggests a degree of convergence that is absent in reality. So important are these points that they must be explored in more detail.

THE CHRISTIAN UNDERSTANDING OF GOD

There was a period when there was some sympathy for the idea that mutual understanding among the world's religions would be enhanced if Christians accepted a kind of "Copernican Revolution," in which they stopped regarding Jesus Christ as of central importance and instead began to focus their attention on God. Being God-centered would be more helpful than being Christ-centered.

In the end, an incarnational Christology is now seen as a serious barrier to interreligious understanding only in the sense that the Qur'an is also a barrier. Both are integral to the faiths in question. To eliminate them is to radically alter the faiths, assisting interfaith reconciliation only to the extent that it destroys the distinctiveness of the religions in question. This may be a hypothetical possibility in academic seminar rooms; in the real world, we must learn to live with conflicts between such defining and distinctive characteristics of faiths, rather than attempt to smooth them down. The religions are not putty to be molded by pluralist ideologues, but living realities that demand respect and honor.

It is a simple matter of fact that traditional Christian theology is strongly resistant to the homogenizing agenda of religious pluralists, not least on account of its high Christology. The suggestion that all religions are more or less talking about vaguely the same "God" finds itself in difficulty in relation to certain essentially Christian ideas—most notably, the doctrines of the Incarnation and the Trinity. For example, if God is Christ-like, as the doctrine of the divinity of Christ affirms in uncompromising terms, then the historical figure of Jesus, along with the witness to him in Scripture, becomes of foundational importance to Christianity. Such distinctive doctrines are embarrassing to those who wish to debunk what they term the "myth of Christian uniqueness," who then proceed to demand that Christianity should abandon doctrines such as the Incarnation, which imply a high profile of identification between Jesus Christ and God, in favor of various degree Christologies that are more amenable to the reductionist program of liberalism. In much the same way, the idea that God is in any sense disclosed or defined Christologically is set to one side, on account of its theologically momentous implications for the identity and significance of Jesus Christ—which liberal pluralism finds an embarrassment. Let us turn to consider these two points.

First, the idea of the Incarnation is rejected, often as a myth.[27] Thus John Hick and his collaborators reject the Incarnation on various logical and commonsense counts—yet fail to deal with the question of why Christians should have developed this doctrine in the first place.[28] There seems to be an underlying agenda to eliminate the sheer *distinctiveness* of Christianity at this point. A sharp distinction is thus drawn between the historical person of Jesus Christ and the principles he is alleged to represent. Paul Knitter is but one of a small galaxy of pluralist writers concerned to drive a wedge between the "Jesus event" that is unique to Christianity and the "Christ principle" that is accessible to all religious traditions, expressed in their own distinctive, but equally valid, ways.

It is significant that the pluralist agenda forces its advocates to adopt heretical views of Christ in order to meet its needs. In an effort to fit Jesus into the mold of the "great religious teachers of humanity" category, the Ebionite heresy has been revived and made politically correct. Jesus is one of the religious options made available by the great human teachers of religion. He is "one of the lads," to use a Yorkshire phrase.

Second, the idea that God is in some manner made known through Christ has been dismissed. Captivated by the image of a "Copernican Revolution"—probably one of the most overworked and misleading phrases in recent writings in this field—pluralists demand that Christians move away from discussing

---

[27]Perhaps most notably in J. Hick, ed., *The Myth of God Incarnate* (London: SCM, 1977).

[28]See Alister E. McGrath, "Resurrection and Incarnation: The Foundations of the Christian Faith," in A. Walker, ed., *Different Gospels* (London: Hodder & Stoughton, 1988), 79–96.

Christ to discussing God. Yet they fail to recognize that the "God of the Christians" (Tertullian) might be different from other divinities and that the doctrine of the Trinity spells out the nature of that distinction. As Robert Jenson has persuasively argued, the doctrine of the Trinity is an attempt to spell out the identity of this God and to avoid confusion with rival claimants to this title.[29] This doctrine defines and defends the particularity and distinctiveness and, ultimately, the *uniqueness* of the "God of the Christians."

This point is of considerable importance. Most Western religious pluralists appear to work with a concept of God that is shaped by the Christian tradition, whether this is openly acknowledged or not. For example, they often appeal to the notion of a gracious and loving God. Yet this is a distinctively Christian notion of God, grounded and substantiated in Jesus Christ. There is no such thing as a "tradition-independent notion of God." Even Kant's idea of God, allegedly purely rational in character and hence independent of culture, is actually ethnocentric, having been deeply shaped by implicit Christian assumptions ingrained into his social matrix. As Gavin D'Costa has pointed out, John Hick's concept of God, which plays such a significant role in his pluralist worldview, has been decisively shaped by Christological considerations, whether he realizes or is prepared to admit this. "How credibly," he asks, "can Hick expound a doctrine of God's universal salvific will if he does not ground this crucial truth in the revelation of God in Christ, thereby bringing Christology back onto center stage?"[30]

Pluralists have driven a wedge between God and Jesus Christ, as if Christians were obliged to choose between one or the other. Assuming that the "god" in question is common to all religious traditions, the pendulum swings towards a theocentric approach. As a result, the Christology of the religious pluralists becomes reduced to something of negligible proportions. Only the lowest possible Christology within the Christian tradition is deemed to be worthy of acceptance in the modern period. The awkward fact that this Christology had been rejected as heretical

[29]Robert Jenson, *The Triune Identity* (Philadelphia: Fortress, 1982), 1–20.

[30]Gavin D'Costa, *John Hick's Theology of Religions* (New York: Univ. Press of America, 1987), 103.

by the early church is ignored. If the pluralists have some infallible source of knowledge about the nature and purposes of God apart from Christ, then what is the point of the gospel? And what kind of God is it who can be known apart from Christ? Are we talking about "the God and Father of our Lord Jesus Christ" (1 Peter 1:3) at all, or of some different deity? An idea of God can only be considered "Christian" if it is subjected to the standard of God's self-disclosure through Jesus Christ, as is made known to us through Scripture.

What is the relevance of this point to our theme? The Christian understanding of salvation involves an altered relationship with God, whether this is understood personally, substantially, morally, or legally. But which God are we talking about? Old Testament writers were clear that "salvation," as they understood it, was not about a new relationship with any of the gods of Canaan, Philistia, or Assyria, but with the one and only covenant God of Israel, whom they knew by the distinguishing personal title of "the LORD" (Yahweh). For Christianity, the notion of salvation explicitly centers on a relationship, inaugurated in time and to be consummated beyond time, with none other than the "God and Father of our Lord Jesus Christ." We are thus dealing with a highly particularized notion of salvation, as I will demonstrate later.

THE PLACE OF JESUS CHRIST IN SALVATION

We have touched on the importance of Jesus Christ in relation to the Christian understanding of God and on the pluralist tendency that ends up, as Harvey Cox puts it, "soft-pedaling the figure of Jesus himself." For Cox, the most appropriate way for Christians to engage in meaningful interfaith dialogue is to begin by recognizing that "Jesus is, in some ways, the *most* particularistic element of Christianity."[31] Cox makes the point here that one must begin from something concrete and historical, rather than from some abstract symbol. And for Christians, this particularistic element is Jesus Christ. Christian theology, spirituality, and, above all, Christian worship are strongly Christ-focused.

---

[31]Harvey Cox, *Many Mansions* (Boston: Beacon Press, 1988), 5–6.

The New Testament, which endorses and legitimates this Christocentrism, does not merely regard Jesus Christ as *expressive* of a divine salvation that may be made available in other forms. He is clearly understood to be *constitutive* of that salvation. In the Christian tradition, Jesus is viewed as more than *Rasul*, "the sent one" (to use the fundamental Muslim definition of the sequence of prophets culminating in Mohammed). He is seen as the one who establishes as much as the one who is sent—a prophet and a Savior. Pluralists have a number of options here, from declaring that the New Testament is simply mistaken on this point (which precludes a serious claim to be Christian) to suggesting that these affirmations may be true for Christians, but have no binding force *extra muros ecclesiae* ("outside the bounds of the church").[32] Yet the New Testament clearly regards Jesus Christ as, at least potentially, the Savior of the world (not simply of Christians), thus pointing to the strongly universal character of his saving work.

THE NATURE OF SALVATION

In an important study, John Hick has argued that there is a common core structure to all religions, which "are fundamentally alike in exhibiting a soteriological structure. That is to say, they are all concerned with salvation/liberation/enlightenment/fulfillment."[33] However, it may reasonably be observed that these concepts of salvation are conceived in such radically different ways and are understood to be established or attained in such different manners, that only someone who was doggedly determined, as a matter of principle, to treat them as aspects of the same greater whole would have sufficient intellectual flexibility to do so. Do Christianity and satanism really have the same understandings of salvation? My satanist acquaintances certainly do not think so. In fact, satanists accept that there is a God but choose to worship his antithesis. This dualism hardly bodes well for a pluralist theory of the religions.

A more neutral observer, relieved from the necessity of insisting that all religions of the world are basically the same,

---

[32]For a survey and criticism of these options, see Pinnock, *A Wideness in God's Mercy*, 64–74.

[33]John Hick, *The Second Christianity* (London: SCM, 1983), 86.

might reasonably suggest that they do not merely offer different ways of achieving and conceptualizing salvation; they offer *different salvations* altogether. The Rastafarian vision of a paradise in which blacks are served by menial whites, the Homeric notion of Tartaros, the old Norse concept of Valhalla, the Buddhist vision of *nirvana*, the Christian hope of resurrection to eternal life—all are obviously different. How can all the routes to salvation be equally "valid" when the goals to be reached in such different ways are so obviously unrelated?

Regarding the enormous variations within religions on the nature of salvation, Christian conceptions of salvation focus on the establishment of a relationship between God (in the Christian sense of the term) and his people and use a variety of images to articulate salvation's various aspects. Underlying these convergent images of salvation is the common theme of "salvation in and through Christ." That is to say, salvation is only a possibility on account of the life, death, and resurrection of Jesus Christ, and salvation is shaped in his likeness.

Despite the vast divergences between religions over the issue of the nature, grounds, and means of attaining salvation, similarities exist at certain points. For example, the distinction between "kitten salvation" and "monkey salvation" within the *bhakti marga* tradition of Hinduism is unquestionably grounded in a doctrine of grace. The mother tigress carries her cubs, whereas baby monkeys have to hang on to their mothers. This is often appealed to as an indication of the "convergence" of the religions over the grace of God. Yet this distinction is not found in any of the foundational documents of Hinduism, dating from the Vedic period (2000–600 B.C.), in which a synthesis between the polytheistic sacrificial religion of the Aryans and the pantheistic monism of the Upanishads took place, nor during the pantheistic period (600 B.C.–A.D. 300). It emerged during the Puranic period (A.D. 300–1200), during which time Syrian forms of Christianity became established in the southern regions of India; it is especially associated with the medieval writer Sri Ramanuja (tc. 1050–1137).[34] So, does "kitten salvation" represent an inherent similarity between Hinduism and Christianity, or

---

[34]The best study remains J. B. Carman, *The Theology of Ramanuja* (New Haven: Yale Univ. Press, 1974).

does it represent the tendency of some Hindu writers to "borrow" ideas from Christianity?[35] Unfortunately, the question cannot be answered because of our lack of knowledge of various aspects of the religious history of the period. But it is a question that must be raised. Similarities may reflect borrowing; they need not reflect fundamental convergence. The strongly syncretistic tendencies of some forms of Hinduism have often been noted; perhaps it is a specifically Christian understanding of grace that has found its way into some strands of the movement.

Differences between notions of salvation are also reflected in the worship of religious communities. Those who are attracted to the Buddhist notion of salvation—or, more accurately, one of the many such options available within the various Buddhist traditions—will hardly want to become Christians. For Christian theology, worship and prayer are closely interwoven with a definite series of beliefs concerning both the person and work of Jesus Christ. Christian worship reflects particular beliefs concerning the nature of both salvation and the Savior. Geoffrey Wainwright and others have emphasized the way in which theology and doxology are closely interconnected, making it impossible to graft, for example, a Buddhist idea of salvation to a Christian worshiping community.[36] In a related context, Muslims continue to be at best highly skeptical and more generally intensely critical of the defining Christian practice of worshiping Jesus Christ. Acknowledging Jesus as the Son of God is generally seen as an instance of the heresy of *ittakhadha*.

With these points in mind, let us address the question, "Is salvation possible outside Christianity?" As a result of the writings of Ludwig Wittgenstein, theologians have become acutely sensitive to the need to establish the context in which words are used.[37] For Wittgenstein, the *Lebensform* ("form of living") to

---

[35]The nineteenth-century writer Rammohun Roy is a case in point. See the useful material assembled by Dermot Killingley, *Rammohun Roy in Hindu and Christian Tradition* (Newcastle upon Tyne: Grevatt & Grevatt, 1993).

[36]Geoffrey Wainwright, *Doxology: The Praise of God in Worship. Doctrine and Life* (New York: Oxford Univ. Press, 1980). For a more recent discussion, see Aidan Kavanaugh, *On Liturgical Theology* (New York: Pueblo, 1984). The Latin formula *lex orandi, lex credendi* is often used to summarize this interrelationship.

[37]A theme explored with considerable skill in Fergus Kerr, *Theology after Wittgenstein* (Oxford: Blackwell, 1988).

which a word refers and within which it is used is of decisive importance in establishing its meaning. Yet the term *salvation* is often used in a loose and undefined manner. For Wittgenstein, the particularities of a way of life or "form of living" are of controlling importance to our understanding of concepts:

> Would it be correct to say that our concepts reflect our life?
>
> They stand in the middle of it.[38]

The Christian *Lebensform* is thus of controlling importance in understanding what the Christian concept of salvation implies, presupposes, and expresses. As Wittgenstein himself points out, the same word can be used in a large number of senses. One way of dealing with this might be to invent a totally new vocabulary, in which the meaning of each word was tightly and unequivocally defined. But this is not a real option. Languages, like religions, are living entities and cannot be forced to behave in such an artificial way. A perfectly acceptable approach, according to Wittgenstein, is to take the trouble to define the particular sense in which a word should be understood in order to avoid confusion with its many other senses. This involves a careful study of its associations and its use in the "form of living" to which it relates.[39] "Salvation" is clearly a case in point. Its use and associations within the Christian tradition, especially in worship, point to a distinctive understanding of what the Christian faith is understood to confer on believers, its ultimate basis, and the manner in which this comes about.

If salvation is understood as "some benefit conferred upon or achieved by members of a community, whether individually or corporately," all religions offer "salvation." All religions—and

---

[38]Ludwig Wittgenstein, *Remarks on Colour*, ed. G. E. M. Anscombe, trans. L. L. McAlister and M. Schüttle (Oxford: Blackwell, 1977), 3:302.

[39]Ludwig Wittgenstein, *Lectures and Conversations on Aesthetics, Psychology and Religious Belief* (Oxford: Blackwell, 1966), 2: "If I had to say what is the main mistake made by philosophers ... I would say that it is that when language is looked at, what is looked at is a form of words and not the use made of the form of words." There is an interesting parallel here with Barth's statement that the expressions that make up the "spoken matter of proclamation" in the Christian faith "acquire their meaning from the associations and contexts in which they are used" (Karl Barth, *Church Dogmatics* 13 vols. [Edinburgh: T. and T. Clark, 1936–75]), I/1, 86.

by no means *only* religions—offer *something*. However, this is such a general statement that it is devoid of significant theological value: All religions, along with political theories such as Marxism and psychotherapeutic schools such as Rogerian therapy, may legitimately be styled "salvific." The statement "all religions offer salvation" is thus potentially little more than a tautology. Only by using the most violent of means can all religions be said to offer the same "salvation." Respect for the integrity of the world's religions demands that "salvation" be particularized. That is to say, the distinctive morphology of a religion's understanding of salvation—including its basis, its mode of conveyance and appropriation, and its inherent nature—must be respected and not coercively homogenized to suit the needs of some particular pressure group within the academy.

The distinctive character of each religion may and must be affirmed: Buddhism offers one style of "salvation," just as Christianity offers another. It is no criticism of Buddhism to suggest that it does not offer a specifically Christian salvation, just as it is not in the least imperialist to state that the Christian vision of salvation is not the same as the Buddhist. It is essential to respect and honor differences here and to resist the ever-present temptation to force them all into the same mold.

In the light of this approach, the following statements may be set out.

(1) Christianity has a particular understanding of the nature, grounds, and means of obtaining salvation.[40] And the Christian understanding of salvation, like the Christian notion of God, is Christologically determined. Just as it is illegitimate to use the term *God* in a vague and generic sense, allowing it to be understood that all religions share this same divinity, so it is improper to use the term *salvation* as if it were common to all religions. When used within the context of a given religion, the English word "salvation" (which often translates Greek, Hebrew, Arabic, Sanskrit, and Chinese terms of considerably greater complexity than is appreciated) takes on specific overtones that prohibit it from designating the same concept in each case. "Salvation" is a particularity, not a universality.

---

[40]On the means of obtaining salvation, the importance of the doctrine of justification by faith through grace must be noted. See Alister E. McGrath, *Iustitia Dei: A History of the Christian Doctrine of Justification*, 2 vols. (Cambridge: Cambridge Univ. Press, 1986).

(2) Christianity is the only religion to offer salvation *in the Christian sense of that term*. This verbally clumsy sentence acknowledges the point, stressed by Wittgenstein, that there is a vital need to make clear the associations of terms and the particular sense in which it is being used. In that the word *salvation* is meaningless unless its context is identified, it is necessary to establish the "form of living" that gives the word its distinctive meaning—in this case, the Christian world of doctrine, worship, and hope, going back to the New Testament and consolidated in the Christian tradition.

(3) Salvation in the Christian sense of that term is proclaimed as a real and attractive possibility for those who are presently outside the Christian community. The entire enterprise of evangelism, now recognized to be of such vital importance to the Christian churches throughout the world, is directed towards the proclamation of this good news to the world.

(4) By responding to the Christian gospel and embracing the salvation it confers, individuals as a matter of fact become members of the church. This is not to say that they necessarily become members of an institutional church or a specific denomination. It is to remain faithful to the theological definition of *the church* as the company of believers, which transcends any of its particular institutional embodiments. As Ignatius of Antioch put it, "Wherever Jesus Christ is, there is also the universal church."[41]

(5) It is thus proper to affirm that, in the often quoted words of Cyprian of Carthage, "There is no salvation outside the church [*extra ecclesiam nulla salus*]." It will be clear from the above analysis that anyone who has accepted salvation in the specifically Christian sense of the term is de facto a member of the Christian church. It must be conceded that Cyprian's maxim has often been interpreted to mean "salvation comes only through the institutional church."[42] However, this is not the only sense in which the term can be interpreted, nor is it the most natural. At its heart, the maxim affirms that there is an unbreakable bond between Christian salvation and Christian believers.

---

[41]Ignatius, *To the Smyrnaeans*, 7. See J. Stevenson, ed., *A New Eusebius* (London: SPCK, 1957), 48.

[42]For useful historical background, see Hans Küng, *The Church* (New York: Sheed & Ward, 1967), 313–19.

CHRISTIAN SALVATION AND THE WORLD RELIGIONS

With these points in mind, let us return to the question of salvation in the religions. All religions are salvific in their own terms, in that they offer a particular conception of salvation. Yet I have stressed that there is a specifically Christian understanding of salvation, which is grounded uniquely in the life, death, and resurrection of Jesus Christ. To affirm that there is a distinctively Christian understanding of salvation is not to deny that other faiths offer salvation in their own terms; it is simply to note that the salvation in question differs from one faith to another. It is particular, not universal. It is perfectly legitimate for the Christian to wish to share his or her experience of and hopes concerning salvation with others; to do so is not to belittle others, but to wish to share the Christian experience. In a free market of ideas, the attractiveness and relevance of the Christian understanding of salvation will determine whether others wish to embrace this understanding of salvation, and by doing so, become Christians.

Salvation in its Christian sense is thus available universally. The Christian proclamation of salvation is not bounded by any geographical, cultural, or social divide. One need not join a Christian denomination to receive God's salvation. By receiving that salvation, one enters the church—not in the sense of a physical building or a denomination, but in the sense of the community of believers down the ages. In no way does Christianity declare that salvation is only a possibility for those inside its bounds. The church may indeed be thought of as the company of the redeemed; nevertheless, those outside its bounds are invited to share in the wedding banquet on condition that they dress accordingly (Matt. 22:1–12). No one is coerced into attending, but the invitation is universal. The particularity of that invitation— in that it rests on the person and work of Christ—does not in any way conflict with its universal proclamation and appeal.

Alongside the unequivocal affirmation of the particularity of God's act of redemption in Jesus Christ, the New Testament states the universality of God's saving will. It is God's wish that all people will be saved and come to a knowledge of the truth (1 Tim. 2:4). God intends to have mercy on all (Rom. 11:32). God does not want anyone to perish, but wants everyone to come to repentance (2 Peter 3:9). A responsible Christian theology must be able to accommodate itself within the creative tension that results from the simultaneous New Testament affirmation of the particularity of the person and work of Christ and the universality of the scope of his mission.[43]

This tension cannot be dissolved simply by adopting a universalist route, declaring that all will be saved in the end.[44] This approach has its attractions, not least because it appears to be more faithful to the idea of a loving God.[45] Yet the idea that all will be saved requires the inclusion of a number of additional beliefs, including that all will *consent* to be saved. What if some, wishing to exercise their God-given faculty of freedom, choose to refuse that offer, preferring to go their own way? In such a situation, the doctrine of universalism asks us to envision a situation in which God imposes salvation on individuals. It is a small step from the optimistic affirmation that "all will be saved" to the authoritarian pronouncement that "all *must* be saved—whether they like it or not." The Christian understanding of the love of God is that of a vulnerable love offered to us through Christ. God offers us himself in the knowledge that we may refuse him. Universalism denies humanity the right to say no to God. Despite its initial attractions, it turns out to have its decidedly darker side, in effect declaring that all are predestined to be saved—raising precisely the same problems relating to divine sovereignty and human responsibility associated with the approach of John Calvin, an approach that is not usually regarded with any great enthusiasm by pluralists.

PARTICULARISM AND THE PREACHING OF THE GOSPEL

We are assured that those who respond in faith to the explicit preaching of the gospel will be saved. We cannot draw

---

[43]In their very different ways, the theologies of Karl Rahner and Karl Barth can be seen as attempts to resolve the tension at this point.

[44]On this approach in Karl Barth, see Alister E. McGrath, "Karl Barth als Aufklärer? Der Zusammenhang seiner Lehre vom Werke Christi mit der Erwählungslehre," *Kerygma und Dogma* 30 (1984): 273–83.

[45]This is the position taken by John A. T. Robinson, *In the End God* (London: Clark, 1950).

the conclusion from this, however, that *only* those who thus respond will be saved. God's revelation is not limited to the explicit human preaching of the good news, but extends beyond it. We must be prepared to be surprised at those whom we will meet in the kingdom of God. In his preaching of the good news of the kingdom, Jesus lists some who will be among its beneficiaries—the Ninevites, the queen of Sheba, and those who lived in the cities of Tyre, Sidon, Sodom, and Gomorrah (Matt. 10:15; 11:22; 12:41–42). By strict Jewish standards none of these had any claim to be in the kingdom of God. Yet God's mercy extended far beyond the human limits devised by this rather narrow-minded section of Judaism. Perhaps there is a danger that today's Christians will repeat this mistake, even with the best of intentions, by placing artificial human limits on the sovereignty, freedom, and love of God.

So what about those who have never heard the gospel? Is the universality of the gospel compromised by the fact that, as a matter of history, the gospel has not been preached to all and its benefits made universally available? There can be no doubt that certain types of evangelical theology have caused considerable anxiety in this respect by their apparent insistence that only those who respond to the explicit verbal proclamation of the gospel will be saved. Pluralists and many others rightly observe that this is to write off the vast majority of those who have ever lived, who are deprived of salvation by matters of geographical and historical contingency. But this is a flawed theology, which limits God's modes of action, disclosure, and saving power. As Stuart Hackett has pointed out:

> If every human being in all times and ages has been objectively provided for through the unique redemption in Jesus, and if this provision is in fact intended by God for every such human being, then it must be possible for every human individual to become personally eligible to receive that provision—regardless of his historical, cultural or personal circumstances and situation.[46]

A human failure to evangelize cannot be transposed into God's failure to save. In the end, salvation is not a culturally condi-

---

[46]Stuart Hackett, *The Reconstruction of the Christian Revelation Claim* (Grand Rapids: Baker, 1984), 244.

tioned or restricted human accomplishment; it is God's boundless sovereign gift to his people. As an old Reformed hymn puts
it:

> I sought the Lord, and afterward I knew
> He moved my soul to seek Him, seeking me;
> It was not I that found, O Savior true;
> No, I was found by Thee.

Where the word is not or cannot be preached by human
agents, God is not inhibited from bringing people to faith in him,
even if that act of hope and trust may lack the fully orbed character of an informed Christian faith. The doctrine of prevenient
grace has been severely neglected in our theology of mission, so
that we have overlooked the simple yet glorious fact that God
has gone ahead of us, preparing the way for those who follow.
In the harshly intolerant cultural climate of many Islamic
nations, in which the open preaching of the gospel is impossible and conversion to Christianity punishable by imprisonment
or death, many Muslims become Christians through dreams and
visions in which they are addressed by the risen Christ. Perhaps
we need to be more sensitive to the ways in which God is at
work and realize that, important though our preaching may be,
in the end God does not depend on it.

Christians are asked to proclaim the good news of the love
of God for his people in the sure knowledge that there are no
barriers of culture, race, language, gender, or status to its acceptance. Yet we must never think that it is by preaching the gospel
that we are somehow making salvation available or possible. It
is God who makes salvation possible through the work of Christ
and who uses the preaching of the gospel as a means of actual-
izing that salvation. But it is not the only means. God's saving
work must never be exclusively restricted to human preaching,
as if the Holy Spirit was silent or inactive in God's world, or as
if the actualization of God's saving purposes depended totally
on human agencies. The Creator is not dependent on his creation
in achieving his purposes. We must never, by our inadequate
theological formulations, imply that God's work of salvation is
somehow dependent on us. This confuses the notion of human
responsibility toward God with the different idea of the total
abrogation of divine sovereignty, in which God abandons his

oversight and involvement in his work and delegates it in its totality to his creation.

It is here that a Reformed approach to the question of the religions has its particular merits, especially in its vigorous insistence that God's sovereignty will never permit the will of God to be frustrated by human failure.[47] Christians may have failed to make the good news available to all; this does not mean that God will fail in his intention to make salvation a universal possibility. In the end, a Reformed perspective on this question rests on its total commitment to the inherent goodness of God, expressed in the great rhetorical question of Abraham: "Will not the Judge of all the earth do right?" (Gen. 18:25). A conviction that God will do what is right and that this will be achieved through exercising his sovereign rights over his creation underlies and nourishes a Reformed approach to this question. We may not fully understand the issues; nevertheless, we firmly believe that we may rely on the wisdom, righteousness, and goodness of God—embodied supremely in Jesus Christ—as we consider the question of salvation and other religions.

---

[47]For a brief exploration of the role of God's sovereignty in salvation, see I. John Hesselink, *On Being Reformed* (New York: Reformed Church, 1988), 90–92.

RESPONSE TO ALISTER E. MCGRATH

John Hick

Alister McGrath's chapter contains both a polemic against religious pluralism and a positive discussion of salvation, and I would like to comment briefly on both.

MCGRATH'S POLEMIC

I found his polemic disappointing, in that he often attacks caricatures created for the purpose of being destroyed rather than the arguments of real people. For example, several times he attributes to religious pluralists the idea that all religions are the same and that they are all saying the same thing. If he were to read contemporary pluralist theologians—such as Driver, Gilkey, Kaufman, Knitter, Pieris, Race, Ruether, Samartha, Cantwell Smith, Swidler, or myself—he would not find these absurdly simplistic ideas in any of them. I can correct several of McGrath's misapprehensions by quoting from the one book of mine that he appears to have read, and from the same page as that from which he quotes something else. I pointed out that the pluralistic hypothesis

> has the merit that it does not lead us to play down the differences between the various forms of religious experience and thought. It does not generate any pressure to think that God the Father and Brahman, or Allah and the Dharmakaya, are phenomenologically, i.e. as experienced and described, identical; or that the human responses

which they evoke, in spiritual practices, cultural forms, life-styles, types of society, etc., are the same. The theory—arrived at inductively by observation of the range of human religious experiences—is that the great world faiths embody different perceptions and conceptions of, and correspondingly different responses to, the Real or the Ultimate from within the major variant cultural ways of being human. Such a theory, I would suggest, does justice both to the fascinating differences between the religious traditions and to their basic complementarity as different human responses to the one limitless divine Reality.[1]

But McGrath ignores what does not fit into his own caricature—a procedure that has the effect of misleading his readers.

Again, he rightly criticizes an "excessive reliance on Western categories" in discussing religion, but he attributes this fault to religious pluralists, ignoring the fact that the classic work that first deconstructed the traditional Western concepts of "religion" and "the religions" is Wilfred Cantwell Smith's *The Meaning and End of Religion*.[2] I have myself suggested that the concept of religion is a Wittgensteinian "family-resemblance" concept, so that there is no essence of religion, but a wide network of partly overlapping phenomena.[3]

Again—and this is a matter of professional courtesy in debate—McGrath twice quotes from articles written by others specifically in criticism of my own writings, but does not mention my own replies in subsequent issues of the same journals. He does not say, "Hick responded that . . . , but. . . ." But it would be tedious, as well as disagreeable, to go on about McGrath's tendency to create "straw men" rather than engaging in serious debate with properly delineated positions.

One further point in McGrath's polemic deserves to be mentioned before turning to the question of salvation. He refers to the ancient Indian story of the elephant and the blind men. This may well have been used, particularly in popular exposi-

---

[1]John Hick, *The Second Christianity* (London: SCM, 1983), 86.

[2]Wilfred Cantwell Smith, *The Meaning and End of Religion* (Minneapolis: Fortress Press, 1991 [orig. 1962]).

[3]John Hick, *An Interpretation of Religion: Human Responses to the Transcendent* (New Haven, Conn.: Yale Univ. Press, 1989 / London: Macmillan, 1989), 3–5.

tions, as a picture of religious pluralism, though I and others have pointed out its inadequacy. It is inadequate, and indeed misleading, because the pluralistic hypothesis is not an a priori dogma, presupposing a cosmic standpoint, but a hypothesis built up from ground level to explain the facts of the religious life of humankind. Starting from within a particular tradition— in the case of the authors and readers of this book, Christianity—one is committed to the faith that religious experience within this tradition is not purely projection, but, while including an element of projection, is at the same time a cognitive response to a transcendent divine reality. One also notes the transforming effect of Christian experience in the lives of believers, producing the fruit of the Spirit that Paul listed as "love, joy, peace, patience, kindness, goodness, faithfulness, gentleness and self-control" (Gal. 5:22–23). One then notes, as I have indicated in my own chapter, that this fruit is also evident, apparently to more or less the same limited extent, in the lives not only of Christians, but also of people of other faiths whose religious experience is different from ours. Thus we have to extend the principle of the responsive rather than purely projective character of religious experience to these other traditions.

We then need—if we are theologians—a comprehensive theory that makes sense of this situation. We need, in other words, a religious interpretation of religion in its plurality of forms. The theory that seems to me most promising is this: Because all experience is concept-laden, the great world religions constitute different ways of conceiving and experiencing ultimate reality, and hence different forms of life in response to that reality. This hypothesis does not presuppose any privileged universal vision; it is proposed simply as the best explanation of the data. In contrast to this, however, Christian absolutism, in McGrath's as in other forms, does claim a privileged position from which it is able to locate all non-Christian traditions as either errors or potential preparations for itself. It says, in effect, that we know the elephant as it is in its fullness while the people of other faiths know, at best, only some particular limited aspect of it. If there is an "immensely arrogant claim of one who sees the full truth," that "one" is not the pluralist but the Christian absolutist—a term for which "Christian particularist" is a more reader-friendly synonym.

THE QUESTION OF SALVATION

I turn now to the central issue of salvation. I have argued in some detail in *An Interpretation of Religion* that each of the great postaxial religions (in distinction from preaxial religious life) is concerned with a radical change from a defective and unhappy state to a limitlessly better state in relation to ultimate reality. The defective state is differently diagnosed as fallenness, spiritual blindness, or immersion in *maya* or in *dukkha*. And the limitlessly better state is variously conceptualized as eternal life, peace with God, illumination, liberation, awakening to *nirvana*, or, on a more mystical level, attaining *satori*, or *mukti*, or the Vision of God. What these different conceptualities have in common is that in each case what is offered is a transformation of the human person, through his or her response to the ultimately real, from natural self-centeredness to a new orientation centered in that ultimate reality. The central fruits in human life of this salvific transformation are love, compassion, peace, joy, kindness, and concern for others.

In Christianity the salvific transformation consists in turning away from self and, in the words of the *Theologia Germanica*, becoming to the Eternal Goodness what one's own hand is to oneself. In Islam it consists in a total self-surrender to God, the only Lord of the universe, who is always *Allah, rahman rahim* ("God beneficent and merciful"). In Judaism the hoped-for redemption from present evil into a radically better state has generally consisted in a corporate rather than purely individual life in accordance with the Torah—though it is also individual, as in the other traditions it is also corporate. In Hinduism, to quote Radhakrishnan,

> The divine consciousness and will must become our consciousness and will. This means that our actual self must cease to be a private self; we must give up our particular will, die to our ego, by surrendering its whole nature, its consciousness and character to the Divine.[4]

In Buddhism it consists in the transcendence of the ego's point of view, which is the cause of suffering and anxiety. In the words

---

[4]S. Radhakrishnan, *The Principal Upanishads* (New York: Humanities Press, 1969 / London: Allen & Unwin, 1969), 105.

of Masao Abe, a leading exponent of Buddhism to the West, "Buddhist salvation is . . . nothing other than an awakening to reality through the death of the ego."[5] Because this conception of a transformation from self-centeredness to Reality-centeredness occurs in different forms in all the great traditions, it seems to me appropriate to use the hybrid term "salvation/liberation."

Thus, it is true that Christianity does not speak of *nirvana* or *moksha*, Buddhism and Hinduism do not speak of the kingdom of God, and Jews and Muslims do not follow Christ in order to attain fullness of life in submission to God. Thus far it is clear that different religious concepts are used and different spiritual paths followed within the various traditions. But the important question is whether these conceptualities are different ways of understanding essentially the same salvific transformation, and whether these alternate spiritual paths lead to essentially the same transformed state. In my view, Christian, Jewish, Muslim, Hindu, and Buddhist saints (though variously labeled as saints, jivanmuktas, arahats, mahatmas, or bodhisattvas) have in common a radical transcendence of self and a radical recentering in ultimate reality as manifested to them through their own tradition. As William Penn, the founder of Pennsylvania, wrote, "The humble, meek, merciful, just, pious and devout souls are everywhere of one religion; and when death has taken off the mask, they will know one another, though the divers liveries they wear here make them strangers."[6]

It is, I think, a mistake to conceive of salvation/liberation as something that is to happen after death. It continues, of course, and is completed beyond this life; but each of the great traditions constitutes present good news for suffering humanity because each teaches that the radically better state can begin to be entered now, in this present life. As to its postmortem completion, each tradition has its own stock of images and pictures, pointing beyond itself to a final state that exceeds our present earthly powers of imagination.

McGrath asks, "Do Christianity and satanism really have the same understandings of salvation?" and points out that "the

---

[5]Masao Abe, in Frederick Franck, ed., *The Buddha Eye* (New York: Crossroads, 1982), 153.

[6]William Penn, *Some Fruits of Solitude* (London: Constable, 1926 [orig. 1693]), 99–100.

Rastafarian vision of a paradise in which blacks are served by menial whites, the Homeric notion of Tartaros, the old Norse concept of Valhalla, the Buddhist vision of *nirvana*, the Christian hope of resurrection to eternal life" are obviously different. If this is intended as a response to the view I propounded about the great world religions, we can immediately take out the references to satanism, Rastafarianism, and the Homeric and Norse concepts. Furthermore, the Buddhist concept of *nirvana* and the Christian hope of resurrection to eternal life belong to different categories, in that *nirvana* is a state to be attained in this present life whereas resurrection is to a state beyond this life. The Christian equivalent of *nirvana* is the eternal quality of life that is available to be experienced now. As they are made visible in the lives of Christian and Buddhist saints, they both consist in a universal compassion or love, although this, of course, takes different cultural forms within the different traditions.

RESPONSE TO ALISTER E. MCGRATH

Clark H. Pinnock

How refreshing to read a theologian who appreciates the boundless grace of God! It represents the difference of night and day as far as hope for humanity is concerned. Towards the end of his chapter, McGrath waxes eloquently about God's desire to save the world and, unlike the traditional evangelical position as represented by Geivett/Phillips, does not fall into the error of the fewness of salvation. Indeed, he decries restrictivism as "a flawed theology, which limits God's modes of action, disclosure, and saving power." McGrath believes that salvation is possible for non-Christians, that God can bring the unevangelized to faith in this life, and that prevenient grace is present to every soul seeking God. He maintains that God's saving work is not restricted to preaching but that God can also actualize his plans apart from it. Citing inclusivist philosopher Stuart Hackett, McGrath believes there is a universal access to salvation. Those who do not hear the gospel may attain salvation if they respond to God's presence by faith. Though not called inclusive, the essay is soteriologically inclusive.

At the same time, it is exclusive when it comes to other faiths. That is, it differs from inclusivism in its assessment of the role of religion in salvation. Like an exclusivist, McGrath does not look to religion as a locale of prevenient grace. He sees God's Spirit working in the whole world but not in that sphere. Therefore, his concern is to stress the uniqueness of the Christian message against the pluralist attempt to mix religions in a blender and homogenize them. He stresses the differences among religions, not any commonalities. Though soteriologically inclusive, McGrath is exclusivist in regard to the role of religions in salvation.

Terminology is a bit of a problem, because the editors of this book did not insist on a uniformity of terms. *Particularism* is not the term I would use to describe McGrath's view (or Geivett/ Phillips', either) because it is so general—it can be applied to every chapter in this book except Hick's, since we all (except for him) believe that salvation comes from the redemptive particularity that is Jesus Christ. It would be better to call McGrath's position nonrestrictive exclusivism: "nonrestrictive" because of his wider hope and "exclusivist" because he sees no saving value in other religions. One contribution this book makes is that it presents two varieties of exclusivism, not just one—a restrictive and a nonrestrictive kind. This distinction is crucial, and the book does not overlook it.

I like McGrath's soteriological inclusivism and appreciate his reply to theological pluralism. While Hick faces a phalanx of three voices against his, he is well able to handle it. McGrath makes the uniqueness of the Christian message clear and warns powerfully against the myth that religions believe pretty much the same thing. I agree. Where I am less satisfied is his reluctance to see any truth or light in other faiths. To do so would not have compromised the uniqueness of Christianity but would have supplied points of contact and built useful bridges.

PREVENIENT GRACE AND OTHER RELIGIONS

In distinction from McGrath, inclusivism agrees about the uniqueness of the Christian message but does not refuse to see prevenient grace operating in the sphere of human religion. It is a both/and, not an either/or proposition. There can be similarities *and* differences, not just differences among the religions. As an inclusivist, I believe in uniqueness *and* common ground, similarities *and* differences. Having spelled out differences, I wish McGrath would go on and build redemptive bridges between Christianity and other faiths for the sake of mission.

I know it is typical of exclusivists not to do so. They like to affirm general revelation and say that God calls persons to himself everywhere, but when it comes down to God's presence in the context of religious life other than Christian, they back off and seldom say anything positive. Their emphasis is always on the inadequacy and the differences. They can only see other religions as signs of human self-effort in salvation and never as indicating the activity of divine grace. They see the other religions marked only by human sin and error. They think that other religions are fundamentally wrong and do not offer positive features to which we can appeal as common ground in mission.

Their unrelieved negativity creates a strange picture—they say that God's Spirit is everywhere at work in the world, illuminating hearts and revealing God, and yet salvation is never possible in the context of religion. Why would God be everywhere present to save in the whole world except in one important sphere, the sphere of human religion? It does not add up. Why would God deliberately absent himself from the one area in which people normally seek for meaning and hope? The Second Vatican Council had a better approach in their watching for divine activity in religions and in rejecting nothing that is true and holy in them but rather building on it.

It is hard to be satisfied with exclusivists when they say that non-Christians can be saved but that it is a complete mystery how it occurs. If, as they acknowledge, the Spirit is everywhere at work drawing people to God, why do they disregard the possibility of the Spirit's working in the sphere of religion? If the problem with the position of Geivett/Phillips is a failure to believe in the universal prevenience of grace, the problem with McGrath is that the exclusivists who believe in it keep it on a very short lead. Surely the life-giving and gracing activities of the Spirit take place in the entire created order—in the flourishing of life, in the moral order, *and* in the religious sphere. I believe that grace is universal, and religions *may* thematize the offer of God's love and direct the faithful toward the mystery of existence. I believe that the Spirit is striving to orient all humanity toward God and the coming of God's blessings.

I am not making this up—the Bible itself gives us permission to think in these terms. God was at work in Melchizedek, priest of Salem, to whom Abram paid tithes and from whom he received a blessing. It is as if God had the father of Israel meet this pagan saint in order to teach Abram that his election did not give him or his progeny an exclusive handle on God. Religion is a dynamic piece of human culture that requires a nuanced view. Even though there is often darkness in it, we must not be blind to the possibility of God's presence there. I wish that McGrath's soteriological inclusivism could be opened up in a fuller inclusivism.

MCGRATH'S REFORMED REFORMED THEOLOGY

Near the end of his essay, McGrath extols the virtues of Reformed theology in connection with his nonrestrictive exclusivism. He thinks it may help us because of its emphasis on divine sovereignty, the idea that God does not give up seeking sinners or allow himself to be defeated by unbelief. I am not so sure Reformed theology is helpful, unless reformed itself.

First, McGrath's thinking is not Reformed in a classical sense. If he really believed that God uses his power to stop sinners from frustrating his salvific will for them, he would be a universalist; but from other comments he makes, we know that he is not one. According to McGrath, sinners can freely decline God's offer of salvation. What happened to the idea in Calvinism that saving grace is irresistible? If we add to that his concept of universal prevenient grace and the universal "possibility" of salvation, the impression is confirmed that he is more Arminian than Reformed in these matters.

Second, Reformed theology loses some of its luster when one remembers Calvin's notion of double predestination, which bears much responsibility for getting us into the mess of restrictivism in the first place. According to this doctrine, God does not love those whom he has not chosen to save, a view that gives a perfect justification for soteriological restrictivism. Why should we worry about the unevangelized when the likelihood is that God does not love them anyway? If God is sovereign, has he not "providentially" placed them in places where they would not hear the gospel? If he had intended to save them, would he not have supplied the means? The logic of Reformed theology is more in keeping with Geivett/Phillips than with McGrath.

Third, although Calvin did uphold general revelation and postulated a knowledge of God beyond Scripture, he did not think this would result in salvation for anyone. It is not a saving knowledge. In fact, Calvin maintained that general revelation is so distorted by sin that it can only result in further condemnation.[1] McGrath is not really a Calvinist on this topic.

The mystery of invoking Reformed theology as an asset can be explained. Most Reformed believers in Europe, including McGrath, have accepted what was enshrined in the *Agreement of Leuenberg* (1973), which involved a drastic revision of Calvin's thought. It tossed out double predestination and spoke of God's election of humankind in Jesus Christ, as Barth does. In a nutshell, McGrath is Reformed like Hendrikus Berkhof or Vincent Brummer but not paleo-Reformed like James I. Packer or R. C. Sproul. This is a good thing and explains why he can invoke "Reformed" theology as an asset. I am grateful to Reformed theology for having reformed itself—though I wish more evangelicals in North America would get the message.

---

[1]John Calvin, *Institutes*, 1.4; 1.5.11–15; 1.6.1.

RESPONSE TO ALISTER E. MCGRATH

R. Douglas Geivett and W. Gary Phillips

In the first main section of his chapter, McGrath develops a case against religious pluralism and discusses the values and aims of interreligious dialogue. In the second section he sketches his own Christian theology of world religions, which he calls "a particularist approach." Our remarks focus on his critique of religious pluralism and his version of Christian particularism.

MCGRATH'S CASE AGAINST PLURALISM

Religious pluralists have much to gain by fostering the impression that Christian awareness of other faiths is a novelty. It certainly is not. Nevertheless, while the phenomenon of religious diversity is nothing new, it has unprecedented significance in today's cultural and intellectual climate. Western Christians of the past two centuries have tended to ignore the religiously pluralistic context within which Christianity was inaugurated. The irony is that the early Christians were aware of this phenomenon from the beginning and probably even were attracted to Christianity because of the unsavoriness of pluralism, whereas Christians today are often overcome with disillusionment by the presence of alternative religious perspectives. Thus, it is imperative to expose the sociological conditions that aid and abet the pluralist agenda. Much of the first part of McGrath's essay is devoted to this task.

Unfortunately, there are shortcomings in his critique of representative pluralists. First, McGrath accuses religious pluralists of "potential arrogance" for imagining that they possess the correct account of the relationship between the world's religions. But it is not clear that this charge can be avoided by anyone who makes religious truth claims, including Christian particularists like McGrath (and ourselves, for that matter). We prefer not to think of this posture as arrogant. It is, rather, a matter of being justified or unjustified in one's conclusions. A particular expression of this posture should not be condemned as in principle immoral or dogmatic, but as inadequate to the evidence. The pluralist's arrogance is manifested, not by his claim to know, but by his occasional suggestion that the particularist who disagrees with him is simply naive or obtuse (as Hick does in his chapter). One can claim to know and be wrong without being supercilious.

Second, while it is helpful to recall Wittgenstein's observation that "the particularities of a way of life or 'form of living' are of controlling importance to our understanding of concepts" as employed by a religious community, there does not seem to be much question among some pluralists that orthodox Christian communities function with different and definitely particularist concepts. The pluralists' question is whether it is *rational* for them to continue doing so. We applaud McGrath's desire to honor the real differences that exist between religious traditions. It must be emphasized, however, that each *style* of religious practice and belief makes sense only within a larger conceptual framework. If that conceptual framework is *incorrect* (that is, false), then it does not matter whether a particular account of salvation makes sense *within* that framework. John Hick's pluralist conception of the nature of salvation might make sense within his own larger conceptual framework. But that conceptual framework has to be rejected on the evidence. In contrast, the larger conceptual framework within which the particular beliefs and practices of orthodox Christianity make sense is well supported by the evidence, as we argue in our chapter.[1]

---

[1]There is an application of Wittgenstein's point that is perhaps more significant. John Hick has criticized the Council of Chalcedon for employing sterile and abstract philosophical terminology in its definition of the Incarnation (see John Hick, *The Metaphor of God Incarnate: Christology in a Pluralistic Age* [Louisville: Westminster/John Knox, 1993], 45, 47–48). But this complaint ignores the fundamental continuity between the *Lebensformen* of both the early Christian community, which relied

Third, McGrath misunderstands the soteriological criterion in terms of which John Hick compares the various religions. Hick does not insist that the value of all religions must be appraised in terms of their soteriological component, for he distinguishes between preaxial and postaxial faiths. Hick does not deny the religious nature of preaxial traditions, nor does he fail to see some value in their perspectives, despite the fact that they cannot be assimilated to a soteriological account of religion.[2] Moreover, Hick explicitly condemns certain modern religious practices and beliefs for their failure to satisfy the soteriological criterion. In this way, for example, he repudiates the Jim Jones cult; presumably the phenomenon of satanism suffers a similar fate. In Hick's hands, the soteriological criterion is a device for "grading" the religions.[3]

MCGRATH'S PARTICULARISM

What does McGrath, a particularist, say about the unevangelized? As he points out, the fact that *all* who respond in faith to the explicit preaching of the gospel will be saved does not entail that *only* those who respond in faith to the explicit preaching of the gospel will be saved. This point is logically impeccable. Consider the following two propositions:

(1) All those who respond in faith to the explicit preaching of the gospel will be saved.

(2) Only those who respond in faith to the explicit preaching of the gospel will be saved.

Clearly, (1) does not entail (2). Let us then make this our third proposition:

---

directly and exclusively on the materials of the New Testament for its understanding of the Incarnation, and fifth-century Chalcedonian Christians, who sought to be faithful to the biblical materials while using appropriate metaphysical language then at their disposal. The point is, since both generations of Christians practiced a form of life that sought to be faithful to the same testimony of the New Testament, there is a fundamental continuity between them in their conceptions of the Incarnation, despite differences of language.

[2]See John Hick, *An Interpretation of Religion: Human Responses to the Transcendent* (London: Macmillan, 1989), 21–35.

[3]Ibid., 217.

(3)   Proposition (1) does not entail proposition (2).

So far, so good. But consider a fourth proposition:

(4)   Some who do not respond in faith to the explicit preaching of the gospel will be saved.

It would be a logical mistake to infer (4) from (3). The fact that (1) does not entail (2) does not itself entail (4). So (2) might still be true.

Of course, (2) and (4) are incompatible; they cannot both be true. If (2) is true, then (4) is false; if (4) is true, then (2) is false. Now how does one decide which is true or which to believe? By going back to the primary source for our belief in proposition (1), namely, the Bible. In other words, the problem cannot be solved using logic alone. More data is needed. The main source of data we have on this question is the Bible.

Now suppose proposition (2) is underdetermined by the biblical data, so that there is not enough evidence in the Bible to guarantee the truth of proposition (2). Does it follow that (4) is true? No. Does it follow that one ought to believe that (4) is true? No. If one concludes that propositions (2) and (4) are both underdetermined by the biblical evidence, then what ought one to believe?

As it happens, the choices are not just between believing (2) or believing (4). One might withhold belief in (2) and withhold belief in (4). This is an initially attractive option. But it is still a difficult choice, for the choice between (2) and (4) is momentous. Our behavior as witnesses to the gospel is at stake. For example, if one believes that (4) is true, then one might question the urgency of world evangelism, for it will be supposed that, as McGrath says, "in the end God does not depend upon [our preaching]." Furthermore, one might have different ideas about whether anyone really must believe in order to be saved, depending on whether one accepted (2) or (4).

Since the choice between (2) and (4) is momentous, it would be imprudent for a Christian simply to withhold belief. So what should one believe? As a purely practical matter, it seems the better part of wisdom to hold that only those who respond in faith to the explicit preaching of the gospel will be saved. While belief in proposition (2) is defeasible (a position that may be true but is as yet neither decisively demonstrated nor decisively refuted), it is not obviously false. Nor is proposition (2) less likely to be true than proposition (4).

What does McGrath say on behalf of (4)? First, he observes that a sovereign God is not, in principle, confined to making his salvation available in the way prescribed by (2). He also suggests that God might reveal the gospel to some persons without relying on "the explicit human preaching of the gospel," and he claims that "many Muslims [in Islamic nations closed to Christian evangelism] become Christians through dreams and visions in which they are addressed by the risen Christ."

We really have no idea whether McGrath's first point is true. While we have no doubt that God is sovereign, we know there are certain things a sovereign God cannot do, simply because they are not do-able. For example, even an omnipotent God cannot make a square circle. For all we know, there may be something about the nature of unregenerate human persons which, in conjunction with the requirements of divine justice, limit the ways that God might make his salvation available.[4] Here we confess to being utterly dependent on what God has revealed. Certainly, if God has revealed his method for saving individuals, his veracity limits his flexibility. And do we not have God's own word concerning the specifically human conditions for salvation; namely, proclamation of the good news on the part of the preacher and belief on the part of the recipient of that good news (see Rom. 10:9–15)?

On McGrath's second point, we note that some form of special revelation was apparently required in all the biblical cases cited by McGrath, and all those cases predate the Incarnation. Furthermore, we are not familiar with the evidence for the claim that many Muslims have come to faith in Jesus Christ without the influence of any human agent. Even if dreams or visions are instrumental in the salvation of some, their precise role in the process of salvation would have to be investigated. We would welcome the opportunity to consider the sources of McGrath's knowledge of this phenomenon.

McGrath chides some theologians for "their apparent insistence that only those who respond to the explicit verbal procla-

---

[4]On the question, "Was God obliged to save human persons in the way he has in fact acted to save them?" see Richard Swinburne, *Responsibility and Atonement* (Oxford: Clarendon Press, 1989), 148–62.

mation of the gospel will be saved." Several things need to be said about this. First, we ourselves are not "insistent," if by that McGrath means that we consider our conviction about the matter to be indefeasible. As we point out at the end of our chapter, we allow that the position we present is defeasible. Thus, firm conviction in the matter need not take the form of dogmatism.

Second, McGrath needs to be asked whether he would insist that some people of our generation who never hear the gospel will be saved. He hints that he would when he quotes with approval Stuart Hackett's argument. On first blush, it would appear that Hackett *deduces*, from premises that McGrath apparently accepts, that some who never hear will be saved. But Hackett's argument actually proves little, for both of his premises are stated as conditionals and his conclusion is ambiguous. What he says is that such persons will be *eligible* to receive God's provision of salvation. Does he mean that they actually do receive salvation? At any rate, it would be interesting to know whether McGrath accepts Hackett's general conclusion that "there are certain unidentified persons, involved in very different religious traditions than our own and having their minds clouded in varying degrees by errors quite different from our own—but who are, in spite of these conceptual shortcomings, nevertheless trusting in the true God as genuinely as ourselves."[5] If so, then McGrath's position seems much closer to Pinnock's than to our own.[6]

Third, it is insensitive to suggest that to believe as we do is to "write off the vast majority of those who have ever lived." This implies a lack of concern for the unsaved. We believe, however, that God's own concern extends to all unsaved individuals, including those who do hear and refuse to believe. But his concern does not lead him to revise the conditions he has established for salvation. If a Christian theologian believes that God

---

[5]Stuart C. Hackett, *The Reconstruction of the Christian Revelation Claim: A Philosophical and Critical Apologetic* (Grand Rapids: Baker, 1984), 246.

[6]There are other respects in which McGrath's view parallels Pinnock's. For example, he allows that the unevangelized who are brought to faith in God "may lack the fully orbed character of an informed Christian faith," as if the only thing the evangelist contributes in some cases is a deeper appreciation for an already appropriated reality. But this is not how the goal of evangelism is characterized in the Bible.

has set explicit faith in Jesus Christ as a necessary condition for the salvation of any person of our generation, that theologian is not writing anyone off. Furthermore, that theologian has not set the conditions for salvation. Rather, he has stated what, in his considered judgment, he believes God has established as the conditions for salvation. In addition, there is the real possibility that the need to proclaim the gospel will be written off by those who repose in the confidence that God would not withhold salvation from the unevangelized. As McGrath says, "A human failure to evangelize cannot be transposed into God's failure to save." What does McGrath take to be the significance of our failure to evangelize? How important are we to the process of adding to the kingdom of God?

This brings us directly to the fourth point, for the failure to evangelize is *not* automatically transposed into God's failure to save, *even if it is true that only those who believe will be saved*. The doctrine of middle knowledge may be applied to explain how God might justly withhold salvation from all those who do not believe in Jesus Christ, whether or not they have heard the gospel. For God might have arranged for all those who would believe if they had the opportunity to hear the gospel to actually hear. If that is the case, then anyone who dies without hearing the good news is a person who would not have believed had he heard.[7]

God's sovereignty is such that anyone who *would* believe upon hearing *does* hear. We can agree that the Judge of all the earth will do right (Gen. 18:25), resist the temptation to stipulate what God's righteous action as Judge may or may not include, and still believe that God has revealed much of what he intends to do. We may even have questions about how the actions he reveals comport with our own intuitions about justice. The fact that we do not fully understand all that we would like in this

---

[7]See William Lane Craig, "No Other Name: A Middle Knowledge Perspective on the Exclusivity of Salvation Through Christ," *Faith and Philosophy* 6 (April 1989): 172–88. St. Augustine suggested that "it pleased Christ to appoint the time in which He would appear and the persons among whom His doctrine was to be proclaimed, according to His knowledge of the times and places in which men would believe on Him" ("Letter to Deogratias," par. 14; this quotation is from *A Select Library of the Nicene and Post-Nicene Fathers of the Christian Church*, ser. 1, vol. 1, ed. Philip Schaff [Grand Rapids: Eerdmans, 1974 (orig. 1886)], 418).

area cannot excuse us from accepting what he has revealed and thus has made possible for us to understand. Doubtless there will be disagreement about what God has revealed and what we may therefore be justified in believing. Continued dialogue certainly is desirable.

CONCLUSION

Alister E. McGrath

In what follows, I will engage particularly with Professor Hick, in that his chapter and subsequent responses to other contributors seem to me to be the main point of interest in this book. Although it has indeed demonstrated the diversity of evangelical approaches to religious pluralism, it has also brought out clearly the common evangelical dissatisfaction with the pluralist agenda. In closing, I will relate the evangelical position to the postliberal and postmodern trends that are now so firmly established in the theology of the 1990s.

OUR "POST" CONDITION

As I point out in my *Evangelicalism and the Future of Christianity*, it is a great time to be an evangelical.[1] The old certainties on which the Enlightenment and its intellectual derivatives stand are dying. The old universals—such as "experience," "religion," and "rationality"—are now realized to be strongly particular. The notion of "common human experience" is regarded as little more than an experiential fiction, in much the same way as "universal rationality" is now seen as little more than the idle daydream of reason. The belief in cultural or experiential metanarratives—to borrow from the conceptualities of postmodernism—is acknowledged to be at best flawed and at worst an

---

[1]Alister E. McGrath, *Evangelicalism and the Future of Christianity* (Downers Grove, Ill.: InterVarsity, 1995).

invitation to oppression. Ideas such as "religion" and "culture," which an earlier generation of liberal pluralist writers happily appealed to as constituting universal foundations of nonparticularist forms of Christianity, are now seen to be fictitious constructs, generally reflecting a specifically Western set of presuppositions.

Most significantly, it is no longer regarded as "arrogant" or "imperialist" to suggest that Christian theology concerns the quest for justifiable particularity. The emergence of postliberalism, initially associated with Yale Divinity School, but now exercising a wide influence in Western academic theology, may be regarded as a telling indication that the intellectual and cultural credibility of liberalism has been decisively challenged. For postliberalism embodies a willingness to respect—indeed, to celebrate—the distinctiveness of the Christian tradition and sees Christian theology as concerned with the articulation of the distinctive grammar of the Christian faith.

The basic argument of postliberalism—and one with which evangelicals can easily associate—is that liberal theology feels itself to be under some kind of obligation to ground itself in something in the public arena, such as philosophical concepts or "common human experience." While attempting to render Christianity more intelligible to a secular audience, these extrabiblical terminologies and conceptualities actually suppressed the distinctive character of Christianity. As a result, liberalism ended up becoming the addressee rather than the addresser of a secular culture, making secularism credible to Christianity rather than the other way round.

Postliberalism's attempt to liberate Christian theology from extrabiblical presuppositions should be welcomed by evangelicals. Evangelicals and postliberals share the kind of concerns so frequently expressed by Karl Barth concerning the potential enslavement or debasement of Christian thought through the intrusion of alien assumptions resulting from a deficient theological method, through which ideas originating from outside the church are allowed to assume a controlling influence within it.[2]

---

[2]This indicates that evangelicals can ally themselves, at least to some extent, with postliberalism's emphasis on Scripture as the sole normative source of Christian theology and living. Nevertheless, this does not exclude the apologetic procedure of attempting to identify commonalities between the gospel and human experience,

However, liberal critics of postliberalism have argued that it represents a lapse into a "ghetto ethic" or some form of "fideism" or "tribalism," because of its retreat from universal norms of value and rationality. Yet these same liberal critics seem unable to accept that the Enlightenment is over and that any notion of a "universal language" or "common human experience" is simply a fiction, like (to use Gadamer's famous analogy) Robinson Crusoe's imaginary island. "Foundationalism" of any kind, whether philosophical or religious, is widely regarded as discredited.[3] Postliberalism has comes to terms with the death of the Enlightenment, whereas liberalism, rather like a freshly decapitated farmyard chicken, stumbles pathetically and randomly across the intellectual terrain, looking desperately for an absolutely firm foundation in a world that no longer accepts its existence. The birth of postmodernity seems to have been overlooked by liberalism, which prefers living in the past rather than facing up to the harsh new world of today. It is to the credit of postliberal writers that they have faced up to the cultural abandonment of universal norms and values, even if its liberal critics prefer the cozy nostalgia of the myth of a "universal language" or "public discourse."

As Mary Midgley once commented, the "sad little joke" of "universal languages" is that nobody seems to speak them.[4] To criticize postliberalism for its abandonment of "universal discourse" is like abusing a child who no longer believes in Santa Claus. It may be a reassuring, cozy, and useful illusion—but it is an illusion. And, as postmodernism has emphasized, the illusion of universal norms can all too easily become profoundly oppressive, forcing conformity to the theory and repressing dis-

---

reason or culture, as possible "points of contact" for evangelism. Nor would it involve the rejection of using extrabiblical terminologies and conceptualities in an attempt to explicate or render more intelligible the distinctive character of Christianity to a secular audience. See David F. Ford, "The Best Apologetics Is a Good Systematics: A Proposal About the Place of Narrative in Christian Systematic Theology," *Anglican Theological Review* 67 (1985): 232–53; William Werphehowski, "Ad Hoc Apologetics," *Journal of Religion* 66 (1986): 282–301; Benno van den Toren, "A New Direction in Christian Apologetics," *European Journal of Theology* 2 (1993): 49–64.

[3]On the theological aspects, see D. Z. Phillips, *Faith after Foundationalism* (London: Routledge, 1988).

[4]Mary Midgley, *Beast and Man* (New York: Meridian, 1980), 306.

tinctiveness on the part of, for example, a religion on account of
the prior dogmatic conviction that all are saying the same thing.
The reassertion of the distinctiveness of Christianity reflects both
this reaction against the illusion of universality and a growing
awareness of the genuinely singular character of Christian faith.

There is a growing acceptance within academic theology,
not simply that Christianity *is* distinct and must be accepted as
distinct, but that any worldview that refuses to acknowledge
such distinctiveness must be rejected as seriously at variance
with the observable facts. After all, Jesus Christ was not crucified just for reinforcing what everyone already knew. With the
end of the Enlightenment and its intellectual satellites—including liberalism and pluralism—the embargo on distinctiveness
has been lifted. No longer is the claim to be saying something
different seen as equivalent to being irrational. Jews are special;
they have a special story and a different set of values. In the
same way, Christians are special; they have a special story and
a different set of values.[5] It is against this emerging postliberal
climate that Professor Hick's approach seems increasingly dated
and outmoded.

HICK'S UNDERSTANDING OF RELIGION

Professor Hick dislikes my "polemic against religious pluralism." The use of the word "polemic" is fascinating, in that it
implies a ranting and raving fool hurling abusive and spurious
irrelevancies against a studied and informed position. In fact,
the present volume demonstrates with remarkable clarity how
fatally flawed the pluralist position is. What I have offered is an
informed and scholarly critique of the pluralist position; nothing that Professor Hick says in response to it seems to me to sal-
vage its failure to account for or respect religions as they actually
are, in all their diversity.

To make this point crystal clear to readers, let me ask one
crucial question, if the pun may be forgiven: *Was Jesus crucified?*
In other words, did Jesus die on the cross? It will be obvious that
Christianity is insistent that he did, and that this event is charged

[5]Stanley Hauerwas and William H. Willimon, *Resident Aliens: Life in the Chris-tian Colony* (Nashville: Abingdon, 1989), 18.

with enormous significance for the world, both in terms of our knowledge of God and the salvation of humanity.

Islam, however, happens to take a totally different position. There are, in fact, two major views on this matter within Islam. The orthodox view is that Jesus was neither killed by the Jews nor crucified, "although it seemed so to them" (*shubbiha la-hum*), but that he was translated to heaven, with some other unnamed person taking his place on the cross.[6] The phrase "it seemed so to them" bears the sense of either "the Jews thought that Jesus died on the cross" or "the Jews thought that the person on the cross was Jesus." But the translation of Sura 4:157 in the version of the Qur'an associated with the Ahmadiyya movement, both Lahori and Qadiyani, does not exclude the placing of Jesus on the cross, but explicitly denies that he *died* on the cross.[7] The Ahmadis argue that Jesus recovered from his wounds in the tomb before eventually making his way to Kashmir, where he finally died.[8]

The importance of this point is beyond dispute. It matters fundamentally whether Jesus Christ died on the cross, both as a matter of history and as a matter of theology. The historical aspect of the matter is crucial, in that both the New Testament and Qur'an cannot be right. If one is correct on this historical point, the other is incorrect. For the purposes of stating this point, it does not matter *which* is correct; the simple point is that both cannot be true.[9] The theological aspects of the matter are also beyond dispute. If Jesus did not die on the cross, an entire series of distinctively and authentically Christian beliefs are called into question. As the Ahmadi writer Muhammad Zafrulla Khan (1893–1985) commented, "Once it is established that Jesus did not die on the cross, there was no accursed death, no bearing of the sins of mankind, no resurrection, no ascension and no

---

[6]Sura 4:157. For further exploration of this matter, see Geoffrey Parrinder, *Jesus in the Qur'an* (London: Sheldon Press, 1965).

[7]See Malik Ghulam Farid, ed., *The Holy Qur'an with English Translation and Commentary* (Rabwah, Pakistan: Oriental and Religious Publishing Co., 1969), 232. As the editor comments (n. 697), this translation does not deny that Jesus was placed on a cross; it does, however, explicitly deny that he died on the cross.

[8]See the foundational work by Mizra Ghulam Ahmad (the founder of the Ahmadiyya movement), *Jesus in India* (Tilbury: Islam International, 1989). The Ahmadi tract *Jesus in Kashmir* (London: London Mosque, 1977) should also be noted.

[9]Note especially the comments of Parrinder, *Jesus in the Qur'an*, 116.

atonement. The entire structure of church theology is thereby demolished."[10] Even allowing for the generally anti-Christian tone of Ahmadi writings, the point being made is significant: If Jesus Christ did not die on the cross, there is no Christian gospel.

Here, then, is a simple case of disagreement on a matter— an *important* matter—of history. To deny that such is the case amounts to replacing reasoned argumentation with special pleading and petulant assertion. Honest disagreement is no sin. Furthermore, a willingness to recognize differences removes the fundamental criticism directed against interfaith dialogue—that it is not prepared to acknowledge genuine differences. Only someone of highly questionable intellectual ability and integrity would argue that it is true that "Jesus did die on the cross" and that "Jesus did not die on the cross." Differences *must* be acknowledged and their implications explored.

Professor Hick concedes the empirical distinctions among the religions. His own contribution lies primarily in his interpretation of this distinctiveness—that is, that they are complementary "human responses to the one limitless divine reality." I do not see that my criticisms of this point have been blunted. Let me state three of its central points once more.

(1) Prescriptive pluralism involves a systematic abandonment of the *distinctives* of Christianity—such as the doctrine of the divinity and resurrection of Jesus Christ and the doctrine of the Trinity—so that the "Christianity" being compared with other religions is an artificial construction. This represents a failure to take the religions seriously *as they are*.

(2) This pluralism claims to be able to adopt a tradition- and culture-transcending standpoint in order to view their mutual relationship. Yet this involves breaking free from the limitations of time and space, to impose an unverified and unverifiable framework on the religions. It is a theory, no more. It may happen to resonate with some aspects of contemporary culture— but it remains a theory, and no more.

(3) "Religion" is a *false universal*—that is, the term *religion* has been used uncritically to refer indiscriminatingly to a whole variety of cultural phenomena. A "theory of the religions" is

---

[10]Muhammad Zafrulla Khan, *Deliverance from the Cross* (London: London Mosque, 1978), 89.

therefore dependent on the prior definition of *religion* on which it is based, and there is no consensus on this notion. What one culture regards as a religion, another may regard as an ethical outlook.

HICK'S UNIVERSAL CONCEPT OF RELIGION

In closing, a further point is in order. Hick's agenda is strongly foundational, placing an emphasis on allegedly universal concepts, such as *religion* or *religious experience*. Yet foundationalism has lost its credibility, as the assumptions of modernity have been progressively eroded to the point at which they are being abandoned throughout culture in general and the academy in particular. But the prescriptive pluralism adopted by Hick is inextricably linked to the modernist agenda. His form of pluralism is little more than an intellectual satellite of the Enlightenment, linked with its totalizing and homogenizing agenda.

Modernity may be characterized by two leading features: (1) a "totalizing" urge, which insists that everything must be seen as an aspect of a grand theory or "metanarrative" (to use Jean-François Lyotard's term), and (2) a desire to master raw material—cultural, intellectual, or physical—to fit in with the desires of humanity. Both themes can be discerned within the pluralist agenda. All religions are, we are told, to be seen from the pluralist perspective, which alone allows them to be seen in their proper light. And where religions do not happen to fit in with the assumptions of this particular paradigm, they are forced to conform—in the case of Christianity, by being pressurized to abandon its defining traditional beliefs in the resurrection and divinity of Jesus Christ and the doctrine of the Trinity. This is tantamount to intellectual Stalinism. In making this assertion, I am deliberately pointing up the common modernist agenda and roots that underlie prescriptive pluralism, Nazism, and Stalinism. All three are intellectual colonies of modernism, governed by the same rules and presumptions, even if they may vary in relation to matters of local detail. Postmodernity rejects Enlightenment "metanarratives," of which prescriptive pluralism is simply one example. It has had its day. To understand this point, we may explore the postmodern agenda a little further.

Postmodernity is the general intellectual outlook arising after the collapse of modernity.[11] Modernity believed in a world that, in principle, could be understood and mastered. Postmodernity not only tends to regard the world as ultimately being beyond either comprehension or mastery; it regards such comprehension and mastery as being, in any case, immoral. Postmodernism is characterized by its fundamental disillusionment with the great themes of modernity, which it tellingly places within an insulating skeptical battery of quotation marks. Even at the level of their orthography, postmodern writings on "truth," "reason," "justice," or "reality" make it clear that what were once regarded as universals are now treated as outmoded and questionable. As a result of the influence of Michel Foucault, claims to "universal truth" are now seen as potentially oppressive within postmodernism, with the trauma of the Holocaust being seen as a powerful and shocking indictment of the pretensions and delusions of modernity.[12] It is modernity, especially with its compulsive desire to break totally with the past, that gave rise to the Nazi holocaust and the Stalinist purges. There has been a general collapse of confidence in the Enlightenment trust in the power of what are now realized to be false universals—such as "reason," "experience," or "religion"—to provide foundations for a universally valid knowledge of the world, including God.

In the end, therefore, the criticisms directed by postmodernity against modernity apply with equal, if not greater, force to prescriptive religious pluralism: It is actually profoundly oppressive. The belief that all religions are ultimately expressions of the same transcendent reality is at best illusory and at worst oppressive—illusory because it lacks any substantiating basis, and oppressive because it involves the systematic imposition of the

---

[11]On these general themes, see Diogenes Allen, *Christian Belief in a Postmodern World* (Louisville: Westminster/John Knox, 1989); Thomas C. Oden, *After Modernity ... What? Agenda for Theology* (Grand Rapids: Zondervan, 1990). On the distinction between "modern" and "postmodern" theologies, see Nancey Murphy and James W. McClendon Jr., "Distinguishing Modern and Postmodern Theologies," *Modern Theology* 5 (1989): 191–214.

[12]See Michael Mahon, *Foucault's Nietzschean Genealogy: Truth, Power, and the Subject* (Albany, N.Y.: SUNY Press, 1992); Zygmunt Bauman, *Modernity and the Holocaust* (Cambridge: Polity Press, 1989).

agenda of those in positions of intellectual power on the religions and those who adhere to them. The illiberal imposition of this pluralistic metanarrative on religions is ultimately a claim to *mastery*—both in the sense of having a Nietzschean power to mold material according to one's own will and in the sense of being able to relativize all the religions by having access to a privileged standpoint. As my Oxford colleague Terry Eagleton has pointed out,

> post-modernism signals the end of such "metanarratives" whose secretly terroristic function was to ground and legitimate the illusion of a 'universal' human history. We are now in the process of awakening from the nightmare of modernity, with its manipulative reason and fetish of the totality, into the laid-back pluralism of the post-modern, that heterogeneous range of life-styles and language games which has renounced the nostalgic urge to totalize and legitimate itself.[13]

Perhaps prescriptive pluralism ought to confront these questions.

The attraction of pluralism lies not in its claims to truth, which are remarkably elusive and shallow, but in its claim to foster tolerance among the religions. Yet this claim was made by modernity. The ideology underlying Lessing's parable *Nathan the Wise* reemerges in Stalinism. For Lessing, the ideology fostered the toleration of the religions; for Stalin, it held the key to their suppression and elimination. Prescriptive pluralism runs the same risk. Toleration is more likely to result from showing respect to other religions than from forcing them into an artificial framework that suppresses their distinctiveness in an attempt to make observation conform to theory.

So I would urge my reader to do two things. First, show respect to other faiths. Try to understand and appreciate their distinctive positions and beliefs without indulging in patronizing generalizations. This is far more likely to foster religious toleration than the bland generalizations of pluralism. Second, realize that Christianity is distinctive! The days when it was possible to regard Christianity as simply a local manifestation of a

---

[13]Terry Eagleton, "Awakening from Modernity," *Times Literary Supplement* (February 20, 1987).

universal category of "religion" are long gone, despite the fact that this view is maintained on life-support systems throughout religious studies faculties in North America! Christianity is distinct, with distinct—and, I will add without apology, *unique*—understandings of the person of the Savior and the nature of salvation. There is no inconsistency, arrogance, or difficulty in any religion, whether Christianity or Buddhism, claiming to be different. As Aloysius Pieris comments, "that Jesus is unique is obvious even to Buddhists."[14] The central crucial question, which Christianity has always been obliged to address, is the nature of that uniqueness, and the manner in which it is to be justified and articulated. Christian theology must thus be characterized by an awareness of its own *distinctiveness* and a commitment to its own *integrity*. I believe that evangelicalism possesses such a commitment, and for that reason it will be a major force in the theology of the future.

---

[14]Aloysius Piers, in J. Hick and P. Knitter, eds., *The Myth of Christian Uniqueness* (Maryknoll, N.Y.: Orbis Books, 1988), 171. I am increasingly convinced that the title of this volume is seriously misleading; the editors indicate that they have no intention of denying Christian uniqueness; their concern is to "interpret it anew" (see Paul Knitter's "Preface," p. vii). Note also John Mbiti's emphatic assertion that, in an African context, the "uniqueness of Christianity is in Jesus Christ" (*African Religions and Philosophy* [London: Heinemann, 1969], 277).

Chapter Four

A PARTICULARIST VIEW: AN EVIDENTIALIST APPROACH

R. Douglas Geivett and W. Gary Phillips

A PARTICULARIST VIEW: AN EVIDENTIALIST APPROACH

R. Douglas Geivett and W. Gary Phillips

Anyone looking for a religious answer to the human condition is faced with a bewildering variety of religious positions from which to choose. There is now throughout the world a greater awareness of the presence of numerous conflicting religious traditions. And the menu of apparently incompatible religious options is so exotic that many, feeling powerless to make a reasonable choice, simply withhold religious commitment. Others remain nominally attached to the tradition with which they are most familiar (for example, the tradition of their primary culture), though the proliferation of religions has for them so trivialized religious commitment that their particular religious affiliation plays almost no role in the organization of their lives.

Though these are, perhaps, understandable responses to the phenomenon of religious diversity, the question naturally arises: Among the many religious traditions, is there a uniquely correct one?

On the continuum of possible approaches to religious diversity there are three broad views within contemporary Christendom. At one end of the spectrum, the Christian exclusivist or particularist maintains that Christianity embodies the uniquely authentic response to divine reality. At the other end of the spectrum, the pluralist supposes that a wide range of mutually contradictory human responses to divine reality are all authentic and capable of bringing about the right sort of human transformation. Christian inclusivism lies somewhere between these poles with its suggestion that while the Christian tradition bears a uniquely or paradigmatically accurate testimony to divine truth, alternative traditions may somehow mediate divine grace.

The position we adopt is particularist. But it is possible to define Christian particularism broadly or narrowly. A broad definition, encompassing the views of both the exclusivist and the inclusivist, simply emphasizes *God's role in saving humanity*: People are not saved apart from the work of Jesus Christ on the cross, whether or not they ever place explicit faith in Jesus (indeed, whether or not they have even heard the gospel). But some Christians are uncomfortable with the idea that inclusivists are particularists, for they do not seem to be particularist enough. A narrower definition therefore limits particularism to the exclusivist view. In that case the particularist element is further associated with what is regarded as *the appropriate human response to God's saving initiative*. That is, except perhaps in very special circumstances, people are not saved apart from explicit faith in Jesus Christ, which presupposes that they have heard about his salvific work on their behalf.[1]

We hold that individual salvation depends on explicit personal faith in Jesus Christ. Thus, our position is a version of Christian particularism that is sometimes called *exclusivism* or *restrictivism*. Since these labels tend to have misleading negative connotations—especially in suggesting a kind of unwarranted dogmatism—we will simply refer to our position as particularism. Both religious pluralism and Christian inclusivism are at odds with this view.

AN EVIDENTIALIST STRATEGY FOR DEFENDING PARTICULARISM

In one broad sense, the discussion in this book is intramural, for all participants regard themselves as Christians. But different controls on a Christian conception of faith and practice

---

[1]Some exclusivists have suggested that some appropriate response by an unevangelized person to general revelation is a sufficient human condition for salvation. Others believe a person might be saved on the basis of what God foreknows would be that person's response if he or she had, contrary to fact, heard the gospel. Still others conclude that the person in this situation will not be saved in any case. (The mentally incompetent and those who die in infancy represent a logically dis-

are accepted by the participants in this dialogue, reflecting profound disagreement about what a Christian is. Thus, in addition to the problem of how to conduct interreligious dialogue itself, there is the question of how members of approximately the same religious community (e.g., Christianity) are to dialogue about interreligious dialogue. And answers to this question will depend on who the dialogue partners are and on their respective definitions of Christianity.[2]

When dialogue partners share the conviction that the Bible is the inspired Word of God, they naturally find themselves comparing notes on the interpretation of specific passages of Scripture. But when those who accept the divine authority of the Bible turn to dialogue with religious pluralists who do not countenance the special authority of Scripture, biblical investigation will not resolve these issues. Thus, the dialogue must broaden to include the relevant extrabiblical evidence.

As a result, it is helpful to distinguish between a *first-order intramural debate* and a *second-order intramural debate* concerning the significance of religious diversity. The *first-order* debate takes place between Christian particularists and Christian inclusivists. Sparring partners in this debate agree against religious pluralists that Jesus Christ is the unique Savior of men and women. When participants in this debate are evangelicals, they will tend to agree about the nature of Scripture and its value as a divinely inspired control on our religious beliefs. Religious pluralists, because they tend to reject this view of the nature of Scripture, are excluded from this first-order debate. Constructive dialogue with them shifts to a *second-order* debate that focuses instead on extrabiblical sources of religious knowledge.

Since there are other reliable sources of religious knowledge besides the Bible, it turns out that constructive dialogue with religious pluralists is possible. Christian theologians have traditionally distinguished between *general revelation* and *special revelation*

---

tinct class of individuals who never have the opportunity to exercise explicit faith in Jesus Christ.)

[2]For a defense of the thesis that interreligious dialogue should include polemics, see Paul J. Griffiths, *An Apology for Apologetics: A Study in the Logic of Interreligious Dialogue* (Maryknoll, N.Y.: Orbis, 1991), and his essay, "Why We Need Interreligious Polemics," *First Things* 54 (June/July 1994): 31–37.

as sources of religious knowledge. By means of general revelation, God communicates his existence, aspects of his nature, and many of the ways he is related to the world, as well as the pattern of human moral obligation. Sources of general revelation include the entire order of created reality, whether physical or nonphysical, human conscience, and the pattern of human history. The activity of organizing this data into a systematic body of knowledge is called *natural theology*. The Christian tradition recognizes two primary sources of special revelation: the Old and New Testaments of the Bible and the Incarnation of Jesus Christ. These sources refine our awareness of God's concern for humanity and reveal his plan for saving individuals, including any conditions he expects them to meet. It is the task of *revealed theology* to organize the data of special revelation into a more complete account of religious truth.

Our strategy, then, is to begin with natural theology, in order to show how Christian particularism might be defended against religious pluralism without relying exclusively on revealed theology. On that intial level we are primarily engaged in second-order dialogue with religious pluralists like John Hick. Following our sketch of natural theology, we will concentrate on revealed theology. There we will engage in first-order disagreement with evangelical inclusivists concerning the teaching of Scripture.

CHRISTIAN PARTICULARISM
AND NATURAL THEOLOGY

Christian particularists naturally turn to the Bible as the chief source of evidence in support of their view, for the branch of Christianity that fosters belief in particularism represents itself as a revealed religion. But, perhaps unlike some Christian particularists, we hold that the Bible is not the only source of evidence on behalf of particularism. And since individuals come to the Bible with differing sets of background beliefs and assumptions, the plausibility either (1) of using the Bible as a source of religious knowledge, or (2) of interpreting the Bible one way (e.g., in particularist fashion) rather than another (e.g., in inclusivist fashion), depends to a great extent on the plausibility of background beliefs one brings to the Bible. Background beliefs most relevant to the significance of the Bible as a source of knowledge have to do, first, with the existence and nature of God, the contours of the human condition, the relation between God and human persons, and the available evidence concerning all of these matters. Beliefs about the reliability of the historical content of the Bible and the plausibility of its miracle claims constitute another set of background beliefs relevant to the reliability of the Bible as a source of religious knowledge.

To illustrate, if the atheist is right and God does not exist, then clearly the Bible does not speak with divine authority about the human condition. If God exists but has little or no concern for human affairs, as the deist holds, then it is difficult to imagine what role God might have played in the production of the Bible; the Bible is, on such a view, a dubious source of religious knowledge. If, as religious pluralists like John Hick have maintained, the universe is "religiously ambiguous," so that we must remain finally agnostic about the existence and nature of God, then again the Bible will not function as a source of knowledge in our area of concern. Rather, the Bible will be regarded as a record, not of God's self-revelation, but of some authentic human responses to the Transcendent.[3]

But if, as we shall argue briefly, it is reasonable to believe that God is the personal, wise, and benevolent Creator of the universe, to whom we owe our existence as persons, then it is also reasonable to expect that God would address, in a concrete and religiously satisfying way, the specific contours of the human condition—particularly its darkest aspects where divine aid, if it is available, is most needed. On this view, the evidence of God's general pattern of activity as found in the whole panorama of created reality, both physical and nonphysical, instructs us to keep an eye out for some indication of God's specific intentions to rescue humans from that self-inflicted peril known to theologians as sin and its effects. In other words, general revelation

---

[3]See John Hick, *An Interpretation of Religion: Human Responses to the Transcendent* (London: Macmillan, 1989). For useful critical discussions of religious pluralism from a particularist point of view, see R. Douglas Geivett, "John Hick's Approach to Religious Pluralism," *Proceedings of the Wheaton Theology Conference* 1 (Spring 1992): 39–55; Ronald Nash, *Is Jesus the Only Savior?* (Grand Rapids: Zondervan, 1994); Ramesh P. Richard, *The Population of Heaven* (Chicago: Moody, 1994); and Brad Stetson, *Pluralism and Particularity in Religious Belief* (Westport, Conn.: Praeger, 1994).

supports the expectation of special revelation.[4] General revelation also teaches us where and how to look for a revelation from God that addresses concrete human spiritual needs, so that the divine remedy can be recognized and appropriated by human persons.

Thus, an indistinct but real form of particularism is supported by extrabiblical evidence. The specific character of natural theology generates the expectation that this indistinct particularism will undergo further refinement in a concrete revelation from God. One expects to find the specific dimensions of God's particular diagnosis of and solution to the human condition to be revealed in some manifest way that further confirms the general particularist expectation.

At the very least, the argument we present supports particularism in the following ways. (1) The object of religious devotion (that is, God) is discovered to be a being with certain determinate properties. The resulting conception of God entails that the metaphysical commitments of many religious traditions concerning the nature of "the Transcendent" are false. (2) God himself becomes the source of our knowledge about the nature, scope, and conditions of his grace or mercy. Whatever we may know about the operation of God's saving grace will depend on his revelation to us. Apart from revelation we can do little more than speculate, though we should suppose that meeting unrevealed conditions will hardly be necessary. (God may establish conditions that look from our point of view to be particularist and leave it to us to wonder how certain tensions are to be resolved.) (3) The argument we present in this section does not, perhaps, entail Christian particularism, but it does (a) entail some form of religious particularism and (b) rebut important objections to *Christian* particularism raised by religious pluralists.

Theologians used to speak of the "scandal of particularity." But particularism is not scandalous to the spiritually needy person who has been looking for God's precise remedy to the specific ills of humanity. The only truly scandalous particularism is a counterfeit particularism, which misdiagnoses the human condition and prescribes a fateful remedy. If Christian particular-

---

[4]On the relationship between general and special revelation, see R. Douglas Geivett, "General Revelation and the God of the Bible," *Bible-Science News* 32 (June 1994): 1–5.

ism is true, then religious pluralism is no less scandalous than non-Christian particularisms. It would, indeed, be scandalous if Christianity were not particularist, for, if we are right, particularism is a mark of religious truth.

We propose *to begin*, then, not with the Bible, but with evidence for the existence of a God who might be mercifully disposed to take note of the human condition and to address its most fundamental needs and aspirations, and *to proceed* with evidence that God has in fact revealed a plan to meet these needs—a plan that requires our cooperation on several levels. We shall then be in a position to investigate directly the biblical data concerning widespread religious diversity.

The Religious Impulse

In reasoning about the existence, nature, and dispositions of God, we face something of an embarrassment of riches, made more acute here by the limitations of space. We must stress this since the sketch we provide might be taken by some readers to be a comprehensive account of the available evidence.[5]

The religious impulse among human persons is characterized by a singular desire to make sense of human existence within the larger framework of reality.[6] We wish to understand the general point of our existence—if, as we hope, it even has a point. There are also particular features of human existence that we find especially puzzling. There is the fact that we live our lives under the impression that they have moral significance, though we find it difficult to ascertain with confidence what our moral duties amount to and even more difficult to abide by those we think we understand. Also, we meet with great setbacks to our aspirations: war, pestilence, plague, and, finally (or perhaps not so finally), death. And we ponder inconclusively both the personal and the cosmic significance of all these evils. We reflect on our selves and intuit that we are both wonderful and tragic at the same time. We seem to ourselves to be great specimens of design in both body and soul. But we recognize

---

[5]We refer the reader to the footnotes for sources containing more detailed developments of specific points.

[6]The phenomenon of religious diversity itself attests to the human propensity to seek order in these dimensions of human life by religious means.

also a dark side to our selves—an aspect we should like to eradicate if we could. Such, in brief, is the human condition. And it is humanity's awareness of its own condition that prompts religious inquiry in the first place.[7]

A Personal Creator of the Universe

Under the pressure of this universal concern to make sense of human existence, humans have naturally turned their attention to the larger whole of which they are a part, that is, to the universe itself, and have asked: Why is there anything at all, rather than nothing?

It would appear that the universe had a beginning, that there was a temporally first state of the universe.[8] Many of our scientists have inferred that the universe exploded abruptly into existence with a big bang, and that it is likely eventually to pass out of existence. Advances in observational astronomy in recent years have made it increasingly difficult to think of the universe as infinite in duration. Observation of the red shift of distant galaxies, indicating that the universe is expanding, together with the discovery of background radiation, has led many cosmologists to infer a primeval state of the universe that is infinitely dense. Moreover, since the rate of expansion of the universe continues to decelerate over time, it would appear that the universe originated in the remote but finite past, approximately sixteen to twenty billion years ago.[9]

---

[7]For other descriptions of how the religious impulse is tied to the concern to make sense of the human condition, see David Hume, *The Natural History of Religion*, ed. H. E. Root (Stanford, Calif.: Stanford Univ. Press, 1956); Ernest Becker, *The Denial of Death* (New York: The Free Press, 1973); Michael Green, *Evangelism in the Early Church* (Grand Rapids: Eerdmans, 1970), 144–65; Wolfhart Pannenberg, *Metaphysics and the Idea of God*, trans. Philip Clayton (Grand Rapids: Eerdmans, 1990), 167–70.

[8]By "universe" we mean the familiar array of galaxies, stars, and other entities that make up physical reality; we are not referring to "all that exists."

[9]Our source for this assigned age of the universe is science. Of course, if the universe owes its existence to God, then the universe might well be younger than it appears. In that event, we would be dependent on revelation to know the actual age of the universe. Some Christian theists hold that the Scriptures imply a younger age for the universe. The philosophical argument that the universe had a beginning implies nothing about the actual age of the universe.

Anyone who doubts that we should place so much stock in science on this point should consider the following philosophical argument that the universe had a beginning. Think of the universe as a temporally sequenced series of events. If the universe has always existed, and if time has no beginning but stretches into the infinite past, then infinitely many events must have passed before you started reading this book. There is, then, no limit to the number of events that must have occurred before you began reading this book. This is odd, for it would seem that if infinitely many events had to occur before you could begin reading this book, you would never get around to reading it. But surely there can be no doubt that you are now reading this book. So all of the events that must have occurred before you could begin reading have occurred. Thus, what has no end, an infinite sequence of events making up the total history of the universe prior to your reading this book, came to an end as you began reading. The moment you began reading this book you set an absolute limit on the sequence of events that occurred before you began reading. But an infinity of events, arranged in temporal sequence, can have no limit.

It is difficult to avoid the conclusion that the number of events that make up the history of the universe is not infinite after all but finite; that is to say, the universe had a beginning. The beginning of the universe marks the first in a finite series of events making up the history of the universe, whether that event was a big bang or not.[10]

Now if the universe had a beginning, it must have had a cause, for all events have causes. It will not do to object that the first event of the universe might be an exception. An event without a cause is a brute fact that simply has no explanation. So we must choose between looking for a cause of the beginning of the

---

[10]This type of argument has been called the *kalam* cosmological argument. For detailed expositions and defenses of the argument, see William Lane Craig, *The Kalam Cosmological Argument* (London: Macmillan, 1979); William Lane Craig and Quentin Smith, *Theism, Atheism, and Big Bang Cosmology* (Oxford: Clarendon Press, 1993); R. Douglas Geivett, *Evil and the Evidence for God* (Philadelphia: Temple Univ. Press, 1993), 90–124; and J. P. Moreland, *Scaling the Secular City* (Grand Rapids: Baker, 1987), 15–42; see also Dallas Willard, "The Three-Stage Argument for the Existence of God," in *Contemporary Perspectives on Religious Epistemology*, ed. R. Douglas Geivett and Brendan Sweetman (New York: Oxford Univ. Press, 1992), 212–24.

universe or settling for no cause at all. But what good reason could one have for preferring no explanation over some available explanation?

Perhaps it will be argued that the first event in a causal sequence needs no cause because it can have no cause, since the only thing that could be the cause is some prior event, and there can be no event prior to the first event. But this argument is not convincing. For the series of physical events in the universe is not the only causal series with a first term. Causal sequences are regularly and effortlessly initiated whenever a human agent performs a free act. We know ourselves to be agents with free will directly and introspectively, and together with the knowledge of our freedom comes the knowledge of the reality of first-cause causation, or "agent-causation."[11]

This is an important consideration for our purposes, since we are now in a position to see what sort of cause is responsible for getting the universe going: It must be an agent on the order of personal being, yet surpassing human persons in greatness.

The fact that we owe our existence to a personal Creator of great power can be cause either for great concern or for great expectation. Our lives are set within a context whose initial conditions were established by the Cause of the beginning of the universe. As the apostle Paul remarked to the Athenians gathered on Mars Hill, "'For in him we live and move and have our being.' As some of your own poets have said, 'We are his offspring'" (Acts 17:28). If we are not helpless, we surely are vulnerable.[12]

---

[11]For developments of this idea, see Roderick Chisholm, "Human Freedom and the Self," in *Free Will*, ed. Gary Watson (Oxford: Oxford Univ. Press, 1982); idem, *On Metaphysics* (Minneapolis: Univ. of Minnesota Press, 1989), 3–15; Geivett, *Evil and the Evidence for God*, 114–22; Stewart C. Goetz, "A Noncausal Theory of Agency," *Philosophy and Phenomenological Research* 44 (December 1988): 303–16; William L. Rowe, *Thomas Reid on Freedom and Morality* (Ithaca, N.Y.: Cornell Univ. Press, 1991); idem, "Two Concepts of Freedom," *Proceedings of the American Philosophical Association* 61 (suppl.) (September 1981): 43–64.

[12]What we may make of ourselves, spiritually and otherwise, is conditioned by the arrangement and patterns of reality set up by our Creator. It can hardly matter that we might have a preference for a different arrangement. It is best that we seek to know the actual arrangement of reality so that we can arrange our own lives in a realistic manner.

The Structure of Human Existence

It is instructive to survey the structure of human existence with awareness of its causal dependence on God in the background. Two dimensions of our existence deserve independent attention: the *physical* and the *nonphysical* parameters of our existence.

When we consider the physical conditions set for our lives, we find a remarkable confluence of life-sustaining features in the universe. If the conditions of our universe were not what they are, within a very small margin of flexibility, no life of any kind would be found in this universe. While the universe is a fit habitat for human and other forms of life, the initial probability of there being such a universe is small.[13] This confluence of so-called "cosmic constants" would be improbable enough, were we to assume that the universe is uncaused and undesigned; it is even more improbable on the supposition that our Creator has it in for us. If our lives are special, and if what makes our lives special has anything to do with the physical conditions in which we came to have the lives we have, then the good of human life depends on the Creator as well.

Our bodies, then, locate us in a physical world of astonishing complexity, apparently ordered to the goal of our physical well-being. But we are more than our bodies. We are also spiritual beings; we have souls. We exercise free will, we deliberate, we have emotions, we act in ways that are worthy of praise or blame, we are directly aware of a difference between the movements of our bodies and the events of our own minds, and so on. All attempts to reduce mental events to physical processes that take place somewhere in our bodies are highly implausible. We have first-person awareness of our own mental states that does not depend on empirical observation. It will always be the

---

[13]This claim constitutes an appeal to what philosophers call "the anthropic principle." For detailed discussions of this principle, see John D. Barrow and Frank J. Tipler, *The Anthropic Cosmological Principle* (New York: Oxford Univ. Press, 1986); M. A. Corey, *God and the New Cosmology: The Anthropic Design Argument* (Lanham, Md.: Rowman & Littlefield, 1993); John Leslie, *Universes* (London: Routledge, 1989); Hugh Ross, "Astronomical Evidence for a Personal, Transcendent God," in *The Creation Hypothesis: Scientific Evidence for an Intelligent Designer*, ed. J. P. Moreland (Downers Grove, Ill.: InterVarsity, 1994), 141–72.

case that, if a cognitive scientist's description of the mental states of another person (given in strictly physicalist terms) conflicts with the firsthand reports of the person himself, it is the description proposed by the cognitive scientist that should be revised. For example, if a patient honestly reports having a visual sensation of the color blue, it will be ridiculous for a brain physiologist to insist that the patient is wrong simply because her report contradicts the conclusions the brain physiologist has reached on the basis of observing physical events going on inside the patient's head. So even if we had a complete or nearly complete science of the brain—and we are a long way from that—a person's private access to his or her own mental states would require a nonphysical explanation.[14]

Now, among the phenomena of our mental life are various desires that we have. Some of these desires are spiritual in nature. As C. S. Lewis observed, "If I find in myself a desire which no experience in this world can satisfy, the most probable explanation is that I was made for another world."[15] The trouble is, we have no direct awareness of the means to obtain a passport to that world. So we have a natural desire to flourish as persons that we cannot reliably arrange to satisfy on our own. One's desire to flourish as a person includes both a desire to be a good person and a desire for immortality. We also desire to be on good terms with all or most other persons and to know some persons intimately. Among the persons many of us aspire to know well, there is the Person to whom we owe our existence. We are, however, estranged from our Creator.

Is it necessary that God should remain a stranger to us? One should think not, for both we and God are persons. As persons, we and God are equipped to experience intersubjective relationship. Indeed, it would seem that human persons have capacities for relationship that are more expansive than would

---

[14]See W. S. Anglin, *Free Will and the Christian Faith* (Oxford: Clarendon Press, 1990); Richard Swinburne, *The Evolution of the Soul* (Oxford: Clarendon Press, 1986); J. P. Moreland and David Ciocci, eds., *Christian Perspectives on Being Human* (Grand Rapids: Baker, 1993); J. P. Moreland and Gary Habermas, *Immortality: The Other Side of Death* (Nashville: Thomas Nelson, 1992). For a comparison between Christianity and Buddhism on the nature of the self, which illustrates the religious significance of differences in the metaphysics of personhood, see Griffiths, *Apology for Apologetics*, 85–108.

[15]C. S. Lewis, *Mere Christianity* (New York: Macmillan, 1952), 106.

be needed for even very intimate relationships with other human persons. But, for meaningful interpersonal contact between ourselves and God, it apparently is not sufficient that we and God are persons, for God remains a stranger to us. That we and God are persons does, however, suggest what other conditions there might be for our entering into relationship with God. When desirable interpersonal relationships occur between human persons, it is because the persons involved have opened themselves up to one another. Each one has become, as it were, voluntarily transparent in the presence of the other. Many relationships fail for lack of transparency on the part of the other.

Now, the estrangement that many feel between themselves and God has a striking quality about it. They do not feel that they are perfect strangers in relation to God. The term "estrangement" seems apropos because it suggests a deterioration of some prior relationship, an interruption in fellowship between human persons and God. It is alienation experienced as a departure from something that was meant to be, and perhaps once was. Thus, the human desire to know God may well be ambivalent. But to the degree that it is sincere, the desire to know God also includes a desire to understand the cause of alienation from him and the conditions for reconciliation. This includes the conditions that can only be met by God as well as those that can only be met by humans (assuming that there are such conditions). In this situation, God seems to occupy a superior position both to know and to determine the necessary conditions for reconciliation. So, presumably, our confidence concerning the conditions for reconciliation will depend on God's initiative in revealing them to us.[16]

This leads us at once to expect that a particular revelation, answering to the specific needs of the human condition, might be provided by God. Any religious tradition that withholds the

---

[16]For more on the religious implications of the structure of the soul and of the desires of the human heart, see Dallas Willard, *The Spirit of the Disciplines: Understanding How God Changes Lives* (San Francisco: Harper & Row, 1988); C. Stephen Evans, *Existentialism: The Philosophy of Despair and the Quest for Hope* (Grand Rapids: Zondervan, 1984); James Houston, *The Heart's Desire: A Guide to Personal Fulfillment* (Oxford: Lion, 1992); Peter Kreeft, *Heaven: The Heart's Deepest Longing* (San Francisco: Ignatius, 1989); Calvin Miller, *A Hunger for Meaning* (Downers Grove, Ill.: InterVarsity, 1984); Rebecca Manley Pippert, *Hope Has Its Reasons: Surprised by Faith in a Broken World* (San Francisco: Harper & Row, 1989).

hope of a particular revelation from God seems unduly pessimistic; it can also be dangerously misleading. In any case, the
possibility of a particular revelation from God cannot be ruled
out a priori.[17]

The Provision of Special Revelation

There remains, then, the question of whether a particular
revelation from God has been provided. Here the best policy is
to examine historically-situated divine revelation claims, to see
how well any of them answers to the needs of the human
predicament and what support they enjoy from relevant types
of evidence.[18] From what has been said thus far, at least the following three criteria for evaluating revelation claims seem
appropriate: (1) A revelation claim must be compatible with
what is revealed about God independently of that particular revelation claim; (2) a revelation claim must embody a message
suited to the human needs that prompt the expectation of a particular revelation in the first place; and, (3) a revelation claim
must, when possible, be corroborated by external signs (i.e., miracles) in order to distinguish a genuine revelation from spurious
revelation claims.[19]

We believe that, in terms of these three criteria, the Christian revelation claim enjoys the greatest support among the alter-

---

[17]See Philo's closing statement in David Hume's *Dialogues Concerning Natural Religion*, part 12 (Norman Kemp Smith's 2d ed. [Indianapolis: Bobbs-Merrill, 1947]), 227–28.

[18]It must be noticed that, on the whole, theists have distinguished themselves as "peoples of the Book." That is, they have embraced some form of propositional revelation. Orthodox Jews consider the Hebrew Scriptures to be uniquely inspired. According to the Islamic tradition, God or Allah in effect dictated his word to his prophet Mohammed, producing the Qur'an. And Christians acknowledge the unique divine authority of the Old and New Testaments of the Bible. It is rare for a theist to hold that no form of special revelation has been given.

[19]As we observed in the previous note, revelational theisms differ in their judgment concerning the precise locus of propositional revelation from God. The evidence of miracles is therefore useful for adjudicating between competing revelation
claims. For more on the significance of miracles for corroborating revelation claims,
see Richard Swinburne, *Revelation: From Metaphor to Analogy* (Oxford: Clarendon
Press, 1992), chs. 5 and 6; R. Douglas Geivett, "The Interface of Theism and Christianity," *Ratio* 1 (Fall 1993): 211–30. See also Anglin, *Free Will and the Christian Faith*,
186–208.

natives. (1) God is represented in the Christian Scriptures as the personal Creator of the universe, a being of great power and intelligence who takes an active interest in the affairs of the universe and who exhibits special concern for the finite persons who inhabit our neighborhood of the universe. Thus, the basic metaphysical presuppositions of the Bible dovetail with the results of natural theology.

(2) What of the hope that God has good news for human persons? If we take existing religious traditions to represent the possibilities, it is hard to imagine better news than what we find in the gospel of Jesus Christ.[20] The precise nature of the human predicament in relation to God is diagnosed with unparalleled psychological and spiritual realism in terms of moral rebellion against God. Furthermore, this need is met by God's merciful initiative. That initiative takes the peerless form of the incarnation of God in Jesus Christ, the atoning death of Jesus on behalf of human beings, whose sin has separated them from God, and the resurrection of Jesus to new life as the guarantee of eternal blessedness for all persons who believe in Jesus Christ.

(3) The truth of this good news is confirmed by historically well-attested miracles, especially the resurrection of Jesus Christ from the dead.[21] According to the best historical evidence, we have no less than four reliable accounts (namely, the Gospels of the New Testament) of the main events of the life of Jesus and of his self-understanding as God. We agree with Christian philosopher Hugo Meynell, who writes that "suggestions as to how these narratives might have come into existence, which imply that the historical Jesus was radically different from the figure presented to us, have not on the whole stood the test of time."[22]

---

[20]The term "gospel" simply means "good news."

[21]The miracles of Christianity serve at least two vital purposes: They attract attention to the Christian revelation claim, and they corroborate the Christian revelation claim.

[22]Hugo A. Meynell, "Faith, Objectivity, and Historical Falsifiability," in *Language, Meaning and God*, ed. Brian Davies (London: Geoffrey Chapman, 1987), 158–59. For sophisticated defenses of the historical reliability of the New Testament Gospels, see Craig Blomberg, *The Historical Reliability of the Gospels* (Leicester, England: Inter-Varsity, 1987); R. T. France, *The Evidence for Jesus* (Downers Grove, Ill.: InterVarsity, 1986); Royce Gordon Gruenler, *New Approaches to Jesus and the Gospels* (Grand Rapids: Baker, 1982); E. L. Mascall, *Theology and the Gospel of Christ* (London:

The event of the resurrection of Jesus is confirmed by historical evidence that Jesus' tomb was found empty just days after he was buried and that, following his death and burial, Jesus appeared bodily alive to his disciples and others for a period of about forty days. The resurrection is further confirmed by the overwhelming improbability of the genesis of the Christian church within a few weeks of Jesus' ignominious death.[23] Few other religious traditions can trace their history back to their inception with as much accuracy as Christianity.[24] And no other religious tradition is as dependent on its associated historical events as Christianity. Thus, Christianity has little value as a religious story or myth if its record of the events surrounding the life, death, and resurrection of Jesus is not historically accurate. Christianity cannot be accommodated to the hypothesis of religious pluralism without such great distortion that it ceases to be Christianity.

There is one further point to make about the Christian revelation claim. In the Bible, the Old and New Testaments, we have a permanent deposit of divine revelation in propositional form. Jesus Christ, who both claimed to be God and corroborated his claim by rising from the dead (see Rom. 1:4), also affirmed the divine authority of the Christian Scriptures.[25] On the strength of Jesus' authoritative witness to the divine origin of Scripture, Christians today can rely on the Bible as a source of religious knowledge. We turn next, therefore, to the witness

SPCK, 1977); Michael J. Wilkins and J. P. Moreland, eds., *Jesus Under Fire: Modern Scholarship Reinvents the Historical Jesus* (Grand Rapids: Zondervan, 1995). See also Joel B. Green, Scot McKnight, and I. Howard Marshall, eds., *Dictionary of Jesus and the Gospels* (Downers Grove, Ill.: InterVarsity, 1992).

[23]See William L. Craig, *Knowing the Truth about the Resurrection* (Ann Arbor, Mich.: Servant, 1981), and his more exhaustive study *Assessing the New Testament Evidence for the Historicity of the Resurrection of Jesus* (Lewiston, N.Y.: Edwin Mellen, 1989); also Gary R. Habermas, *Ancient Evidence for the Life of Jesus* (Nashville: Thomas Nelson, 1984).

[24]See Christopher Dawson, *Religion and the Rise of Western Culture* (Garden City, N.Y.: Image/Doubleday, 1958), 12.

[25]See John W. Wenham, *Christ and the Bible* (Downers Grove, Ill.: InterVarsity, 1972); Bernard Ramm, *Special Revelation and the Word of God* (Grand Rapids: Eerdmans, 1961), 110–11, 115–18. On the notion of "propositional revelation," see Paul Helm, *The Divine Revelation* (Westchester, Ill.: Crossway, 1982), 21–27; Leon Morris, *I Believe in Divine Revelation* (Grand Rapids: Eerdmans, 1976), 113–18; Ronald H. Nash, *The Word of God and the Mind of Man* (Grand Rapids: Zondervan, 1982), 35–54.

of Scripture concerning God's provision of salvation, including its scope and its conditions.

CHRISTIAN PARTICULARISM AND SPECIAL REVELATION

The considerations of the last section are especially important to the second-order intramural debate with religious pluralists, who deny the unique divine authority of the Bible. But if, as we have argued, it is reasonable to expect that a particular revelation, answering to the specific needs of the human condition, might be provided by God, and if the authenticity of the Christian revelation claim is historically well-supported, then it behooves us to consider the biblical data concerning the nature and scope of salvation. Our investigation of the specific data of the Bible involves us in a first-order intramural debate with evangelical inclusivists concerning the significance of religious diversity.

In contrast to theologically liberal pluralists, evangelical inclusivists are concerned to show that their views, if they do not arise from Scripture, are at least compatible with Scripture. Clark Pinnock, for example, has acknowledged that, as an evangelical, he believes "there is a truth deposit in Scripture which needs to be guarded (2 Tim 1:14)."[26] So we now move to a "first-order intramural debate" with these inclusivists regarding the picture of salvation presented in the Bible. Which view best fits the biblical data, inclusivism or particularism? What are the conditions of salvation on the human side? Is there anything that one must believe in order to be saved? Does Scripture teach that salvation is dependent on an explicit trust in Jesus Christ and his work? Or does Scripture teach that salvation is available outside of an explicit faith in Jesus and that somehow culture and alternative traditions may mediate divine grace? In this section, we will examine the chief texts that particularists consider most relevant on these questions. In the following section, we will respond to common inclusivist arguments.

---

[26]Clark H. Pinnock, "Response to Delwin Brown," *Christian Scholar's Review* 19 (September 1989), 78; see also Clark H. Pinnock and Delwin Brown, *Theological Crossfire: An Evangelical/Liberal Dialogue* (Grand Rapids: Zondervan, 1990), 36, 37–57, 255.

230 | Geivett and Phillips

Acts 4:12

Early in the history of the church, as Peter and John were entering the temple one day, Peter healed a lame beggar "in the name of Jesus Christ of Nazareth" (Acts 3:6). He then explained to the Jewish witnesses to this healing that faith in the name of Jesus had made the man whole (3:16). Although large numbers believed Peter's message (4:4), both Peter and John were arrested and tried the next day before the religious authorities (4:3ff.). In their defense before the Sanhedrin, Peter repeated his position: "Know this, you and all the people of Israel: It is by the name of Jesus Christ of Nazareth, whom you crucified but whom God raised from the dead, that this man stands before you healed" (4:10).[27] To reinforce and extend his point, he added, "There is salvation in no one else, for there is no other name under heaven given among mortals by which we must be saved" (4:12 NRSV). On examination, the two clauses of verse 12 provide a forcible case for particularism.

In the first clause, Peter excludes the possibility of any basis of salvation or any person through whom salvation might come other than Jesus: "There is salvation in no one else." But the second clause—"for there is no other name under heaven given among mortals by which we must be saved"—is stronger and more precise. As the word "for" indicates, this clause is added in order to explain Peter's initial claim. Let us briefly examine four terms in this clause that, taken together, suggest Peter was a particularist.

(1) Peter uses the broad phrase "under heaven" to indicate how extensive his exclusion of all other names actually is.

(2) Peter does not restrict the scope of those to whom this name is given. As he says, the name is "given among mortals," not "given to you" or "given to the Jews."[28] Although the particularist should not rest his case on this point alone, it does imply that the requirement of salvation by belief in Jesus' name is universal.

---

[27]In Acts 2:36 Jesus the Nazarene had been identified with the messianic title "Christ."

[28]The word "given" is a perfect participle, implying that the name, once given, permanently remains as God's only means of salvation.

(3) Consider the easily overlooked term "must" (δεῖ). Almost all uses of δεῖ (or ἔδει) within Luke-Acts are related, either directly or indirectly, to Jesus Christ as the one who fulfills God's sovereign plan to save sinful humanity. As Walter Grundemann observes, in Luke "Jesus sees His whole life and activity and passion under this will of God comprehended in a δεῖ."[29] Jesus told Nicodemus, a Jewish man, that he must (δεῖ) be born again (John 3:7). Paul and Silas, when asked by the Gentile jailer what he must (δεῖ) do to be saved, replied: "Believe in the Lord Jesus, and you shall be saved" (Acts 16:30–31).[30] If salvation could come apart from knowledge about Jesus, Paul and Silas seem confidently oblivious of that option. Indeed, they almost appear to answer in unison, as if it were a well-established fact that the gospel—to all people—is the good news about Jesus. The point is, it is difficult to argue that Peter allows that the salvation of which he speaks in Acts 4:12 did not require knowledge of the person of Jesus. Indeed, the inclusivist notion of "ontology—but not epistemology" violates the usage of the term δεῖ.

(4) This understanding of the passage is strengthened by the presence of a fourth term, "name." This use of the name of

---

[29]Walter Grundemann, "δεῖ, δέον ἐστί," *Theological Dictionary of the New Testament*, ed. Gerhard Kittel and Gerhard Friedrich, trans. Geoffrey Bromiley (Grand Rapids: Eerdmans, 1964), 2:22. Grundemann continues (22–23),

Over Him there stands a δεῖ which is already present in His childhood. This is the δεῖ of divine Lordship (Lk. 2:49). It determines His activity (Lk. 4:43; 13:33; 19:5). It leads Him to suffering and death, but also to glory (Lk. 9:22; 17:25; 24:7, 26; Ac. 1:16; 3:21; 17:3). It has its basis in the will of God concerning Him which is laid down in Scripture and which He unconditionally follows (Lk. 22:37; 24:44). His disciples, apostles and community are also laid under this δεῖ which derives from the will of God. Claimed by the divine will, they are shaped and determined by it down to the smallest details of their lives (Lk. 12:12; Acts 9:6,16; 14:22; 19:21; 23:11; 27:24). ... The δεῖ, which as an expression of the will of God is at all these points an expression of His saving will, finally reveals to man his state of loss and thus demands faith in God's act of salvation (Acts 4:12; 16:30).

We should note that ἔξεστι, as an alternative to δεῖ, might have served Peter's purpose better if he had embraced an inclusivist perspective on salvation.

[30]Given the form of the jailer's question, the reply of Paul and Silas seems to have the force: "In order to be saved, you must believe in the Lord Jesus."

Jesus refers to the authoritative fullness of the being and work of Jesus.[31] That the term *name* includes specific knowledge concerning Jesus as Savior is supported by its usage elsewhere in the New Testament. Descriptions of missionary activity following the flight of the church from Jerusalem are consistently given in terms of bearing witness to "the name" of Jesus. For example, Philip identifies the gospel expressly with "the name of Jesus Christ" (Acts 8:12, 35). Paul's vocation is to carry Jesus' name to Gentiles as well as to Jews (Acts 9:15; cf. 9:27). Indeed, he indicates a definite preference to conduct his ministry among those who did not know of Christ, as if it is urgent that this name be known as a condition for salvation (Rom. 15:20).[32] When God's ministers are sent out, it is "for the sake of the Name" (3 John 7). Furthermore, the persecutors of the early church properly and routinely associated the message of salvation preached by the church with "the name of Jesus" (Acts 4:17–30; 5:28–33, 40; 26:9). Thus, the name of Jesus is the focal point of conflict between believers, as representatives of God's salvation, and unbelievers, as opponents of God's witness. In addition, there was such close association of the content of the gospel of Jesus with the name that in some cases the terms "Jesus" and "Name" are used interchangeably (Acts 5:41; 9:34; 3 John 7). Finally, the subjection of demons is apparently dependent on making direct reference to the name of Jesus (Acts 19:13–15; cf. Matt 7:22).[33]

We conclude that "name" refers to the focus of God's universal redemptive plan in the person and work of Jesus Christ, who must be the object of explicit faith by those who want to be saved. Peter does not appear to be referring to Jesus merely as the ontological ground of salvation—that is, as the sole *source* of atonement. Rather, he is indicating what must be acknowledged

---

[31]Hans Bietenhard, "ὄνομα, κτλ.," *Theological Dictionary of the New Testament*, 5:242–83, esp. 270–83.

[32]Ramesh Richard observes that "'calling upon the *name* of the Lord' is the pre-Flood (Gen. 4:26); post-Flood (Abraham, Gen. 12:8); Israelite (Jer. 33:3); Christian (Rom. 10:13); and eschatological (Joel 2:32) condition for deliverance" (*Population of Heaven*, 33). See also 1 Kings 18:24–26.

[33]See Richard, *Population of Heaven*, 60. He observes that it is difficult to argue that the demons were subject to Jesus only in the ontological (and not the epistemological) sense.

about Jesus before one can be saved. Everyone—whether Jews or Gentiles, including the ranking authorities in both groups—must grapple with the theological truth expressly associated with Jesus' name. Paul concurs, for as he says, a day is coming when "at the name of Jesus every knee should bow, ... and every tongue confess that Jesus Christ is Lord" (Phil. 2:10).[34]

Inclusivists sometimes argue that Acts 4:12 does not support particularism, claiming that the verse does "not say one has to know about that work [of Jesus Christ] in order to benefit from the work."[35] From what we have said above, we take this to be a misreading of the text. Moreover, inclusivists hold that this text is silent about the precise fate of the unevangelized or of adherents to other religions, and they warn against any tendency to generalize beyond the immediate context of Acts 3–4.[36] Of course, we agree that the unevangelized are not specifically mentioned. But neither is the doctrine of the Trinity expressly identified as such in any of the texts from which it is properly deduced. The presumably universal scope of such phrases as "no one else," "under heaven," and "given to men," and the usage of both "$\delta\varepsilon\hat{\iota}$" and "name" throughout Luke-Acts strongly imply that the total expression in Acts 4:12 functions as a controlling statement with prescriptive force for anyone who wants to be saved.

---

[34]We may also observe that in Acts 4:12, when Luke employs the phrase "no one else" in the first clause, the word "else" translates ἄλλος in the Greek, whereas the word "other" translates ἕτερος in the second clause. There is no one like or comparable to Jesus who can bring salvation (first clause), and there is no different name by which salvation comes (second clause). As Hermann Beyer observes, "The new which has come in Jesus Christ is something quite *different* from what preceded to the degree that it excludes everything else as a way of salvation" ("ἕτερος," *Theological Dictionary of the New Testament*, 2:703). This is not only an argument against pluralism, but—because the second clause elaborates upon the first, and particularism is supported in the second clause—this would be a converging argument against inclusivism.

[35]John E. Sanders, "Is Belief In Christ Necessary for Salvation?" *The Evangelical Quarterly* 60 (1988): 246. This is Sanders' way of handling both Acts 4:12 and John 14:6.

[36]See, for example, Clark Pinnock, "Acts 4:12—No Other Name Under Heaven," in *Through No Fault of Their Own?* ed. William V. Crockett and James G. Sigountos (Grand Rapids: Baker, 1991), 107–15.

John 3:16, 18

In the familiar story of John 3, the Jewish leader Nicodemus is informed that God's universal salvific will is matched by a particular divine arrangement for the salvation of humanity. God the Father ordained the death of his Son on the cross in order that life might come to those who fulfill a specific condition: belief in *him*. Verse 18 warns that the one who does not believe in Jesus' *name* is judged already.

> For God so loved the world that he gave his one and only Son, that whoever believes in him shall not perish but have eternal life. ... Whoever believes in him is not condemned, but whoever does not believe stands condemned already because he has not believed in the name of God's one and only Son. (John 3:16, 18)

Some inclusivists are strangely silent concerning this illuminating passage; others dismiss it as applying only to the evangelized—an interpretive distinction not found within the passage itself.

Ironically, inclusivists must insist that in verse 18, believing in "the name" excludes Christological awareness, which would require dubious exegesis in the context of John 3. In any case, inclusivists must hold that *something* is the proper object of saving faith. Since these verses stress belief—and belief always has an object—what is the object of faith, if not Jesus?

Romans 10:9–15

The heart of the apostle Paul beat with the passion of a pioneer evangelist. He was compelled to preach the gospel (1 Cor. 9:16), and in particular to bring the knowledge of Christ to those who had never heard (Rom. 15:20–21). He introduced the letter to the Romans, his great treatise on salvation, with the claim that it is the gospel of Jesus Christ that brings salvation to every individual who believes (1:16–17).[37] In this letter, the need for salvation is discussed in detail. All humans without exception are

---

[37]In the apostle's vocabulary, the terms "Jew" and "Gentile/Greek" cover all unredeemed persons. See 1 Cor. 10:32 for Paul's threefold classification of humanity: "Jews, Greeks [and] the church of God."

guilty sinners and are therefore deserving objects of God's wrath (1:18–20; 2:1; 3:9–24; 5:12–21). Individual faith in Jesus Christ removes one's guilt and satisfies God's wrath (3:21–31; 5:1–11; 6:23).[38]

It is not surprising, therefore, that as Paul closes the doctrinal portion of the letter, he stresses the urgent purpose of mission—that the mouths of the *as yet* unevangelized can confess the name and lordship of Jesus:

> If you confess with your mouth, "Jesus is Lord," and believe in your heart that God raised him from the dead, you will be saved. For it is with your heart that you believe and are justified, and it is with your mouth that you confess and are saved. As the Scripture says, "Anyone who trusts in him will never be put to shame." For there is no difference between Jew and Gentile—the same Lord is Lord of all and richly blesses all who call on him, for, "Everyone who calls on the name of the Lord will be saved."
>
> How, then, can they call on the one they have not believed in? And how can they believe in the one of whom they have not heard? And how can they hear without someone preaching to them? And how can they preach unless they are sent? As it is written, "How beautiful are the feet of those who bring good news!" (Rom. 10:9–15)

Indeed, it is difficult to account for the evangelistic mandate, and for the sufferings God's witnesses are called upon to endure, on the supposition that the unevangelized do not need to hear in order to be saved. To be saved, a specific confession has to be made, and a specific set of truths must be believed (10:9–10). Hearing the gospel is, therefore, a natural prerequisite for the satisfaction of this condition. Jews and Gentiles alike need to hear about and believe in Jesus (10:14). But inasmuch as many are unable to "call on the name of the Lord" (10:13)—who is here identified as Jesus (10:9)—because they have not heard

---

[38]This point counts against those inclusivists who maintain that the basis of human condemnation is not sin but the rejection of Jesus Christ. Surely this could not be the case, for then the Bible would be teaching the universal salvation of the unevangelized.

about Jesus, an evangelist must be sent. Only then may the unevangelized hear, believe the gospel, call on the name of the Lord, and so be saved (10:13–15).

The most natural assumption to make about this passage is that apart from the faithful labor of the human evangelist the unbeliever will have no opportunity to hear that which must be believed in order to be saved.[39] No alternative means of salvation for the unevangelized is alluded to. If there were another alternative that offered the wide hope of the inclusivist, Paul's argument here might seem misleading, if not deceptive.

John 14:6; 17:20

Jesus' Upper Room Discourse (John 13–17) is the centerpiece of John's Gospel. It records Jesus' last will and testament to his disciples prior to his crucifixion. In it he promises them the Holy Spirit and reminds them of essential teachings, emphasized by the repeated formula, "These things I have spoken to you" (NASB).[40] As Jesus prepares the disciples with the news that he is about to return to the Father, he reminds them that they know "the way" (14:4). When Thomas queries, "Lord, we don't know where you are going, so how can we know the way?" Jesus replies: "I am the way and the truth and the life. No one comes to the Father except through me" (14:5–6).

The first thing to notice about John 14:6 is the "I am" statement identifying Jesus equally with "the way and the truth and the life." Jesus claims not merely to *know* but to *be* the way, truth, and life. Since he adds that "no one" ($o\dot{v}\delta\epsilon\hat{\iota}\varsigma$) comes to the Father except by this way, we infer that anyone who wants to come to the Father must find that way that uniquely leads to the Father, namely, Jesus himself.[41] And there seems to be no reason for the

---

[39]See C. K. Barrett, *The Epistle to the Romans* (New York: Harper, 1957), 204–6.

[40]In Greek, $\tau\alpha\hat{v}\tau\alpha\ \lambda\epsilon\lambda\dot{\alpha}\lambda\eta\kappa\alpha$ (see John 14:25; 15:11; 16:1, 4, 6, 25, 33). The use of the perfect tense stresses the abiding nature of the words Jesus has spoken, which later the Holy Spirit will help the disciples to recall (14:26).

[41]"Way," referring to the path to the Father, is central to the verse. "Truth" and "life" enjoy supporting roles in the clarification of the nature of that way to the Father. Jesus is the way to God precisely because he is the truth of God (John 1:14) and the life of God (1:4; 3:15; 5:26; 11:25). Thus, life is associated with truth. See D. A. Carson, *The Gospel According to John* (Grand Rapids: Eerdmans, 1991), 491. Notice

definite article that accompanies each of the three terms—the way, the truth, and the life—except that all others who may claim to be the truth and the life are thereby exposed as untrue and without life. In the early church, belonging to "the Way" became an identifying mark by which Christians distinguished themselves from those who did not believe in Jesus (Acts 9:2; 19:9, 23; 24:14, 22).[42]

A few hours later, in the context of his high priestly prayer, Jesus prays for believers and their witness in the world. There is no indication that he prays for those who would not be saved. In fact, he remarks, "I am not praying for the world" (John 17:9). He does, however, pray for those "who will believe in me *through their message*," that is, through the apostolic word (17:20). This implies a direct link between the future salvation of those who are not of his immediate Jewish fold (10:16) and the explicit proclamation of the apostolic word.[43]

Other Biblical Considerations

Much more might be said to support the view that particularism is more naturally evident throughout the Bible than inclusivism.[44] Several broader biblical themes deserve to be mentioned. First, in both Testaments other religions are viewed at best as nonredemptive, and at worst as partaking of the domain of darkness (e.g., Ex. 20:3–6; 2 Chron. 13:9; Isa. 37:18–19; 40; Jer. 2:11; 5:7; 16:20; Acts 26:17–18; Col. 1:13). As for those Gentiles who remain apart from Jesus Christ, God's wrath abides on them (1 Thess. 2:16). By implication, before their conversion to Jesus Christ, adherents of other religions held to what was dead and false. But with their conversion they "turned to God from

---

that Jesus' statement in 14:6 is not restricted to his disciples; he does not say οὐδεῖς ἐξ ὑμῶν ("none among you").

[42]Clearly, to refer to oneself as a traveler on "the Way" might be regarded as exclusivist, and therefore offensive to many. Opponents of first-century believers adopted "Christian" as a term of opprobrium (Acts 11:26; cf. 1 Peter 4:14–16).

[43]Note the authoritative role of the apostles in Acts 1–12. The apostolic word was later inscripturated in the New Testament (see John 14:26; 16:12–16; etc.). See W. Gary Phillips and William E. Brown, *Making Sense of Your World* (Chicago: Moody, 1991), 106–112.

[44]See especially John 1:12, 14, 18; 5:23; 1 John 2:23; 5:11–12.

idols to serve the living and true God" (1 Thess. 1:9). Other religions are considered devoid of salvific truth and reality (Acts
19:26; 1 Cor. 1:21; 8:4–6; 10:19–20; Gal. 4:8; 2 Thess. 1:8; cf.
1 Thess. 2:13). They are not treated as merely inferior but as simply wrong, as dangerously identified with the domain of darkness, because there is only *"one* hope . . . , *one* Lord, *one* faith, *one*
baptism; *one* God and Father of all" (Eph. 4:4–6; italics added).

Second, the Bible presents a consistent pattern of "fewness"
in redemption and "wideness" in judgment. For example, in the
Flood of Genesis 6–8, only eight people were considered righteous enough to be spared.[45] All others perished, presumably
whether they overtly rejected Noah's preaching, just passively
ignored it, or never even heard his specific salvific message
(Heb. 11:7). The Flood is not an isolated case in the history of
God's dealings with humanity. Clearly, there have been other
periods of history during which few were saved or many were
judged.[46] And in the New Testament, Peter interprets the Flood
as a pattern for the eschatological judgment (1 Peter 3:20–21;
2 Peter 3:6–7).

Third, there are cases in the Bible of individuals who, even
though they had received some special revelation, were required
to believe further redemptive truth in order to be saved. This
was true for the Samaritans (John 4:9, 24), for "devout" Jews
from every nation (Acts 2:5, 38 NASB), for all zealous Jews (Rom.
10:1–3), and for "God-fearing" Gentiles (Acts 9:2; cf. 10:33, 43).[47]
Much of what these groups already believed was true, but what
they knew apparently was not enough for their salvation. It is
difficult to escape the impression that the biblical writers them-

---

[45]Even those who do not take the Flood narrative to describe a universal flood
must acknowledge an unmistakable emphasis on the fewness of the remnant that
was saved.

[46]For example, Babel, the Sodomite cities, Pharaoh's Egypt, the Canaanites,
Assyrians, Babylonians, etc. (Would an inclusivist allow that God was less loving in
the Old Testament?) See Paul Helm, "Are They Few That Be Saved?" in *Universalism and the Doctrine of Hell*, ed. Nigel M. de S. Cameron (Carlisle, U.K.: Paternoster
/ Grand Rapids: Baker, 1991), 257–81; William Lane Craig, "'No Other Name': A
Middle Knowledge Perspective on the Exclusivity of Salvation through Christ," *Faith
and Philosophy* 6 (April 1989): 172–88.

[47]The obsolescence of the belief of the disciples of John the Baptist (Acts 19:4–
5) shows that even in a transition between biblical epochs it was urgent to make
known whatever was novel in special revelation.

selves were particularists. The burden of proof weighs heavily on the shoulders of the inclusivist.

INCLUSIVISM AND THE BIBLE

Evangelical inclusivists join particularists in holding that the Bible is an authoritative source of religious knowledge. Yet they disagree about the significance of religious diversity and in their assessment of the fate of the unevangelized. A difference in "control beliefs" between the parties to the first-order intramural debate goes far in explaining why particularists and inclusivists reach different conclusions in this vital area of soteriological concern.

God's Universal Salvific Will

Much inclusivist optimism regarding the possibility of salvation apart from knowledge of Jesus Christ is based on biblical references to God's universal salvific will. Second Peter 3:9 (the Lord does not want "anyone to perish, but everyone to come to repentance") and 1 Timothy 2:4 (God "desires everyone to be saved" NRSV) are often cited.

The irony is that these verses, when studied in their contexts, support particularism more than they do inclusivism. (1) Second Peter 3:1–2 anchors the discussion of salvation in 3:9 solidly within special revelation. (2) This same passage offers an illustration of fewness, not wideness, in salvation (3:6). (3) One should consult the book of Acts for Peter's own account of the relation between "repentance" and belief in the name of Jesus (e.g., Acts 2:38).

As for 1 Timothy 2:4, the passage identifies the target of God's desire with *two* infinitives—for all "to be saved," and for all "to come to knowledge of the truth." This implies that God's universal salvific will is for salvation to come *through* knowledge of "the man Christ Jesus" (v. 5), not apart from knowledge of him. Furthermore, verses 5–6 observe that there is one God and one mediator, "who gave himself a ransom for all." Finally, assuming that God's will is coextensive with his salvific plan, inclusivists would, it seems, be compelled to argue that 1 Timothy 2:4 teaches universal *salvation* (that is, universalism) and not merely universal *access* to salvation. As has been observed, inclusivists confuse God's wider heart with wider hope.

The "Faith Principle"

When asked how universal access to salvation is accomplished, inclusivists often appeal to the so-called "faith principle," which they believe is expressed in Hebrews 11:6. According to this principle, saving faith has a theocentric focus rather than a Christocentric object. Inclusivists see this principle operating in the Old Testament on the part of those who were redeemed apart from special revelation—for example, Melchizedek, Job, Jethro, and others. The inference is that the same principle operates today in connection with the unevangelized.

This line of reasoning faces certain difficulties. First, those saved prior to the Incarnation were always the recipients of special revelation to which they had responded in faith. Clearly, the individuals identified by inclusivists in defense of their proposal had received special revelation: Enoch (Gen. 5:22); Job (Job 39–42); Noah, "a preacher of righteousness" (2 Peter 2:5); Melchizedek, the king of righteousness; Jethro, father-in-law of the one to whom Yahweh was revealed (see Ex. 18:11); Naaman (2 Kings 5:15); the Queen of Sheba (2 Chron. 9:8); Nebuchadnezzar (Dan. 4:34–37); even the inhabitants of Nineveh (Jonah 3:5). Thus, these figures are not among the untold, strictly speaking. Again, anyone who believes otherwise owns a weighty burden of proof.[48]

Second, Hebrews 1:1–2 states, as the thesis of the letter, that at a particular moment in history the focus of special revelation has narrowed to the incarnate Son. Thus chronology cannot be dismissed. The point is that now salvation is available only through an explicit faith in Jesus Christ.

---

[48]The inclusivist faces further difficulties. Supposing that Hebrews 11:6 teaches a "faith principle," one would still have to insist at the very least on belief in the existence of a personal God. Thus, the sincere Hindu and Buddhist, as well as the ethical agnostic or atheist, would still not be eligible for salvation. Furthermore, inclusivists cannot accuse particularists that allow for the possibility of infant salvation of inconsistency, because infants do not fall within the scope of the application of the inclusivist faith principle. See Richard, *Population of Heaven*, ch. 5.

The "Logos Doctrine"

Inclusivists argue further that the second eternal Person of the Trinity is the unique Logos. The evangelical inclusivist, Clark Pinnock, writes, for example:

> Though Jesus Christ is Lord, we confess at the same time that the Logos is not confined to one segment of human history or one piece of world geography. . . . God the Logos has more going on by way of redemption than what happened in first-century Palestine.[49]

Because the Logos "gives light to every man" (John 1:9), one can be saved by the universal Logos apart from specific knowledge of the incarnate Logos.

This is mistaken. The verb "gives light" ($\phi\omega\tau i\zeta\epsilon\iota$) cannot refer to successfully causing salvation, for that would imply universalism, since the light goes into all the world.[50] Nor does it seem to refer to inner illumination. What then does the verb mean? D. A. Carson argues persuasively that John has in mind the Incarnation. The light is a divine invasion that divides the human race, forcing distinctions (John 3:19–21; 8:12; 9:39–41) as it shines on every person—regardless of whether he or she sees it or receives it (1:13–14).[51] Thus, it is in the Incarnation that this light comes to the world.

In any case, John's entire point is that the Logos became incarnate (1:14), not that there is salvation through the nonincarnate and universal Logos $\check{\alpha}\sigma\alpha\rho\kappa o\varsigma$.[52] John's Logos is not dimly theocentric; it is brightly Christocentric.[53]

---

[49]Clark H. Pinnock, *A Wideness In God's Mercy: The Finality of Jesus Christ in a World of Religions* (Grand Rapids: Zondervan, 1992), 77.

[50]Perhaps the clearest passage on the effectual cause of salvation is Rom. 1:16, where that cause is identified as belief in the gospel.

[51]Carson, *Gospel According to John*, 124.

[52]See James E. Bradley, "*Logos* Christology and Religious Pluralism: A New Evangelical Proposal," *Proceedings of the Wheaton Theology Conference* 1 (Spring 1992): 190–207.

[53]On the Incarnation as a modality of revelation, see Ramm, *Special Revelation and the Word of God*, 106–22.

Alleged "Wideness" Texts

Inclusivists also frequently cite texts that seem to them to reflect God's benign or even optimistic attitude toward other religions. Acts 10:35 is often identified as a clear statement of wide salvific hope, since God "accepts men from every nation who fear him and do what is right."[54] However, verses 34–35 clearly emphasize God's impartiality in his provision of salvation. That is, anyone, regardless of nationality, may believe and be saved.[55] Furthermore, we believe that when the "wideness" passages are studied in context, they do not support the inclusivist position. Acts 10:43, appearing in the context of 10:35 but generally ignored by inclusivists, indicates the sort of fear that results in divine approval: "everyone who believes *in him* receives forgiveness of sins *through his name*."

The "Cornelius Paradigm"

Finally, inclusivists often suggest that the case of Cornelius should serve as a paradigm of God's redemptive pattern among the unevangelized. According to John Sanders, "Cornelius was already a saved believer *before* Peter arrived, but he was now a Christian believer."[56] Clark Pinnock writes that if anyone could be saved on the basis of spiritual character ("direction of the heart") apart from further revelation, it would seem to be Cornelius the God-fearer. But does this case support the inclusivist claim that salvation is available prior to receiving information about Jesus Christ?

To be sure, Cornelius was a devout man, a man of prayer, a man respected for his integrity in a culturally diverse society. However, the Cornelius case does not support the inclusivist position regarding the salvation of the "untold." (1) The point

---

[54] See, for example, Pinnock, *Wideness in God's Mercy*, pp. 32, 96, 105, and 165; and, John Sanders, *No Other Name: An Investigation into the Destiny of the Unevangelized* (Grand Rapids: Eerdmans, 1992), 28, 223.

[55] We should add that other alleged "wideness" texts may not envision salvific blessing, for God's blessing on humanity is not limited to saving persons from their sins. God is indeed the benevolent Father of all (Matt. 5:45; Acts 14:15–17; 17:28–29; James 1:17). See Richard, *Population of Heaven*, 41 (cf. p. 61).

[56] Sanders, "Is Belief in Christ Necessary for Salvation?" 254.

of the entire episode was to show to everyone the ongoing and far-reaching mission mandate of God (Acts 1:8). Peter and the church needed to learn that salvation was also for the Gentiles. (2) Cornelius's salvation was regarded as still future: "you will be saved" (11:14). (3) That salvation was tied to special revelation: This "God-fearer" received a vision with instructions to send for Peter and await his message (10:1–6, 22, 33; 11:14). (4) The result of Cornelius's action was not more information only, but redemption as well (11:15). (5) The focus of Cornelius's new faith was explicitly Christological (10:43, 48; 11:17). If anything, Cornelius is an example of a sinner, even a God-fearing one, who responded to special revelation concerning Jesus so that he might be saved.[57]

In short, inclusivists adopt strained interpretations of selected texts and then impose them as controls on the meanings of those texts that strongly support particularism.[58] It is characteristic of inclusivist hermeneutics that once a *logically possible* "wideness" interpretation of Scripture is conceived, it comes to term as a *probability* and is born and celebrated as a virtual *certainty*. If inclusivists own the burden of proof, it appears that they have not shouldered the burden well.

CONCLUSION

We have presented a particularist position regarding the significance of religious diversity. In our view, Christianity is uniquely true, and explicit faith in Jesus Christ is a necessary condition for salvation. Our commitment to the singular truth of Christianity distinguishes us from religious pluralists. Our conviction that the Bible presents faith in Jesus Christ as a necessary condition for salvation distinguishes us from inclusivists.

---

[57]See John 6:45.

[58]For example, on Jesus' statement regarding the small gate and the narrow road (Matt. 7:13–14), Pinnock remarks that "at the time when he spoke this warning the number of disciples was few" (Pinnock, *Wideness In God's Mercy*, 154; see also his comments on Rev. 1:7, p. 153). This implausibly suggests that the "narrow way" statements are no longer applicable today. John Sanders argues unconvincingly that when Peter mentions "those who fear God" in Acts 10:2, he is referring to "those who trust and obey God to the extent of the revelation they have" (Sanders, "Is Belief in Christ Necessary for Salvation?" 254; see also his *No Other Name*, 66).

Our approach is "evidentialist" in the sense that we believe that particularism is the position best supported by the available biblical and extrabiblical evidence. We have surveyed a portion of that evidence, beginning with reasons to believe that there is a personal Creator of the universe who takes an interest in the human condition and proceeding to the biblical data concerning the conditions God has set for the salvation of persons.

In conclusion, we wish to clarify our view of the strength of particularism as compared with the main alternative attitudes towards religious diversity. When weighing a position like ours, it is not enough to consider the positive support it enjoys. The full strength of our position can only be appreciated as it is compared with the hypotheses of religious pluralism and inclusivism. Very little of what humans have come to believe is entirely immune to criticism. A position that may be true but is as yet neither decisively demonstrated nor decisively refuted is sometimes said to be "defeasible." We hold that all the positions presented in this book are defeasible in this sense. This consideration leads us to make the following observations.

First, contrary to popular belief, particularism does not entail dogmatism. While some defenders of Christian particularism have sometimes spoken in a strident and dogmatic tone, pluralism and inclusivism have their dogmatic exponents as well. But critics of particularism need to keep in mind that conviction about the truth of one's position is compatible with awareness of the defeasibility of one's position. Many have insisted that interreligious dialogue must take the exclusive form of seeking to understand one another. We believe there is also room within appropriate interreligious dialogue for trying to convince one another.[59]

Second, even if we assume epistemic parity for particularism, inclusivism, and pluralism—where the question would then be too close to call on the available evidence—it would seem more *prudent* to adopt the particularist position over that of either the inclusivist or the pluralist.[60] One way to appreciate

---

[59]See Griffiths, "Why We Need Interreligious Polemics."

[60]If we assume epistemic parity for these three positions, then, by the nature of the case, Christian particularism is at least as reasonable as either inclusivism or pluralism. Some defenders of exclusivism have relied almost entirely upon this type of consideration. See, for example, Alvin Plantinga, "A Defense of Religious Exclu-

this point is to ask: What are the stakes if both pluralism and inclusivism happen to be wrong and particularism happens to be right? If the pluralist is right, there is little danger in promoting either inclusivism or particularism. If the inclusivist is right, there is little danger in promoting particularism, though it would be risky to promote pluralism. But if the particularist is right—and, on the supposition of epistemic parity, he is about as likely to be right—then there is great danger in promoting either inclusivism or pluralism. If particularism is true, then pluralism and inclusivism offer dangerously misleading assessments of the human condition and of the prospects for resolving the human predicament. The inclusivist should want to have especially good evidence for his or her position before reposing in it and commending it to others, given the risks involved if that position is wrong—and the religious pluralist even more so.

Third, we doubt that Christian particularism stands in epistemic parity with either pluralism or inclusivism. From where we stand, religious pluralism seems to be seriously defective in light of the abundant evidence for the existence of a personal, self-revealing God of biblical proportions. And inclusivism seems to be suspect in light of the biblical data. It is not as if the Bible is so unclear that we have no idea what God plans to do with the unevangelized.

In sum, we have not argued merely for the coherence of our position; we have argued that it is true. It does not follow from this that we are not aware of the defeasibility of our postion. Still, we recommend it as more than an interesting logical possibility that can meet common criticisms. Viewed as a hypothesis, Christian particularism seems to us to offer the best explanation of a wide range of facts about God and human existence. If there are unresolved difficulties for all three positions, and if the evidence is not "conclusive" in the strongest sense of the term, Christian particularism offers the most intellectually and spiritually satisfying account of the available evidence with a minimum of difficulty.[61]

---

sivism," in *Philosophy of Religion: An Anthology*, ed. Louis P. Pojman, 2d ed. (Belmont, Calif.: Wadsworth, 1994), 529–31.

[61]We wish to thank William Lane Craig, J. P. Moreland, Steve Porter, Ernie Ricketts, and David Talley for helpful comments on portions of the material we have written for this volume.

RESPONSE TO R. DOUGLAS GEIVETT AND W. GARY PHILLIPS

John Hick

Geivett/Phillips have given an exposition of full-blooded Christian exclusivism[1]—yet not quite, for they prefer to avoid the accurate term "exclusivism," adopting instead the less harsh-sounding, though meaningless, term "particularism." This term is meaningless because everything is particular, so that to describe Christianity as particular is to say nothing particular about it! I see their revised language, however, as a good sign. They are conscious that a frank exclusivism, which accepts the implications of their view that "individual salvation depends on explicit personal faith in Jesus Christ"—namely, that the large majority of the human race are condemned by God to eternal perdition—is so morally and religiously revolting that they cannot bring themselves to say it explicitly. But I will return presently to the moral impossibility of Christian exclusivism.

NATURAL THEOLOGY

Let me comment first on Geivett/Phillips' natural theology. I must begin by correcting their reference to my own view that the universe is religiously ambiguous, "so that we must remain firmly agnostic about the existence and nature of God." This is a

---

[1]For the sake of convenience, I will use the composite Geivett/Phillips in responding to R. Douglas Geivett and W. Gary Phillips.

misapprehension. As I have argued in *An Interpretation of Religion*, that the universe is religiously ambiguous means that it is capable of being consistently and comprehensively interpreted, from our present position within it, in both religious and naturalistic ways.[2] This does not mean that it cannot be interpreted in either way, so that one has to be agnostic about it. Nor does it mean that the universe has no definite character or structure, so that neither interpretation is in fact correct. If the religious interpretation is correct, its truth will be verified in the eschaton. To borrow an image from John Bunyan, the believer and unbeliever are like two people walking along a road, one convinced that it leads to the Celestial City and the other that it leads nowhere. Although the issue between them cannot be settled until they turn the last corner, it will then be apparent that one of them was in fact right all the time and the other wrong.

This conception of the religious ambiguity of the universe is based on the judgment that all the philosophical arguments both for and against the existence of God are inconclusive, both individually and collectively. This includes Geivett/Phillips' argument that the universe must have a beginning and therefore a personal Creator. The strong reasons at present to think that the universe as we now observe it began with the Big Bang of some ten to twenty billions years ago do not entail that the Big Bang was an absolute beginning. One model under discussion in scientific cosmology is that of a beginningless and endless series of expansions and contractions. Geivett/Phillips seek to rule this out by the philosophical argument, advocated by William Craig, that if the universe as a whole is eternal, with no beginning, the present moment could not exist because an infinite series of moments would have to have transpired before it; and since an infinite series can never be completed, the present moment could never be arrived at. This argument seems to me completely unconvincing. If the universe comprises an infinite series of moments, each "present moment" is one of them! From a given moment—such as when you began to read this book— the series of past moments stretches back endlessly. But this series of past moments does not have to be finite for this or any

---

[2]John Hick, *An Interpretation of Religion* (New Haven: Yale Univ. Press, 1989 / London: Macmillan, 1989), Part 2.

other present moment to exist. Thus the Craig/Geivett/Phillips argument is in my opinion fallacious.

Having argued on logical grounds—but mistakenly, as I have suggested—that the universe must have an absolute beginning, Geivett/Phillips' claim (and here I agree with them) that *if* it had an absolute beginning, there must have been a pre-existing cause to bring it into existence. But, of course, if their premise of an absolute beginning has not been established, their conclusion is also not established. And their further argument that such a cause must be "an agent on the order of personal being, yet surpassing human persons in greatness" is, in my opinion, again fallacious. Their argument is that we human beings act as first causes whenever we initiate a free act. But in doing so, we only act as relative first causes, requiring the existence of the world in which we act, and not as the absolute first cause that began the universe—if it did indeed have a beginning. There is no true analogy here to the creation of the universe out of nothing. So far as we can know purely by philosophical reasoning, the Big Bang that began what we call our universe may have been an incident in the history of a temporally more extensive universe of which ours is a phase.

It thus seems to me that Geivett/Phillips' philosophical arguments are such as to convince only those who already believe their conclusion. They would never convince a thoughtful agnostic. Of course, in arguing against arguments for the existence of God I am not arguing against the existence of God! Philosophical considerations can show the real possibility of divine existence and can thus open the door to religious belief; however, it is not philosophy but religious experience that propels anyone through the door. The appropriate apologetic is thus not an argument directly for the existence of God, but an argument for the rationality of forming beliefs on the basis of experience, including religious experience. But that is another discussion.

THE AUTHORITY OF SCRIPTURE

I now turn to Geivett/Phillips' use of the New Testament, which is that of the ultra-conservative wing of Christianity, far removed from contemporary mainline biblical scholarship. It is impossible in this context to do more than note this and alert a conservative readership to the fact that there is a vast gap between Geivett/Phillips' use of the texts and that which they would find in such acknowledged centers of scholarship as Harvard, Yale, Chicago, Princeton, Vanderbilt, Duke, and Claremont.

For example, Geivett/Phillips speak of "Jesus Christ, who both claimed to be God and corroborated his claim by rising from the dead," and say that "according to the best historical evidence, we have no less than four reliable accounts (namely, the Gospels of the New Testament) of the main events of the life of Jesus *and of his self-understanding as God*" (italics mine). But even conservative New Testament scholars, who are personally orthodox in their beliefs, are agreed today that Jesus did not teach that he was God. I have quoted some—including Moule, Dunn, and Archbishop Ramsay—in my own chapter in this book, and I need not repeat that here. Geivett/Phillips write as though they thought of the four Gospels as contemporary eye-witness reports. But the earliest Gospel, Mark, is generally dated around 70 A.D., forty years after Jesus' death, with Matthew and Luke in the 80s and John in the last decade of the first century. None of the writers was among Jesus' original disciples, and none was present at the events they describe. Each is dependent on oral or written sources embodying traditions that had developed over several decades, and each works his material up from his own individual point of view. The most recent major lives of Jesus—John Dominic Crossan's *The Historical Jesus* (1991) and *Jesus* (1994), and E. P. Sanders' *The Historical Figure of Jesus* (1993)—do not support the Geivett/Phillips' picture of Jesus at all. It is impossible to go here into detailed questions of New Testament exegesis; but it is important to note that the Geivett/Phillips line flies in the face of most modern biblical scholarship.

THE MORAL DIFFICULTY WITH PARTICULARISM

Finally, the exclusivist (renamed particularist) view that salvation is confined to those who explicitly take Jesus as their Lord and Savior has such horrifying implications that it is hard to believe that Geivett/Phillips have thought these through. They do not do so in their chapter. The implication is that the large majority of the human race thus far have, through no fault of their own, been consigned to eternal perdition, and that in the future an even larger proportion will meet this fate, for while the number of Christians in the world is increasing, the proportion of Christians within the human population is decreasing. In 1960 the Congress on World Mission at Chicago said, "In the years since the war [i.e., since 1945], more than one billion souls have passed into eternity and more than half of these went to the torment of hell fire without even hearing of Jesus Christ, who He was, or why He died on the cross of Calvary."[3] Today the number of the damned must, in the dark imagination of Christian fundamentalists, be much greater. But can it possibly be the will of the loving heavenly Father of Jesus' teaching that only that minority of men and women who have the luck to be born into a Christian part of the world can enter eternal life? This would not be the work of a God of limitless and universal love, who values all human beings equally, but of an arbitrary cosmic tyrant, more fit to be reviled as the devil than to be worshiped as God.

---

[3]J. O. Percy, ed., *Facing the Unfinished Task: Messages Delivered at the Congress on World Mission* (Grand Rapids: Eerdmans, 1961), 9.

RESPONSE TO R. DOUGLAS GEIVETT AND W. GARY PHILLIPS

Clark H. Pinnock

One reason for writing *A Wideness in God's Mercy* (1992) was to stimulate restrictivists, who predominate in the leadership of evangelicalism, to explain their position better and to join the wider debate over religious pluralism. I wanted to discover whether a more moderate version of Christ-centered theology in relation to the unevangelized in other religions (inclusivism) might win the acceptance among theologians that it is gaining among evangelical people. I was hoping that a more lenient position might come to prevail, knowing what a burden restrictivism can be for sensitive souls. A response has been forthcoming—witness this chapter and the two book responses by Ronald Nash and Ramesh Richard cited, to which can be added *The Other Side of the Good News* by Larry Dixon.[1] A number of scholars are mounting a defense of the view expressed in this chapter, which I call soteriologically restrictive exclusivism. Two issues are intertwined here—salvation and the role of religion in God's plan. As regards salvation, Geivett and Phillips are restrictivists; as regards the role of other religions, they are exclusivists.

This is not their preferred terminology. They call themselves particularists who conduct themselves in an evidentialist way. Theirs is unusual terminology, and not a little misleading, since

---

[1] See footnote 3 in the Geivett/Phillips chapter; see also Larry Dixon, *The Other Side of Good News* (Wheaton, Ill.: Victor Books, 1992).

McGrath and myself are particularists also—confessing Jesus Christ as the one Mediator between God and humanity. Nevertheless, terminology aside, they present a coherent point of view and one distinct from the three other offerings. Their fourth option is a restrictivist variant of exclusivism.

The Geivett/Phillips' chapter employs the two-stage format of classical apologetics, beginning with theistic arguments and going on to historical evidence. In the first phase, theism is defended as the best worldview over against other options—in this case, Hick's view of the undifferentiated Real; in the second, historical evidence is adduced to confirm Christianity as the truest form of theism, in order to show against my position that restrictivism and not inclusivism enjoys the strongest biblical foundations. This is a large double-barreled task. Their confidence in human reason to achieve it marks the approach as modern as well as classical.

As a person interested in apologetics, I am sympathetic with what they are trying to do with general revelation in the first phase. Reminiscent of Pannenberg's program, they want to show the rationality of belief in God, in order to put the core of the Christian message on a firm intellectual footing. This aim suffers, however, from a major disadvantage, because owing to restrictions of space, they are compelled to pass over major steps in the argument. They are able to offer only a brief sketch of their rather bold position, which is situated within a densely argued field of inquiry. Every move invites an extensive response. As a result, they cannot really claim to have proved much here. All they have done is declare that they believe such a proof can be formulated if only they had the pages. Ironically, John Hick has written extensively about these matters in the philosophy of religion and is not likely to be persuaded by this sketch.

Another facet of this phase interests me. Exclusivists do not normally emphasize general revelation so strongly. This is because it might seem to imply that God, having revealed himself to all persons, might actually be trying to save sinners outside the church, something they usually deny. For this reason, Karl Barth, the foremost exclusivist, would have nothing to do with general revelation, because to allow such a category would be to admit a possible rival to revelation in Jesus Christ. One might begin to think that God has other plans afoot for saving humanity before the gospel arrives. Barth was wrong to deny general revelation but right to sense the implication. General revelation points to the mercy of God graciously providing all people with a revelation of himself, supporting the model of inclusivism.

The odd thing here is that you have general revelation without grace. We are told to believe that special revelation is gracious, but general revelation itself is not. It is as if God reveals himself to all people in such a way that the revelation is incapable of helping them to be saved, even though they lack any other possibility. What a strange circumstance!

As for special revelation in the second phase of the chapter, it is interpreted to be saying that although Christ has achieved salvation for the world, access to this benefit is limited. It seems that one who lacks access to the message and cannot exercise faith in Jesus before death cannot be saved, even though he or she is included in the atonement (1 John 2:2). There is no provision for them, God having neglected to supply prevenient grace to help those who did not hear through no fault of their own. As a result, our authors acknowledge that only a few will be saved and that exceptions to the scenario will be rare. If God does not use general revelation to help people, obviously he does not use other religions either. It requires only a couple of lines to state that the Bible views religions other than Christianity as nonredemptive at best and as demonic at worst. What this amounts to is that there is no opportunity of salvation for the majority of the human race. Although this imposes an appalling moral difficulty, we are assured that God's Word teaches it and that we are required to believe it.

Fortunately, these assertions are not so. Relief comes in the form of pieces of evidence that the evidentialists have not reckoned with. Most important is the evidence that speaks of the boundless grace of God. Jesus tells us that God loves to be generous beyond what anyone would expect (Matt. 20:15–16). The restrictivists do not grasp the large dimensions of the divine love (Eph. 3:18). They miss the rainbow of hope around the throne of God (Rev. 4:3). Yes, in Paul's words, God has imprisoned all sinners in disobedience, but in order that he might have mercy on them all (Rom. 11:32). In a nutshell, God desires all to be saved and to come to a knowledge of the truth (1 Tim. 2:4). The reason restrictivism is in decline in the churches is that Christians, more than previously, understand the primacy of the universal salvific will of God and will not accept a theology that tells them God allows most to perish without lifting a finger to help.

This failure to grasp the extent of God's mercy prevents our authors from noticing other pieces of relevant data from special revelation that indicate wider hope. The entire Old Testament record is a problem for them because it describes countless pagans and Jews who were saved by faith without knowing Jesus or calling on his name—all saved by faith even though they had no Christian theology. Unless we assume that God is stricter and less generous after Easter than before (a strange assumption indeed!), we must suppose that God responds to all sinners who call on him, whether they employ Christian language or not. As Peter puts it, God "accepts men from every nation who fear him and do what is right" (Acts 10:35).

Insensitivity to divine mercy also blocks their sight of the positive side to the witness in Scripture about human religion. Melchizedek, Abimelech, and Job were all godly men of faith in regions beyond Israel, men of ancient Near Eastern culture and religion. The magi who came from the East to worship Jesus were astrologers, and it was a Roman centurion who had the kind of faith that Jesus longed to find among his own people. Cornelius too was a devout and God-fearing man, who had a good relationship with God and with whom God had dealings prior to Christian conversion. We do not deny that the Bible condemns evil in human religions. But it also testifies to the truth and nobility that can be found there by the grace of God. I fear that restrictivism may prevent people from seeing truth and goodness that result from God's grace working in other people and hide from them the spirit of Jesus, who regards deeds of love done to the poor as done for him (Matt. 25:40). He has a generous spirit and can detect the seed of faith evidenced in good works in those who are unaware of any relation to himself.

There is an attempt in the Geivett/Phillips chapter to use isolated proof texts to cover over the unwanted evidence. The reader may judge what is right. I maintain that Peter does not address the issue of the unevangelized in Acts 4:12 and that Paul does not address it in Romans 10. Both apostles are speaking about messianic salvation, which has come as the fulfillment of, not as a negation of, revelation that came before. They are celebrating the beauty of the gospel of Christ, not decrying earlier forms of the gracious divine working on which people had to depend before the gospel came.

Let me close with a hard question: "Is God's grace limited to the relatively few who, often through accidents of time and geography, happen to have responded to the gospel?"[2] No, certainly not.

---

[2]Ronald Nash, *Is Jesus the Only Savior?* (Grand Rapids: Zondervan, 1994), p. 24.

RESPONSE TO R. DOUGLAS GEIVETT AND W. GARY PHILLIPS

Alister E. McGrath

The Geivett/Phillips' chapter is a lucid statement of a particularist approach to the issue of religious pluralism. I was impressed by the way in which several strands of argument were woven together, bringing out both the inherent rationality and the explicative potential of the Christian faith. It is clear that this type of approach is attractive to many evangelicals, and this well-argued and thoughtful chapter makes the reasons for this attraction clear. There are many minor points over which I would greatly like to interact with the writers. However, I think it may be of more use to readers of this volume if I identify a single major question that formed in my mind as I read and reflected on this paper.

The question that emerged is simply this: Is the knowledge of God that can be had from general revelation *saving?* The general thrust of the argument presented by Geivett/Phillips is that a number of general factors, none of which can be considered to be "particular revelation," lead us "to expect that a particular revelation, answering to the specific needs of the human condition, might be provided by God." In other words, there are adequate "pointers" in the natural order to enable an individual to realize that a saving particular revelation is to be expected. That is, one can expect that there is a "focus of God's universal redemptive plan in the person and work of Jesus Christ, who must be the object of explicit faith by those who want to be saved."

The difficulty I have with this approach is primarily apologetic in orientation. I believe it is a significant observation, as it highlights the considerable difference between the approach of Geivett and Phillips on the one hand, and that of Pinnock on the other. What happens to those who, through no fault of their own, are not granted the possibility of hearing of Jesus Christ and are thus unable to place *explicit* faith in him? I fully concede that Geivett and Phillips have laid a firm foundation for their argument that natural revelation points to the means of redemption being available. But what if that means is denied through the force of historical circumstances? A similar point is made by Augustine:

> Now the inhabitants of Tyre and Sidon would have believed, if they had seen Christ's wonderful signs. However, because it was not given to them to believe, the means of believing were also denied them [*quoniam ut crederent, non erat eis datum, etiam unde crederent est negatum*]. From this, it seems that certain people have naturally in their minds a divine gift of perception, by which they may be moved to faith, if they hear the words or see the signs compatible with their intellect [*si congrua suis mentibus*]. But if, by virtue of a hidden divine judgment, these people have not been separated from the mass of perdition by the predestination of grace, then these divine words or deeds—through which they would have been able to believe, if they had heard or seen them—are not inviting them.[1]

In other words, the inhabitants of Tyre and Sidon would have been able to come to a saving faith, if only they were allowed to hear of Christ.

The issue is primarily apologetic in that it raises a fundamental question concerning the *fairness* of God. I am sure that a similar concern may underlie the position of John Hick and other pluralists, who raise questions concerning the finality and the salvific efficacy of the Christian faith that they consider are not adequately answered by some Christian theologies. In a period of evangelical history when evangelization has once more

---

[1]*De dono perseverantiae*, 14.35; in *Oeuvres de Saint Augustin*, ed. J. Chene and J. Pintard (Paris: de Brouwer, 1962), 680–82.

come to the fore, apologetic questions remain of major importance. What does one say to a young Chinese student who has become a Christian, and yet whose parents, back in the rural heartland of the Peoples' Republic of China, have never heard of Christ? He is naturally concerned for their spiritual welfare and destiny. I think it is this kind of pastoral concern that makes me a little hesitant concerning the approach taken by Geivett and Phillips.

Perhaps the issue is simply one of space, in that the limitations understandably imposed on the authors by the editors of this volume have prevented Geivett and Phillips from dealing with this issue in any depth. Yet it is a real question for many. It also raises a major theological question: Does salvation depend on human preaching of the gospel? In other words, are God's human servants in a position to determine whether or not someone is saved by virtue of whether they preach the gospel or not? This issue focuses on the interaction of human responsibility and divine sovereignty.[2] I found myself wondering if the approach offered in this chapter, with its distinctive emphasis on the need for an explicit faith, ended up making God a hostage to human weakness. But let me stress that this question is not fully addressed by Geivett and Phillips, and it is possible that they may be able to accommodate this anxiety in an apologetically and theologically acceptable manner.

I have raised this issue partly because I believe it to be important in its own right, but also because I am aware that concern over the apologetic questions it raises are known to have been of considerable influence in moving some towards pluralism (in the belief that it has a better answer to this "fairness" question than evangelicalism), and particularly in causing some evangelicals to explore alternative options within the Christian tradition, such as the concept of the *logos spermatikos*. I would suspect that this difficulty would be noted by Clark Pinnock, who is clearly sensitive to this consideration and has attempted to forge a response that remains faithful to Scripture, yet addresses this concern.

---

[2]This issue is thoroughly explored by James I. Packer, *Evangelism and the Sovereignty of God* (Downers Grove, Ill.: InterVarsity, 1961).

CONCLUSION

R. Douglas Geivett and W. Gary Phillips

REPLY TO MCGRATH

Alister McGrath singles out one major question regarding our approach to particularism. He asks, "Is the knowledge of God that can be had from general revelation *saving*?" He realizes, of course, that we have offered a tentative negative answer to this question. But McGrath is concerned that our position erects a needless obstacle to the progress of the gospel among others concerned about divine fairness. And he seems to think that God does save at least some who never have the opportunity to hear.

McGrath's own example, cited also by Augustine, is of the inhabitants of Tyre and Sidon, who "would have been able to come to a saving faith, if only they were allowed to hear of Christ" (see Matt. 11:20–24). This is an interesting example, for, if it is literally true and not simply hyperbolical, it hardly supports McGrath's thesis. Apparently, the denizens of Tyre and Sidon were never saved. On a strictly literal reading of Jesus' words, these were people (1) who did not hear but (2) would have believed had they heard and yet (3) did not experience salvation. That is, this kind of literalism itself implies that their salvation was forfeited through the sheer force of historical circumstances.

Our own view is that Jesus' reference to the people of Tyre and Sidon is hyperbolical. His point is not that they would actually have believed if they had been in the same situation as his first-century audience, but that his first-century audience was even more obstinate than these ancient peoples who were known for their rebellion against God.

McGrath anticipates that Pinnock and Hick will raise similar concerns about the fairness of God's judgment of the unevangelized. Since they do indeed stress this point, Pinnock calling it "an appalling moral difficulty" and Hick judging it to be a "moral impossibility," we address this issue in our replies to them.

REPLY TO PINNOCK

Clark Pinnock divides his critical comments into two parts. In the first part he raises two objections to our sketch of an argument for the existence of a personal Creator of the universe who takes an interest in the spiritual concerns of his human creatures.

His first objection is that our natural theology is so sketchy that someone like John Hick "is not likely to be persuaded." But we do not consider Hick's resistance to this strategy to be an index of its value. (Our reply to Hick addresses his specific objections.) As for Pinnock himself, we notice that he offers no specific objections. While we agree that our presentation is concise, we do not think we have passed over any major steps. Of course, we do not expect anyone to think we have attempted a complete natural theology within a few pages. Our objective was the more modest one of illustrating how a program of natural theology might support the exclusivism that is traditionally and correctly associated with Christianity. Certainly, our confidence in the possibility of natural theology at least partially explains our own commitment to Christian particularism.

Pinnock's second objection is that the availability of general revelation implies the provision of salvation apart from special revelation, and that we fail to acknowledge that implication. Pinnock has not made it easy to detect the implication, however. We hold that general revelation is epistemically valuable, even if not soteriologically efficacious. Furthermore, we have not denied that general revelation is gracious, as Pinnock avers. God's provision of grace need not be limited to soteriological objectives. There are numerous ways in which general revelation evinces the grace of God without producing the salvation of the unevangelized. And we doubt that the possibility of a rich natural theology makes it more likely that Pinnock's inclusivism is true.

In the second part of his response, Pinnock challenges our presentation of the biblical evidence in support of our version of particularism. We make five observations in response. First, unlike the other contributors (including Pinnock), we have patiently examined a series of Scripture texts that seem obviously to bear on the central question of this book. Yet we are accused of "proof-texting." Pinnock's own terse handling of texts is to our minds more indicative of this questionable approach to Scripture. (We invite readers to stop right now and read Revelation 4:3 to see if they can figure out what this text has to do with Pinnock's inclusivist thesis.) At any rate, we agree with several lessons he draws from Scripture. For example, it is certainly true that "God loves to be generous beyond what anyone would expect" (Matt. 20:15–16). We suppose, however, that the love of Christ *for every individual saint* is "wide and long and high and deep" (Eph. 3:18), and that the specific number of the redeemed is not a measure of this love.

Second, Pinnock must be careful in his appeal to such texts as 1 John 2:2 and Romans 11:32, lest he be hoist by his own petard. Unless he holds that universalism is true—that all human persons will be saved—how can he be sure that his way of making sense of the final judgment of some is not available to the exclusivist, who holds that there are few who will be saved? Pinnock claims that God's mercy extends to all, and we agree. But on Pinnock's own account of what this offer of mercy involves, it is unclear how any can remain unsaved.

Third, he speaks of "those who did not hear through no fault of their own." Presumably, Pinnock is referring here to a possible class of persons who never hear the Christian gospel but would believe if they did hear. But we doubt that Pinnock knows that there actually are such persons. If there are no persons who never hear but would believe if they did hear (because all who would believe have heard), then we fail to see the "appalling moral difficulty" Pinnock envisions. We would not be surprised if the majority of those who do hear withhold belief in Jesus Christ and remain unsaved, nor would we be prepared to blame God for this outcome of human freedom.

Fourth, Pinnock seems not to have noticed that we have addressed his question about Old Testament saints in our essay. It is disappointing that he does not directly address our position on that matter.

Finally, he says he fears that our view "may prevent people from seeing truth and goodness that result from God's grace working in other people and hide from them the spirit of Jesus." But our position does not entail that God's grace is withheld from people of other faiths. There is reason to fear the practical lessons concerning evangelism that people might draw about Pinnock's position, a point we develop in our response to his chapter elsewhere in this volume.

We do not mean to cover over any of the evidence relevant to this important discussion. Rather, we describe the position we think makes the best sense of the total evidence, including those elements Pinnock chooses to emphasize.

REPLY TO HICK

John Hick files three general complaints: (1) Our sketch of natural theology falters on several levels; (2) "Jesus did not teach that he was God"; and (3) Christian exclusivism is "morally impossible." We will respond to each of these.

Hick's Rejection of Natural Theology

Hick has long advocated the general futility of natural theology. Thus it is not surprising that he is unconvinced by our sketch of the evidence for God's existence and his interest in the human condition. But neither do we find Hick's objections impressive.

First, he insists on the viability of an oscillating model of the universe, a model run aground on the shoals of contemporary cosmology. As Chris Isham of The Blackett Laboratory, Imperial College, London, remarks:

> Perhaps the best argument in favour of the thesis that the Big Bang supports theism is the obvious unease with which it is greeted by some atheist physicists. At times this has led to scientific ideas, such as continuous creation or an oscillating universe, being advanced with a tenacity which so exceeds their intrinsic worth that one can

only suspect the operation of psychological forces lying very much deeper than the usual academic desire of a theorist to support his/her theory.[1]

The hypothesis that the universe had an absolute beginning currently enjoys greater support from the available evidence than any other cosmological theory.

Second, Hick proclaims the philosophical possibility of a beginningless universe, and our argument to the contrary is judged "fallacious." But we are not told what fallacy is committed, nor are we treated to an argument that the "series of past moments does not have to be finite for this or any other present moment to exist." The conditional statement, "If the universe comprises an infinite series of moments, each 'present moment' is one of them," looks innocent enough as a statement of what it would mean if the universe did not have a beginning (though there is here the faint hint of a controversial B-theory of time[2]). But we have argued against the truth of the antecedent, and Hick's *assertion* does not answer our *argument*.

Third, our argument for a personal cause of the beginning of the universe is said to be fallacious. Four observations are in order. (1) Notice that Hick does not deny our claim that if the universe had a beginning, it must have had a cause. The question is, what sort of cause would Hick favor? There are basically two possibilities, state-state causation and agent causation. State-state causation is obviously ruled out, for prior to the absolute beginning of the universe there would, by hypothesis, be no physical state of the universe that could cause the Big Bang. This leaves the only other familiar form of causation, namely, agent causation.

(2) While it is certainly true that human agency is presently conditioned by the actual existence of a physical world, human

---

[1]Chris J. Isham, "Creation of the Universe as a Quantum Process," in *Physics, Philosophy, and Theology: A Common Quest for Understanding*, ed. Robert J. Russell, William R. Stoeger, and George V. Coyne (Vatican City State: Vatican Observatory, 1988), 378.

[2]For a helpful introduction to the distinction between the A-theory of time and the B-theory of time, see Richard M. Gale, *The Language of Time* (London: Routledge & Kegan Paul / New York: Humanities Press, 1968), esp. 3–100, and the articles in Section II of Gale's edited volume, *The Philosophy of Time: A Collection of Essays* (London: Macmillan, 1968), 65–167.

persons are nevertheless self-determining creatures. And their acts of genuine agency, though they "require" the existence of the world in which they act, bring about real changes in the arrangement of things in the universe. Is this not a plausible model for divine action in producing the physical world even if such action is not conditioned by the presence of physical constraints?

(3) Furthermore, Hick has not shown that "there is no true analogy" between human agency and divine agency. The difference is that humans are only "relative first causes," whereas God is the absolute first cause. But how is this difference relevant to the success of our analogy? We agree with Hick's claim that there is a difference between human agency and divine agency, but not with his assumption that all agency requires a physical world for its operation.

(4) Finally, according to the Christian worldview, human agency is modeled after divine agency. Indeed, human agency itself is inexplicable apart from a theistic view of the world.[3]

Fourth, Hick asserts that theistic arguments only convince the already convinced and that religious experience is the only plausible basis for religious belief. But we know of individuals, including scientists and other mature intellectuals, who have been converted to theism in response to the sort of evidence we have presented. Furthermore, it is not surprising, given his strict dependence on the vagaries of religious experience, that Hick's own conception of God's nature is highly amorphous. The evidence of religious experience alone does not permit a precise account of the nature of divine reality. Indeed, the religious experiences of different individuals and communities yield conflicting accounts of religious reality. Relying exclusively on the data of religious experience, Hick would construct a frame of reference for understanding the specific nature of religious reality. But he neglects a far wider range of evidence, also presented in experience, that proves relevant to forming a religious view of reality. One measure of a person's religious convictions, based

---

[3]See J. P. Moreland, *Scaling the Secular City* (Grand Rapids: Baker, 1987), 77–103; Richard Swinburne, *The Existence of God*, (Oxford: Clarendon Press, 1979), 152–75; C. Stephen Layman, "Faith Has Its Reasons," in *God and the Philosophers: The Reconciliation of Faith and Reason*, ed. Thomas V. Morris (New York: Oxford Univ. Press, 1994), 94–97.

on personal religious experience, is the prior justification he or she has for the background beliefs brought to the experience. By denying a role for other evidence, however, Hick excludes a category of possible justification for those background beliefs that are so vital for making correct judgments about the value and significance of religious experience.[4]

Fifth, Hick denies that he is agnostic. Of course, we did not suggest that he is "firmly" agnostic but that he is "finally" agnostic. Hick has written elsewhere that the propositions of the various theistic religions should be regarded as "mythologically true" rather than "literally true," since we cannot be justified in claiming that any particular tradition's specific theology is literally true.[5] He sometimes appears to allow that some particular theological tradition (e.g., Christianity) may turn out to be true. But he maintains that, because the universe is "religiously ambiguous," we will not know that a particular tradition is true until we have "eschatological verification" of its truth. This is the sense in which Hick is agnostic. Of course, if he is right, traditional Christianity as we understand it cannot be true, for it envisions the possibility of specific religious *knowledge* in this life.

Jesus' Self-understanding

Hick observes that "even conservative New Testament scholars, who are personally orthodox in their beliefs, are agreed today that Jesus did not teach that he was God." On one of two possible readings, this claim is simply false; on the other, it is irrelevant. If Hick means that all or even the majority of "conservative New Testament scholars" who are "personally orthodox in their beliefs" agree that Jesus did not teach that he was God, then he is mistaken. It is fallacious, for example, to reason from a few examples of otherwise orthodox scholars (such as Moule, Dunn, and Ramsay) to the more general conclusion that their attitude is *representative* of conservative scholarship. Moreover, the conclusion is false. A clear majority of conservative

---

[4]This point is developed further in R. Douglas Geivett, "Is Jesus the Only Way?" in *Jesus Under Fire: Modern Scholarship Reinvents the Historical Jesus*, ed. Michael Wilkins and J. P. Moreland (Grand Rapids: Zondervan, 1995), 177–205.

[5]John Hick, *An Interpretation of Religion: Human Responses to the Transcendent* (London: Macmillan, 1989), 343–70.

scholars holds that Jesus did regard himself as God and that this self-understanding was recognized by those with whom he associated, whether or not they agreed with his self-understanding.[6]

If, on the other hand, Hick means only that there are a few conservative scholars who allow that Jesus did not teach that he was God, then this seems irrelevant. For this ignores what most conservative scholars now believe about Jesus' self-understanding and the reasons they offer on behalf of their views. The alleged fact that some conservative scholars do not share the view endorsed by the majority of conservative scholars does not entail that the majority is mistaken.

Furthermore, there are less conservative scholars who conclude that Jesus Christ did indeed rise from the dead, which we take to be further evidence of his deity even if they do not. For example, Pinchas Lapide, an eminent Jewish scholar of the New Testament, affirms the historical reality of the resurrection of Jesus, though he denies that Jesus was the Messiah of Israel.[7] And Wolfhart Pannenberg, professor at the University of Munich, while unwilling to consider the Gospels as in every respect historically reliable, is confident that "a strong argument in favor of the historicity of the Resurrection of Jesus can be given. . . . There are good and even superior reasons for claiming that the Resurrection of Jesus was a historical event, and consequently the risen Lord himself is a living reality."[8]

Hick seems intent on deciding questions of great spiritual significance by counting scholarly noses. He alludes to an artificial consensus among "contemporary mainline biblical scholars" in order to marginalize the more orthodox sector of the intellectual world, which he saddles with the onerous label "ultra-conservative." He incautiously invokes the authority of

[6]See, for example, Robert L. Reymond, *Jesus, Divine Messiah: The New Testament Witness* (Phillipsburg, N.J.: Presbyterian & Reformed, 1990), 44–126; David F. Wells, *The Person of Christ: A Biblical and Historical Analysis of the Incarnation* (Westchester, Ill.: Crossway, 1984), 32–51.

[7]See Pinchas Lapide, *The Resurrection of Jesus: A Jewish Perspective*, trans. Wilhelm C. Linss (Minneapolis: Augsburg, 1983); idem and Ulrich Luz, *Jesus in Two Perspectives: A Jewish-Christian Dialogue*, trans. Lawrence W. Denef (Minneapolis: Augsburg, 1985).

[8]See Wolfhart Pannenberg's comments on a public debate about the resurrection, in *Did Jesus Rise from the Dead? The Resurrection Debate*, ed. Terry L. Miethe (San Francisco: Harper & Row, 1987), 129, 132, 134–35.

figures at "acknowledged centers of scholarship" without reminding readers that many of these scholars presuppose a picture of the world that excludes the possibility of divine intervention in the world. American philosopher, William Alston, of Syracuse University, issues the following caveat about such appeals to the run of scholarly opinion:

> Let it be granted that the belief in such interventions runs counter to various features of the contemporary mindset. But unless we have reason to think that our age is distinguished from all others in being free of intellectual fads and fancies, of attachments to assumptions, paradigms, and models that far outstrip the available evidence, of believing things because one finds one's associates believing them, and so on, this is hardly of any probative value. I fear that theologians who appeal in this way to the contemporary climate of thought are doing nothing more intellectually respectable than considering what it takes to sell the product, or rather, what would inhibit the sale of the product.[9]

If it was Hick's policy always to adjust his opinion to what the majority of scholars think about a given subject, his own meteoric rise to stardom as a pluralistic revolutionary and revisionist Christian theologian would not have been possible. At any rate, we do not disdain the critical acumen of the numerous evangelical scholars who bear the same academic credentials that Hick celebrates, whether or not they happen to be teaching at centers of scholarship acknowledged by Hick.[10]

In our response to Hick's chapter earlier in this volume, we noted that there are several ways to illustrate Jesus' own self-understanding as God by appealing to the New Testament. Since Hick is so insistent that Jesus did not regard himself as God, we include here an additional line of argument for our position.

---

[9]William P. Alston, *Divine Nature and Human Language: Essays in Philosophical Theology* (Ithaca, N.Y.: Cornell Univ. Press, 1989), 210.

[10]For a recent example of evangelical scholarship regarding the identity of Jesus, see the essays in Wilkins and Moreland, *Jesus Under Fire*. See also Ben Witherington III, *The Jesus Quest: The Third Search for the Jew of Nazareth* (Downers Grove, Ill.: InterVarsity, 1995), and Gregory A. Boyd, *Cynic Sage or Son of God? Recovering the Real Jesus in an Age of Revisionist Replies* (Colorado Springs, Colo.: Bridgeport, 1995).

The radical critics' own tests of authenticity may be applied to certain sayings of Jesus generally excluded by these critics to certify that such sayings both ought to be included and clearly support the traditional view that Jesus regarded himself as God. For example, the "Son of Man" sayings should, by the critics' redoubtable *criterion of dissimilarity*, be judged no less authentic than the other sayings countenanced by those who employ this criterion. All strata of the Gospels tradition—Mark, Q, M, L, and John, which have dozens of instances of the phrase "Son of Man"—place these sayings on the lips of Jesus. Furthermore, the phrase has a distinctive meaning in those sources that attribute its use to Jesus. This meaning is unprecedented in Judaism, and nowhere else in early Christian literature, including the other documents of the New Testament, do we find such persistent appropriation of this phrase as a title for Jesus Christ.

Once we see that the Son of Man sayings belong on the list of authentic sayings of Jesus, we may investigate their significance by considering how Jesus used the phrase "Son of Man." He regularly employed it as a self-referring expression and used it to denote his own deity by associating uniquely divine prerogatives with the activity of the Son of Man, notably the forgiveness of sins (see Mark 2:1–12). Jesus used the phrase to depict both his earthly task as Suffering Servant and Redeemer and his eschatological work as the exalted and unmatched Judge of the world. Jesus evidently considered his own person to be a full explication of the meaning of the reference to the "son of man" in Daniel 7:13, who is portrayed there as a divine figure.[11]

In his own contribution to this volume, Hick speaks sparingly of the Son of Man sayings and focuses instead upon the significance of the title "Son of God." But the Son of Man say-

---

[11]On the significance of the "Son of Man" sayings, see Chrys C. Caragounis, *The Son of Man: Vision and Interpretation* (Tübingen: J. C. B. Mohr, 1986); Oscar Cullmann, *The Christology of the New Testament* (London: SCM, 1959), 137–92; Royce G. Gruenler, "Son of Man," in *Evangelical Dictionary of Theology*, ed. Walter A. Elwell (Grand Rapids: Baker, 1984), 1034–35; Donald Guthrie, *New Testament Theology* (Downers Grove, Ill.: InterVarsity, 1981), 270–91; Morna D. Hooker, *The Son of Man in Mark* (Montreal: McGill Univ. Press, 1967); I. Howard Marshall, *The Origins of New Testament Christology* (Downers Grove, Ill.: InterVarsity, 1976, 1990), 63–82; Reymond, *Jesus, Divine Messiah*, 52–61; Robert H. Stein, "Jesus Christ," also in Elwell, *Evangelical Dictionary of Theology*, 584.

ings are every bit as significant as the Son of God designation. While Jesus actually preferred to refer to himself as the Son of Man, his special filial relationship with God is affirmed in passages where he identifies himself as the Son of Man. So not only is he the Son of God by virtue of being the Son of Man in the special sense he associated with this title, but, in his self-designation as *"the* Son of Man," the sense in which he is the Son of God becomes clearer. While there is a sense in which believers in Jesus are also sons of God (see, e.g., Matt. 5:9, 45; John 3:16, 18; 1 John 4:9), there is no sense in which the designation "Son of Man" applies to them when it includes the definite article.

The Moral Impossibility of Christian Exclusivism

Hick asks, "Can it possibly be the will of the loving heavenly Father of Jesus' teaching that only that minority of men and women who have the luck of being born into a Christian part of the world can enter eternal life?" The question is framed in terms of Hick's own prejudices and assumptions: (1) What part of the world one is born into is a matter of "luck"; (2) only persons born into "a Christian part of the world" ever hear the Christian gospel and are saved in response to it; and (3) if God consigns any person to hell, it is because he wills their eternal perdition. We do not accept these assumptions. The loving heavenly Father of Jesus' teaching is sovereign over all events in the lives of human persons, including the circumstances of their births. And the Great Commission of the disciples by Jesus ensured that many in non-Christian parts of the world would actually hear the Christian gospel. Also, while God wishes the eternal happiness of all human persons (1 Tim. 2:3–4), he honors the freedom of human creatures as they elect their own destinies by their responses to him. Furthermore, it is possible that only a minority of persons born, as Hick says, into "a Christian part of the world" will believe the Christian gospel and be saved, even though most will have heard the gospel.

Suppose we restate the question as follows: Is it possible for the loving heavenly Father of Jesus' teaching to allow that only that minority of men and women who hear and believe the gospel receive eternal life? Certainly this seems possible. We do not know how Hick would argue that this is strictly impossible.

The doctrine of middle knowledge, according to which God knows all free acts any human person would perform in any nonactual states of affairs, safeguards this possibility. Why should not God, who is omniscient, know what a person in some non-Christian land would freely decide if that person were, contrary to fact, to hear the gospel of Jesus Christ? Some who accept the doctrine of middle knowledge hold that there are individuals who never hear the gospel but would believe if they were to hear it and that God saves them on the basis of his foreknowledge of that fact. But it is equally plausible philosophically that God knows that all individuals who never hear the gospel are individuals who would not believe if they were to hear the gospel.

All this suggests that God is far from indifferent about the human situation. Indeed, it would be surprising if it turned out that God manifests no interest in human persons and their concerns. It would not be surprising, however, if God's interest in us and his initiative toward us respected our capacity for self-determination as free creatures. Our moral intuitions are provisional and fallible guides to the specific content of objective morality and to the moral hue of departments of the universe. Christianity is for people who want to find out from God whether their intuitions about hell, for example, are correct; it is not for people who have made up their minds a priori that hell cannot be real.[12] The religious pluralist's insistence that God cannot have arranged for our salvation in the exclusivist way of Christianity presupposes a greater knowledge of God than radical religious pluralists are in a position to have on their own assumptions.

---

[12]For more on these issues, see R. Douglas Geivett, *Evil and the Evidence for God: The Challenge of John Hick's Theodicy* (Philadelphia: Temple Univ. Press, 1993), especially ch. 12.

INDEXES

SUBJECT INDEX

NAME INDEX

SCRIPTURE INDEX